Business Intelligence with Microsoft® Office PerformancePoint™ Server 2007

Business Intelligence with Microsoft® Office PerformancePoint™ Server 2007

Craig Utley

Mc Graw Hill

New York   Chicago   San Francisco
Lisbon   London   Madrid   Mexico City   Milan
New Delhi   San Juan   Seoul   Singapore   Sydney   Toronto

The **McGraw·Hill** Companies

Cataloging-in-Publication Data is on file with the Library of Congress

Business Intelligence with Microsoft® Office PerformancePoint™ Server 2007

1234567890   FGR FGR   0198

ISBN   978-0-07-149370-3
MHID   0-07-149370-0

Sponsoring Editor
Wendy Rinaldi

Editorial Supervisor
Patty Mon

Project Manager
Vasundhara Sawhney,
International Typesetting and
Composition

Acquisitions Coordinator
Mandy Canales

Technical Editor
Allyson Powell Erwin

Copy Editor
Julie M. Smith

Proofreader
International Typesetting and
Composition

Indexer
Kevin Broccoli

Production Supervisor
Jim Kussow

Composition
International Typesetting and
Composition

Illustration
International Typesetting and
Composition

Art Director, Cover
Jeff Weeks

Cover Designer
Pattie Lee

This book is dedicated to my parents, whose support never wanes

About the Author

Craig Utley is a mentor with Solid Quality Mentors and a former program manager for the SQL Server Customer Advisory Team at Microsoft. He has been working with Microsoft's BI products since the SQL Server 7 beta, originally helping to author Microsoft's first data warehousing course and then teaching it at Microsoft and many other companies. Craig now helps companies implement BI solutions using Microsoft and related technologies, covering all aspects from architecture and design to implementation and training. He is a published author, conference speaker, and member of the INETA Speakers Bureau.

About the Contributing Author

Sony Jose, who has a MS in Engineering from Georgia Tech in Atlanta, Georgia, has over 10 years of experience working with Microsoft Business Intelligence tools. As a consultant, he has delivered successful Data Warehouse implementations and OLAP solutions in several industries, including Banking and Finance, Healthcare, Energy, Retail, and Software verticals. Sony served as a member of the team that implemented PPS Planning module at Microsoft prior to its General Availability release. He is currently a mentor with Solid Quality Mentors, and provides training and mentoring in advanced BI solutions to clients across the country. He teaches classes on Microsoft BI tool suite and speaks at BI seminars and conferences. He is also a Microsoft Certified Database Administrator (MCDBA). He lives in Atlanta with his wife Lucy and daughter Anne.

About the Technical Editor

Alyson Powell Erwin is a program manager for Microsoft Corporation (Nasdaq: MSFT). Alyson is responsible for managing customer programs, early product feedback, and deployments for PerformancePoint Server Monitoring and Analytics. Previously, Alyson was a technical product manager for ProClarity Corporation, managing customer programs, product feedback, and early deployments of the ProClarity Analytics family of products. Alyson had previous experience working on the Professional Services team at ProClarity deploying BI solutions, writing and delivering BI training materials, and acting as a Technical Account Manager. Prior to joining ProClarity in 2000, Alyson worked on the SAP team at Trus Joist, a division of Weyerhaeuser (NYSE:WY) and in various development roles for Micron (NYSE: MU) and Logicon, now a division of Northrop Grumman. Alyson holds a Bachelor of Science degree in Mathematics from Idaho State University.

Contents at a Glance

Contents

Acknowledgments

Working on a technical book is something that cannot be done alone. The image of the writer hunched over his keyboard and writing into the wee hours of the morning may be accurate, but it's only part of the tale. Chapters are sent to a technical editor, reviewed, updated, reviewed by a copy editor, updated, typeset (for lack of a better word), reviewed again, and finally they're ready to go. In between, questions fly back and forth between editors, managers, and technical people as the book comes together. Somewhere, one or more artists create professional images from hand-drawn pictures when the author, as in my case, lacks any sort of artistic skill.

I've been extremely lucky to have excellent help on this project. Two people, in particular, are singled out for high praise. The first is Alyson Powell Erwin, a program manager on the PerformancePoint Server team. Alyson was the technical editor for this book and her suggestions were always excellent. Beyond simply being the technical editor, however, Alyson answered many of my often inane questions, provided insight about why some features worked as they did, and offered alternatives to the ways I first presented some of the material in this book. Alyson was my conduit into the PPS team at large and I truly appreciate her as well as her efforts.

The second person to make a major impact on this book is Sony Jose. Sony is a colleague of mine at Solid Quality Mentors, but as of the time of this writing we have not met in person. Sony was lucky enough to be involved with one of the first production installations of the Planning Server portion of PerformancePoint Server; as such, I asked him to write Chapter 7 and he obliged. I found his writing style to merge well with mine, but it was his actual use of the product in a large corporate environment that proved invaluable for seeing how to actually set up and work with models. Sony, thanks a million!

There are many people to thank at McGraw-Hill, of course. Mandy Canales was my acquisitions coordinator and she somehow managed to put up with me and my schedule changes, all the while remaining positive. Wendy Rinaldi, the Editorial Director, first approached me about doing the book and she continued to stay involved.

Wendy helped drive the book to completion and was always professional and friendly. My copy editor, Julie Smith, helped ensure that none of my former English teachers would throw a fit.

Thanks to Russ Whitney of Microsoft for looking over the chapters and providing feedback; I think his team has done a superb job and I expect great things from them in the future. I'd also like to thank Mark Souza, Lubor Kollar, and the rest of the SQL Server Customer Advisory Team who gave me a chance to work directly with the Analysis Services team for over a year.

Naturally there are others who did not have a direct impact on the book, but had to deal with me while I wrote. First and foremost is my wife, Linda, who was supportive from start to finish. My daughter, Alison, continued to grow into a fine young lady while I was busy. My dogs forced me to take breaks every few hours and helped restore some sanity to the late nights of writing. Special thanks go out to Greg Clark, Mark Orgel, Jim Walters, and all the other guys at the RCMC. Doug Churchman was always there to inject some levity into the situation. I'd also like to thank Kevin Heine because my wife told me to. I cannot say enough about my friends at FPG Unlimited. And once again, this book would not have been possible without the help of my good friend, Martha McMahon.

Introduction

I t was a hot and humid day in New Orleans. I was speaking at a conference, presenting a topic on Analysis Services (it might have been OLAP Services; my mind is a little fuzzy on this point). After I finished describing cubes and showing people how to build them, I browsed the cube using ProClarity 2.0. After the presentation, I learned there had been someone from ProClarity Corp. (then called Knosys) in the audience when Tammy Tilzey came up to speak with me. Over the course of a few months, we discussed the product and its future and I ended up writing the courseware for version 3.0.

My familiarity with Microsoft's data warehousing products goes back to the beta days of SQL Server 7 and I've always been a fan of the ProClarity front-end tool. I was fortunate to end up working with ProClarity and see the introduction of their thin-client product, the ProClarity Analytics Server, as well as the ProClarity Dashboard and a few other products firsthand.

I always felt that data warehousing had the power to truly bring benefits to an organization, but that the choice of the proper front end tools was crucial. Therefore, I advocated a mix of scorecards aimed at the top end of the organization, reports for the majority of users, and powerful analytics tools for the analysts and power users. ProClarity could handle some of this, and mixed with SQL Server Reporting Services and Microsoft Office Business Scorecard Manager, businesses had a fairly complete set of tools to deliver value from their warehouse to the entire organization.

In early 2006 I was teaching a data warehousing class to a group at Microsoft, and I mentioned that I wished Microsoft would hurry up and buy ProClarity; a week later the deal was announced. I believed that Microsoft buying ProClarity would be a good thing, but the way that Microsoft would choose to integrate the ProClarity products remained to be seen.

Several months later, Microsoft announced a new product, PerformancePoint Server 2007. This product was to combine Business Scorecard Manager with ProClarity's tools, a move that seemed to make perfect sense. In a bit of a surprise, at least to me, Microsoft also announced the inclusion of a planning module—a new product that would allow businesses to budget and forecast more easily.

Microsoft's goal for PerformancePoint Server was for a unified product that would allow businesses to monitor the business, analyze the data, and plan for the future; plans could then be compared against actuals in the new year as well as performance monitored—thus completing the circle.

I was excited about the prospects for the product. Finally, the ProClarity features I had known for years were growing up and would become part of a larger, integrated suite that would provide business intelligence value at many levels of the organization. While version one of PerformancePoint Server isn't quite as integrated as I'd hoped, it's definitely headed in the right direction and is going to help deliver value to many businesses that have thus far deployed nothing more than Excel.

This book lays out what business intelligence is all about, who the consumers of business intelligence are, and how they consume data. It discusses the business intelligence concepts and shows how they can be delivered using PerformancePoint Server and ProClarity, whether through monitoring, analysis, or planning. I also discuss Excel 2007 and Reporting Services, since both can continue to be used for delivering data in various formats.

As you'll discover from reading this book, I'm a fan of business intelligence in general. I believe it has the power to enable businesses to make informed decisions more quickly. I'm also a believer in a variety of approaches for delivering the data; I find PerformancePoint Server to be on the right path to delivering data to a very broad swath of users. No tool is perfect, but I've found PerformancePoint Server to be the best product yet created to address the various needs of different users to consume data from a data warehouse.

Business Intelligence

The Case for Business Intelligence

Business intelligence is a concept that can cover many technologies. A business intelligence solution usually covers a wide range of processes, software, and techniques, from retrieving the data from source systems to delivering business value to end users. In order to help deliver end-to-end business intelligence, Microsoft has created a suite of products that covers the entire gamut, of which PerformancePoint Server 2007 is an important part. This chapter, however, will focus on business intelligence in general, including the users of business intelligence and the kinds of tasks they'll perform in their daily jobs. In this chapter, I'll first describe business intelligence from a high level, and then define what it is and why it's important. Next I'll describe the various consumers of business intelligence, and as you'll see, it can encompass virtually everyone in an organization. Finally, I'll conclude the chapter with a variety of ways to deliver data to the various classes of users.

What Is Business Intelligence?

Business intelligence (BI) is more of a concept than a single technology. The goal is to gain insight into the business by bringing together data, formatting it in a way that enables better analysis, and then providing tools that give users power—not just to examine and explore the data, but to quickly understand it. Many in the information technology field are familiar with the saying, "Data is not information." This phrase underscores the idea that data points by themselves fail to impart much useful information and that data must be put into context to be meaningful. A list of sales numbers is not helpful unless it includes the products sold, when they were sold, where they were sold, and so on. It is important to include context when looking at data in order to turn it into information.

While obtaining information is important, information is only useful if it is easy to grasp so that people can use it to make decisions. There is much information in books on nuclear physics or Cycladic statuary and burial rites, but without the proper context and training such information can be hard to comprehend. It is therefore the goal to make data easy to comprehend; a quick grasp of the trends, relationships, and relative strengths and weaknesses is essential to delivering a usable system that truly delivers business value.

Building a system that allows users to easily grasp what is presented and turn it into easily comprehended, actionable business information requires a number of steps. First, the business problems to be solved must be identified. Then, the data must be located in the various source systems and consolidated in such a way that it is consistent and accessible. This is the process of building a data warehouse or data mart, and is covered in detail in Chapter 3. This is often a challenging process, with many companies seeming to make the mistake of believing that this is the beginning and end of their BI project. I have personally been into numerous companies that have built warehouses and then provided completely inadequate tools for letting people actually use the information contained in the warehouse. This is like buying a car and then locking it in a garage so it can never be driven; the potential value will never be realized.

After building the warehouse, there must be a mechanism to retrieve the data and present it to business users so that they can understand it and act upon what they see. This is where PerformancePoint Server and ProClarity come in, because they are tools built to provide businesses with the ability to monitor and analyze the data. Much of the ability to easily grasp data is because of visualization capabilities available in the products, such as charts, graphs, scorecards, decomposition trees, performance maps, and so on. The data in warehouses can also be used in traditional reports, which, when viewed online, may include interactivity for performing data analysis.

PerformancePoint Server adds another piece to the mix: modeling. Modeling can encompass planning, budgeting, and forecasting. While these three items can certainly be done without a warehouse in place, the warehouse provides two major benefits: first, historical data is easily accessible and can be examined for trends and past results; second, the budgets and forecast can be put back into the warehouse and actual results can be tracked against the budget or forecast in the warehouse as time moves on.

There are numerous pieces to a business intelligence solution. The term *business intelligence,* or BI, is used in this book to indicate the entire process. The entire process of business intelligence can be broken into the following steps:

1. Identifying the business problem(s) to be addressed by the warehouse and the data needed to address those problems.
2. Identifying the location for all necessary data and extracting it from those sources.
3. Transforming the data from various sources into consolidated, consistent data.
4. Loading the transformed data into a centralized location.
5. Building a data warehouse (or data mart) with the data from the centralized location. The structure being built is called a *cube.*
6. Putting in place commercial products or custom applications that give access to the data in the cubes. There are many different ways of working with cube data, and different approaches make sense for different roles within an organization.

Step 1 requires you to identify the business problems to be solved and is beyond the scope of this book except for casual mention. Steps 2-5 are discussed in some detail in Chapter 3, which addresses the overall process of building a data warehouse (or data mart or cube; the terms are clearly defined there.) Step 6 is what is covered in the rest of the book, including the PerformancePoint Server product and its capabilities. Figure 1-1 shows these various steps in an overall business intelligence process. It should now be obvious that business intelligence covers more than just building a data warehouse; indeed, it includes one or more ways to access and analyze data that deliver value across the business.

While the process of building a data warehouse is critical to the success of the project, it is a subject best handled by books dedicated to the tools used for data warehouse creation: SQL Server Integration Services (SSIS) and SQL Server Analysis Services (SSAS). Books such as *Hands-On SQL Server 2005 Integration Services* and *Delivering Business Intelligence with Microsoft SQL Server 2005* cover these topics in great detail. This book, on the other hand, focuses on the tools that allow companies to use the warehouse and to achieve the benefits of being able to monitor the health of the organization, perform complex analysis of their data, and plan for the future using the strength of the warehouse. In order to better understand these pieces, however, it is important to understand the various roles played by the users of the system.

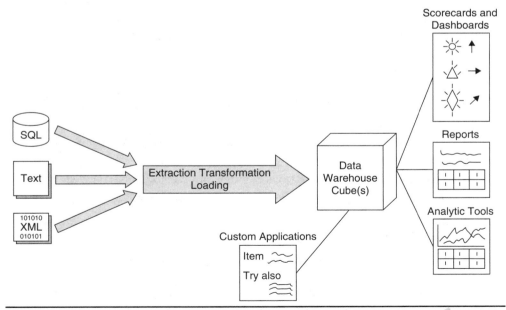

Figure 1-1   *The Business Intelligence process from end to end*

The Consumers of Business Intelligence

People perform vastly different roles within organizations and therefore have varying needs for how and why they consume information. It is important to understand these roles and the business reach and impact they have. After identifying four roles of an organization, I will delve into the ways these roles can interact with data and why there is no one approach that satisfies all business needs.

The four roles that will be examined include

- ▶ Business Decision-Makers
- ▶ Knowledge Workers
- ▶ Analysts
- ▶ Line Workers

Obviously, roles are not always so cut and dry, and one person may well have responsibilities in more than one role. However, it is important to understand the business focus of each role and their corresponding need for information.

Business Decision-Makers

The role of business decision-maker encompasses several titles in an organization: executives, directors, and managers. These various jobs are different in important ways, but all have one thing in common: the need for timely information is critical so that these individuals can make decisions that drive the business.

Executives are those at the top of an organization. Their view is often quite wide; they must understand all facets of the business and how they relate. A CEO is concerned with revenue and expenses, but also with staffing, manufacturing, customer satisfaction, supply chains, and so forth. Executives rarely have much time to dig into the numbers so they need very broad, high-level measures of the overall health of a business. Vice presidents and directors of certain business functions may get more detailed information about their area, but they still take a broad view and need high-level information. Managers often manage at a much more granular level, but are still making business decisions that can impact the profit and loss of their specific areas. When the information upon which a business decision-maker relies can have an impact on the profitability of a functional unit, it is critical that the information be timely and accurate. The presentation of the data must make it very easy to grasp quickly and provide unambiguous information about the health of that information.

The actual data needed by business decision makers varies based on their functional role: A vice president of finance will look at different metrics than the vice president of human resources, for example. Chapter 4 will delve more into different business areas and what some of the key metrics are for various departments within a company.

Knowledge Workers

Knowledge workers make up the bulk of non-management office staff. Software developers, marketing personnel, human resources staff, financial accountants, and other such workers are professional staff that have the need for information, but often do not have the ability to make decisions that have a large business impact. A marketing person, for example, may be tasked with creating marketing materials to sell a new product or service. This person may do research by examining the market place, look at competing products, conduct focus groups, study internal quality control procedures, and more, but the end result is materials that must be approved by management—the money for creation is allocated by someone other than that marketing person.

Such knowledge workers have a real need for data, but often the data needed is at a lower level of detail than that needed by business decision-makers. In addition, the data needed may be completely different for each request, while business decision-makers tend to look at the same set of numbers on a regular basis.

Knowledge workers may need to do some data exploration, but this is often not at a particularly deep level. For example, a sales representative might well need to know the previous sales to a particular client, returns by that particular client, and the projected sales to that client over the next several months. The drivers behind the projection are probably known to the sales representative and might include items such as new products in the pipeline or promotions that are in the works, but the statistical models used to forecast the projected product mix or future sales for that particular client are often of little concern. Such details are often left in the hands of analysts.

Analysts

Analysts are a special breed of knowledge worker who often work directly with business decision makers. Analysts, whether they're business analysts, financial analysts, or some other kind of analyst, often spend time performing very detailed analysis of data. They may delve deeply into vast quantities of information looking for root causes to problems or trying to uncover trends in the data that are not already obvious.

Many analysts employ advanced statistical techniques in order to analyze the data. These models may be used for forecasting purposes or to examine the numbers in relation to norms and standards throughout the industry. One is example is when a business manages pensions or other retirement funds for its employees. The performance of these funds can easily be compared to a number of standard financial indexes, and future performance can be forecasted and compared against future payout forecasts.

Many manufacturing and transportation businesses also employ models that help predict costs based on the price of oil. Some of these models might also have to include currency fluctuations if some of the raw materials are purchased from foreign businesses. These complex statistical models require flexible software that gives analysts nearly unrestricted access to the data. Some of what these analysts do is considered data mining, a technology which uses statistical models to examine data for relationships or make predictions based on existing data.

Line Workers

Line workers are those workers on the front lines and may include assembly line workers in a manufacturing company and cashiers in a retail establishment. Many such workers benefit from business intelligence although they may not realize it. Data derived from a business intelligence process may be integrated into line of business applications that allow line workers to better do their jobs. Cashiers in a retail establishment might be able to recommend complimentary or replacement items based on customer preferences. Call center workers can see the order and return history of customers calling in with questions. Assembly line workers can obtain real-time statistics on the number of units produced, quality control, and inventory levels. Such workers may not know the term "business intelligence" or have any idea that the data they are viewing comes from a data warehouse. Nonetheless, they are still consumers of data and therefore part of the business intelligence process.

Delivering Data to Business Intelligence Consumers

The previous section described four types of consumers of business intelligence information, ranging from executives to sales clerks and assembly line workers. This shows that the end result of a business intelligence project can provide benefits to nearly every facet of an organization. More importantly, a data warehouse can be designed so that a single warehouse can serve the needs of all the consumers, greatly simplifying the creation and maintenance of the warehouse.

While a single warehouse may be able to handle the data needs for many or all consumers, the same is not true of the different methods used to display and navigate that information. In other words, there are many different techniques that can be used to present data to consumers, and thus there are different tools available to provide this data display. It would be great to be able to say that PerformancePoint Server can handle every situation. In fact, PerformancePoint Server and ProClarity combine to provide a wealth of different display methods, although custom applications are sometimes the best way to get information to consumers. This section focuses on different ways to present the data and the ways that users benefit from those different presentations.

Business Scorecards

Business scorecards, sometimes called just scorecards, are a means of quickly showing someone the overall health of the business or a particular division. Scorecards typically show Key Performance Indicators, or KPIs, which are the primary numbers upon which the organization or person is focused. For example, the vice president of manufacturing might be interested in such items as

- ▶ The number of units produced
- ▶ The number of items failing quality control
- ▶ The amount of scrap metal generated
- ▶ Current inventory levels
- ▶ Current raw materials inventory
- ▶ The current price of steel

These items are the KPIs that might appear on a scorecard for the vice president of manufacturing. Each KPI is typically displayed as a symbol indicating the health of that particular number. For example, the number of items failing quality control might be 50. Is this good or bad? It depends on many factors. If the company is making two million items a day and 50 fail the quality control check, this is a low percentage and might be acceptable. If, on the other hand, the company is producing only 75 expensive products a day and 50 fail the quality control check, there is likely a serious issue that needs to be addressed. The idea behind scorecards is not to necessarily display the number, but to provide an icon that indicates whether the number is good or bad. This icon can take the form of colored indicators (green/ yellow/red), smiley faces, gauges, dials, and so forth. This way, at a glance, an individual can determine whether things are good (or not) for each particular KPI without having to see the exact number or translate a number into an indicator of overall health.

In addition to the health of a KPI, many KPIs also have a *trend indicator*, showing whether they are improving or slipping. In the case of the number of items failing a quality control audit, lower numbers are better, so a decline in the number would actually be a positive trend. Because the trend and the health of a KPI are tracked separately, the health might be good but show a downward trend, or a KPI with poor health might be holding steady, indicating that efforts to improve it are not having any impact. Figure 1-2 shows a sample scorecard in PerformancePoint Server.

The name scorecard also implies some form of score. Many organizations do not go through this process, but KPIs can be weighted so that an overall score is generated. This is useful in situations where a company wants to apply the same scorecard to each of several locations. Using a score, it becomes simple to rank each location based on this score.

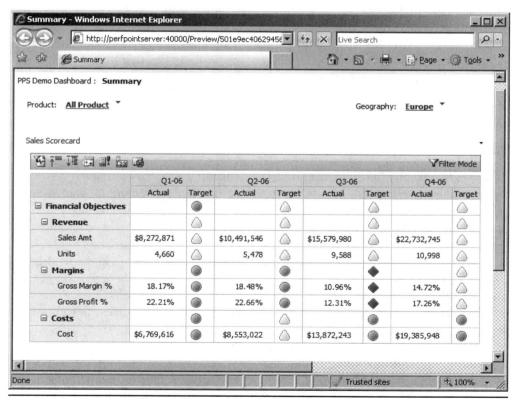

Figure 1-2 *A scorecard created in PerformancePoint Server*

Scorecards can certainly be used by anyone in an organization, as everyone appreciates a quick glance summary of the data. However, scorecards are aimed at higher levels of an organization: the business decision-makers. Executives and others with decision-making authority in an organization are typically very busy people, and they don't have time to plumb the data for hidden gems of information; instead, they need a quick overview of the organization's health. Scorecards work perfectly for this by providing that at-a-glance update on the most important business metrics. If any numbers are off, the business decision maker can sometimes perform some analytics to uncover the cause, but most often they have an analyst on staff that will be given the task for investigating the issue. The analyst has tools far more adept at performing complex analysis than can be done with a scorecard.

Scorecards are often placed on a *dashboard*. A dashboard may contain one or more scorecards, some KPIs independent of a scorecard, reports from Reporting Services, and charts from ProClarity. To add another layer to this, a *portal* is the top of the heap and may contain one or more dashboards as well as a copy of the person's calendar, e-mail, and so forth. Dashboards are what are ultimately deployed by PerformancePoint Server, and the primary deployment target for these dashboards is SharePoint. SharePoint is an excellent tool for bringing together information from multiple applications and displaying it in a centralized location.

The creation of scorecards, as well as some common KPIs, will be examined in depth in Chapters 4 and 5.

Reports

Reports are typically boring collections of numbers in rows and columns. Despite their generally dull nature, reports are still in huge demand across many organizations. Fortunately, reports don't have to be as dull as they have been in the past. Thanks to online report viewing, reports can now be interactive, providing end users with the ability to drill down and obtain additional information, or choose values from a filter list to narrow the scope of what they see in the report. Understand that when discussing reports, the terms *filters* and *parameters* are often used interchangeably, and that will be the case in this book. Figure 1-3 shows a report that allows users to narrow the data using drop-down list boxes, as well as drill into more detail by expanding regions of the report.

SQL Server Reporting Services allows for the creation of reports against a data warehouse, regardless of whether the data are stored in a relational format or in a cube. These reports can be interactive; users can choose values from a parameter list and the reports can allow for limited drill down and other analytic operations. Reports can also link to other reports so that data may be examined in more detail.

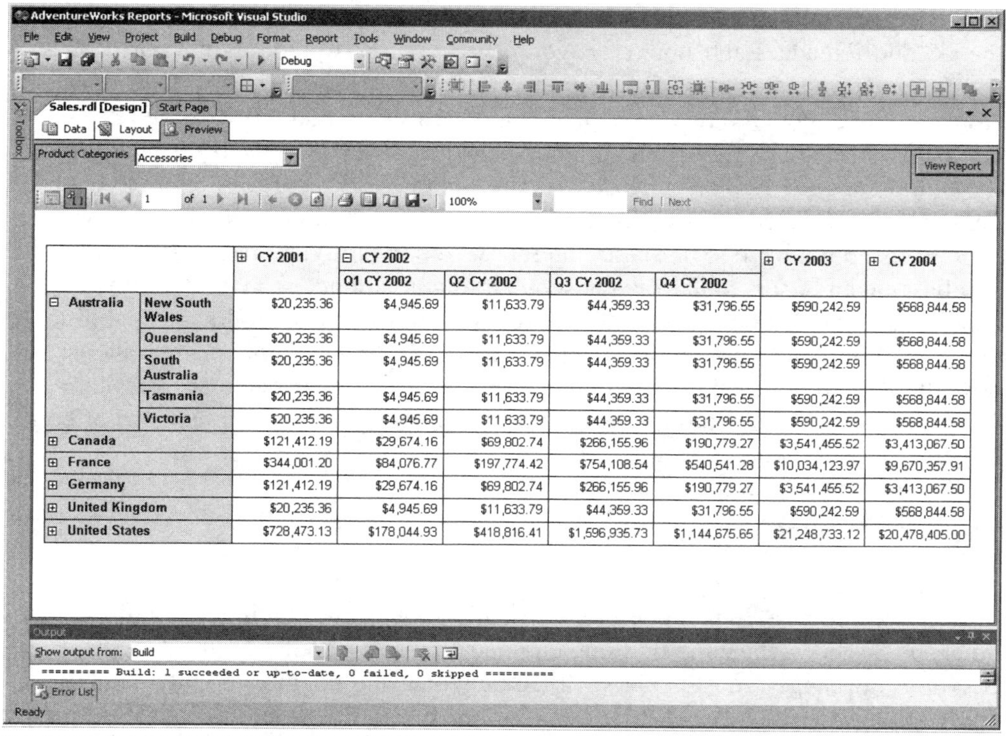

Figure 1-3 *A report showing both filters and drill-down capabilities*

Standard reports are not natively part of PerformancePoint Server, but PerformancePoint integrates well with Reporting Services. Various actions in PerformancePoint can link to reports hosted in Reporting Services, allowing end users to find more detailed information. For example, a KPI in a scorecard might show that employee retention is below desired levels. Clicking on that KPI could open a report that lists each department ordered by the percentage turnover that department has experienced in the last quarter.

Reports do not need to be only a device reached through other tools, however; for many organizations, reports are the only tool widely distributed. Reports are a staple of any organization and—thanks to intranets and ubiquitous connectivity—online reports can be distributed with ease. Anyone can log onto a centralized report server and view real-time reports. In addition, reports can be generated on a scheduled basis and distributed via e-mail or printed and distributed.

For example, imagine a company in the US that has a number of stores throughout the US and Canada. Each store manager has access to six predefined reports. Most store managers start their day by viewing online reports showing how their particular store is doing compared to the other stores in their district and to other stores companywide. These reports are simple, static reports and the managers can flip through them quickly. This is close to being suitable for a scorecard, but the reports contain more detailed information than is normally found in a scorecard scenario.

Reports do not have to be static. Interactive reports provide tremendous flexibility by allowing end users to narrow the scope through parameters by selecting values from drop-down list boxes. In addition, reports can provide drill-down capabilities, either by linking to other reports or providing expanding and collapsing regions directly in the report. Adding such interactivity allows end users to answer many questions themselves without having to learn complex analytic applications or how to perform their own queries.

Analytic Applications

Analytic applications are specialized tools that enabled detailed analysis on data in a warehouse. In this book I specifically about tools that interact with Analysis Services, the cube-building engine Microsoft provides with SQL Server. Surprisingly, most readers will already be using the most popular analytic application, Microsoft Excel. Excel has had the capability to interact with Analysis Services cubes for some time, but Excel 2007 makes a huge leap forward in the capabilities and usability of Excel as a cube browsing tool.

For years, the most popular third-party tool for browsing cubes was ProClarity. ProClarity Corporation created a thick, desktop client called ProClarity Professional, as well as a web-based tool they called ProClarity Analytics Server, or PAS. PAS included a thin client for browsing cubes called ProClarity standard, and it mimicked most, but not all, of the functionality found in ProClarity Professional. With Microsoft's acquisition of ProClarity in 2006, the groundwork was laid to merge the strong analytic tools from ProClarity with some of Microsoft's tools, including the Business Scorecard Manager. The merger of these tools, as well as the addition of a planning piece, has led to PerformancePoint Server.

Analytic applications such as ProClarity are designed for analysts who need to perform complex analysis on data. This doesn't mean that such tools are limited only to analysts—I've have taught numerous ProClarity classes to end users over the years. However, these tools are more specialized than standard reports and therefore don't have the same broad reach. They are designed primarily for someone who wants to work with the data without restrictions and follow any train of thought through iterative analysis of the data.

Many of these tools also include advanced visualizations in the form of different graph and chart types. Figure 1-4 shows an example of some of ProClarity's advanced views of the data and how they can be used to quickly identify problem areas, outliers, and so forth.

In many organizations, the number of people needing a full-blown analytic tool compared to reports with limited analytics is anywhere from 1:5 to 1:10; in other words, one user will need a true analytic tool for every five to ten users that consume reports. However, Excel skews this number by allowing for the creation of canned reports against the data while still allowing for a fairly detailed analysis. Therefore, assume that the line between true analytic tools and more general tools is continually blurring.

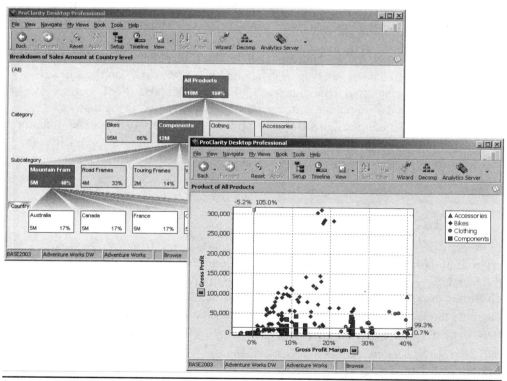

Figure 1-4   *ProClarity provides advanced visualizations which enable users to more quickly analyze and explore data.*

Line-of-Business Applications

Line-of-business applications are not business intelligence tools in a true sense. Instead, they're the applications that allow a business to run its day-to-day operations. However, integrating data from a business intelligence solution into line of business applications can provide line workers with tremendous benefits. Call center employees can immediately see charts or numbers representing all past business from a customer. Online stores can recommend complementary products when a person is making a purchase, based on the customer's previous purchases and the habits of similar customers. A medical center could use statistics covering a wide range of lab values and a large number of patients to identify whether a patient currently being treated might be at an elevated risk for a certain types of disease. Data input applications can validate data in real time against the known universe of good data. It can also flag potentially bad data at the time of data entry, before it makes its way into the system.

This ability to use the data from a data warehouse provides benefits all the way to the workers on the front lines of dealing with customers or products. These individuals may be totally unaware of the existence of a data warehouse, but they know that they use the numbers shown in the applications to get their job done more efficiently. Such integration between data in Analysis Services and line-of-business applications is provided by such enabling technologies as OLE DB, ADO.NET, XML web services, XMLA, and more. This alphabet soup means one thing: accessing the data and bringing it into client applications is well supported in a variety of ways and in many different application formats. Whether a company is using Windows applications or web applications, the data can easily be integrated into the daily workflow of all users.

Real World Examples

In theory, I'm sure all of this sounds well and good to you. However, there's nothing like practical applications of business intelligence for proving the value of the technology in real organizations. The following examples are just a few of the customer stories with which the author has first-hand knowledge and explains how business intelligence has enabled companies to run more efficiently and improve processes, save money, uncover problems, or some combination of all three.

Scorecard for Non-Profit Entity

One company, which will be referred to as Medical Non-Profit here, ran a number of facilities around the United States. These facilities cared for a rather specialized kind of patient and as such, all their money came from federal and state contracts.

Because their cost per patient was fixed, they worked hard to keep occupancy high, but had little actual control over occupancy in most cases. Therefore, nearly their entire focus was on controlling costs. In order for a facility to run smoothly, it had to operate at a profit, for even nonprofit organizations can't operate at a constant loss; nonprofit simply means any profits are reinvested and not held by the company or given away as dividends.

Medical Non-Profit had facilities across the United States, each with its own unique contracts and circumstances. However, at all centers a few things remained the same: people needed to be fed, the lights had to stay on, rent on the building or land had to be paid, and workers at those facilities had to be paid. There were many other expense categories, such as maintenance, water, office supplies, fuel costs, and more, but the four expenses that dwarfed all others were food, electricity, rent, and salaries. All costs were broken down on a per-patient basis and facilities with lower per-patient costs in each category were deemed better than those with higher costs.

NOTE

Please don't think this meant that a facility could starve its patients and achieve lower food costs; these were patients quite capable of complaining loudly if they were underfed.

The people running Medical Non-Profit were interested in determining the facilities that ran well and those that didn't. More than this, they sought to share this information with the facilities themselves without revealing too much information. In this particular area, Medical Non-Profit faced stiff competition, so it was important that the directors of each center not know the money received per patient from federal and state contracts, which was used to help determine profitability. In addition, while the director of each center knew his or her expense per patient, the operators of Medical Non-Profit did not want that information shared with directors of other centers.

Given the desire to rank centers without revealing the exact figures involved, a scorecard seemed to be the perfect answer. A KPI for each expense was established, such as Food Expense, Salary Expense, and so forth, on a per-patient basis. But rather than showing the actual figure, the only thing shown was an indicator: Green for Good, Yellow for Marginal, and Red for Bad. The color of the indicator was based on the expected cost for that item per patient in that facility's location. Now, each facility could immediately see how they were doing against projections in each expense category.

More importantly, weights were put in the different expenses and an overall score per facility was established. This score was then used to rank the facilities from top to bottom. A scorecard at Medical Non-Profit headquarters showed all the facilities ranked in order, and a + sign next to each one could be clicked to display the detailed expense items for each facility. At each facility, the director could see the overall scores for each facility but only expand his or her facility to see the details. This way, a facility director would know where his or her facility stood in relation to others, and could call those doing well to determine what they were doing right and the best practices that might be implemented at his or her facility.

The scorecard used at the time of this project was the first version of the Microsoft Business Scorecard Manager. This product continues to be enhanced and is in its third generation in PerformancePoint Server. The back end was an Analysis Services 2000 cube built from data from the Navision accounting application among other sources.

Where's the Time Going?

One organization—which will be referred to as Where's My Time, Dude?—needed to better analyze the hours being worked and the pay for those hours. This company felt they were getting hit with too much overtime and but were faced with staffing challenges at very inopportune times. Where's My Time, Dude? had a wealth of information about salaries in their accounting system, which seemed to work well and was up to date. Unfortunately, it was fed by a time-entry system that had been purchased long ago and had fallen into the Not My Job category. No one at Where's My Time, Dude? would admit to owning the application or really knowing much about it.

The nature of Where's My Time, Dude?'s business was one of rapid changes. These changes caused departments to sprout up and either change names, merge with other departments, or disappear with amazing speed. Each such change brought about new department and billing codes, of course, and maintaining these was never done quite right, thanks to the black hole of the time-entry system.

Upon first building a warehouse, a lot of data cleansing had to be done, specifically around department codes and mapping those to the codes in the accounting system (which was not a one-to-one match, of course.) When the data was compiled, the Vice President of Operations and her staff were shown the data. Fully 40 percent of the hours were being reported against departments that were closed or to which the employee entering the time did not belong. Needless to say, a task force was created immediately in order to determine how to address issues in the time entry system and to clean up department codes and align them properly with the accounting and payroll system.

Despite the mess with departments, the payroll data provided useful insight to the business immediately. When looking at overtime, one employee rose to the top by earning more in overtime in a year than her base pay. This raised a red flag but after investigation, the business learned that this was in fact the case for this particular employee. More importantly, they began looking at seasonal adjustments to their staffing and overtime levels and began setting boundaries for when such items became too high or too low.

The technology used for this particular engagement was SQL Server 2000 and ProClarity Analytic Server. Reports were created by a few users in Information Technology and published to the internal PAS site. Department managers were trained in how to view the reports and conduct some of their own analysis on the data.

Tracking Retail Sales

A large retail chain in Europe, the Middle East, and Africa (EMEA) wanted to better track and report on sales, as well as perform complex analysis on what sold well in different areas and which combinations of attributes were included in the most profitable items. Sales needed to be collected daily from each point of sale terminal in each store in the chain. This data amounted to literally millions of records being uploaded from the stores each night and loaded into the warehouse.

Each day, business decision-makers and managers of each product line consume reports that show how each item in their product line sold and where. Inventory can be adjusted according to the demands in various areas or even individual stores. These daily reports are relatively high level, represent a snapshot of the previous day's activities across the organization, and are used by everyone in the organization, from the CEO on down. Analysts throughout the company can then perform more detailed analysis using analytic tools against a wealth of data, including analysis of products by various attributes.

As an example, a new dress shirt might sell well one season. However, this shirt is available in a variety of different styles, such as with different fabrics, different collars, different buttons, and so forth. All of the shirts sold well, but did a specific combination of attributes sell better than others? If the shirt with mother of pearl buttons and silk fabric outsells all shirts with either cotton fabrics or plastic buttons, this information can be used for both stocking and pricing strategies.

This particular business intelligence solution builds warehouses out of approximately 15TB of relational data. The relational data is stored in SQL Server 2005, while the cubes are built with Analysis Services 2005. Reports are generated with Reporting Services 2005 and analysis is done with ProClarity.

Summary

As discussed in this chapter, the business benefits of business intelligence are real and working for many companies worldwide. However, it is important to realize there are different kinds of roles in an organization that can benefit from business intelligence, and those different roles often consume data in different ways. Therefore, there are a variety of tools that provide views of the data in the cubes making up the data warehouse. By properly implementing the appropriate tools for the various organizational roles, the benefits of a business intelligence solution can be realized throughout the organization.

Creating a business intelligence application is not a simple process. An organization must decide what business problems it wants to solve and then build a warehouse to support solving those problems. Building the warehouse is discussed in Chapter 3. Delivery of the data throughout the business must be planned and created, and this is covered throughout most of the rest of the book. Coming up, Chapter 2 will take an overview look at Microsoft's new product, PerformancePoint Server, which brings together a number of the tools and provides tools for scorecards, analytics, and planning.

Introducing PerformancePoint Server 2007

IN THIS CHAPTER

Performance Point Server 2007 is a brand new project from Microsoft. However, in reality, it is three products in one, and only one of the products is truly new. PerformancePoint Server 2007 is a tool designed to support the cycle of monitoring the health of the organization, analyzing the organization's data at a detailed level, and planning for the future so that monitoring can continue as the future slides into the present and then the past.

PerformancePoint Server 2007 represents an attempt by Microsoft to bring together tools that provide companies with greatly enhanced business intelligence capabilities. Two of the pillars of PerformancePoint Server provide tools that support different types of users, such as analysts and business decision makers, while the third pillar moves beyond delivering data to the organization to supporting the planning, budgeting, and forecasting efforts of the organization. The budgeting and forecasting data can become part of the process, so that actual performance is compared to the forecasts and so that the health of the business can be monitored. Variances in performance from the plan can be easily analyzed in detail to determine the source of any variances.

What Is PerformancePoint Server 2007?

Microsoft Office PerformancePoint Server 2007 is a concept with a bit of a split personality. First, it is both an application and a platform. In other words, it is an application that can be used as is, but it is also a platform because it can be extended and customized heavily. Second, there are three distinct areas of focus in the PerformancePoint Server: Monitoring, Analysis, and Planning. While there are three pillars, two of them are integrated to some degree, and in other ways, are the most separate. Monitoring and analysis are both integrated into a single tool, and in fact are both installed together, which means that they are tightly integrated; on the other hand, the analysis features in PerformancePoint Server 2007 are not as far along as originally planned, so Microsoft includes a license for a separate analytics application with the purchase of PerformancePoint Server. The planning piece of PerformancePoint uses a separate installation and a separate end-user tool from the monitoring and analysis pieces. There is little doubt that this product schizophrenia will be greatly reduced in future versions of PerformancePoint Server. For now, companies will still have access to the most powerful set of tools yet delivered to business intelligence to the organization.

Monitoring with PerformancePoint Server

PerformancePoint Server 2007 provides monitoring functionality that includes key performance indicators, scorecards, and dashboards. These dashboards are hosted in SharePoint, including either the free Windows SharePoint Services or the definitely not free Microsoft Office SharePoint Server. The monitoring functionality in PerformancePoint Server is the third iteration of technology from Microsoft, replacing Microsoft Office Business Scorecard Manager 2005. Key Performance Indicators, or KPIs, scorecards, and dashboards are covered in detail in Chapters 4 and 5 but are covered from a very high level here.

A rich-client application, Dashboard Designer, is the tool used to create KPIs, scorecards, and dashboards. A KPI is a metric that is tracked by the business to monitor the health of a particular piece of the business. For example, a company might track KPIs for sales, inventory turnover, employee head count, customer satisfaction, market share, employee training, and so forth. Rather than just being numbers, KPIs have the actual value (such as the actual sales), a target (the sales forecast), an indicator (how the actual value compares to the forecast or budget), and a trend that shows whether the KPI is trending up, trending down, or is flat.

Multiple KPIs are placed on a scorecard. A scorecard provides an overview, so in a single glance a person can see how the business or division is performing. The indicators are often graphical images such as colored circles, smiley faces, arrows, or the like, so that users can quickly grasp the meaning without having to concentrate on the numbers themselves. Aside from showing just the KPIs, a scorecard can show scores. A KPI has an actual and a target, and the better the actual compared to the target, the higher the score in most cases. This means that KPIs can be given scores and that these scores can roll up to higher level scores. This also means that different products, locations, or employees can be scored against each other for the purposes of ranking. This is no different from taking the range of grades over a semester for an entire class and ranking students based on their averages, but it provides an impartial way to rank what may be very different products or locations.

Dashboards are containers for one or more scorecards, possibly mixed with reports or other items. Dashboards may have filters that users can change to update one or more of the items on the page. For example, a filter for products would allow users to change from one product to another as well as update a scorecard and the two reports on the dashboard. Figure 2-1 shows an example of a dashboard hosting a scorecard and several reports, both as charts and grids.

One of the elements missing in the first version of the monitoring tool is the ability to click on a KPI and pass parameters to an existing application or report.

Figure 2-1   *This is a PerformancePoint Server dashboard containing a scorecard and multiple reports.*

For example, imagine that a business was looking at the salary expense for a particular location and noticed a particularly low score, meaning that salaries were much higher than expected. A useful feature would allow the user to click on that KPI and then launch the company's time and attendance system, with the location and the time period being viewed automatically passed as parameters. This type of integration may be possible via customizations but it is not a functionality that is available out of the box in this first version of PerformancePoint Server.

The monitoring piece uses Dashboard Designer and works using a disconnected model. This is similar to how Visual Studio 2005 is used to create web applications. The developer can work locally on a development machine, even though the application will eventually run on a server. Visual Studio 2005 allows developers to create web applications on a development machine and test the application fully before deploying it to the server. Similarly, Dashboard Designer allows developers to work on the files on a local machine and preview them using Internet Information

Server before deploying the dashboard to a server running SharePoint. This model will be examined in Chapter 5.

Analysis with PerformancePoint Server

In mid-2006, Microsoft purchased ProClarity Corporation. ProClarity was the creator of the most popular third-party analytics tool for Analysis Services (the most popular tool overall was Excel, but its analytics capabilities fell far short of ProClarity's.) ProClarity actually had several products, the primary two of which were the ProClarity Desktop Professional and the ProClarity Analytics Server. The Desktop Professional application was a Windows application while the Analytics Server was a web application that included a thin client analytics tool that mimicked almost all features of the Desktop Professional.

Soon after ProClarity's acquisition by Microsoft, PerformancePoint Server was announced as the answer to the question for what would happen to the ProClarity Products. PerformancePoint Server was presented as the blending of Business Scorecard Manager and ProClarity into one product, with the addition of a planning module.

In reality, the integration of the powerful analytics from the ProClarity platform did not happen as quickly as expected. The analytic features in PerformancePoint Server 2005 are good at what they do, but they are limited compared to a true analytic application. The analysis features that made it into PerformancePoint Server are wrapped up primarily in two reports: the Analytic Chart and the Analytic Grid. There are other ways of getting additional analysis but they rely on the Office Web Components, which require both an installation of components on the client machine and a client license. The Analytic Chart and Analytic Grid are very good at what they do, allowing users to drill down to explore additional data, as well as use filters to change some of the data, but they are basically limited to this functionality. End users cannot change the dimensions being examined in a report (for example, they can't replace products with customers on the rows). The Analytic Chart and Analytic Grid are mentioned in Chapter 5 and covered in more detail in Chapter 6. Figure 2-2 shows an example of the Analytic Chart and Analytic Grid reports.

In order to address the analytics shortfall in PerformancePoint Server, Microsoft is keeping the ProClarity product line alive for the time being. Customers who purchase a license of PerformancePoint server will also get a license for ProClarity. Customers interested in using PerformancePoint Server for analytics will almost certainly install and use the ProClarity Analytics Server, and Microsoft has added a report type in PerformancePoint Server that ties to a report, called a view in ProClarity Analytics Server.

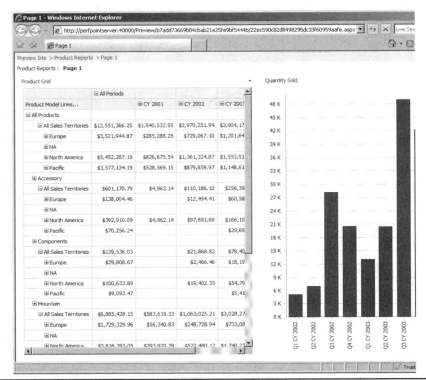

Figure 2-2 *The Analytic Chart and Analytic Grid reports represent the bulk of the analytics functionality in PerformancePoint Server.*

The ProClarity tools represent true analytics applications, offering basically unlimited abilities to work with the data in Analysis Services cubes. The rich graphical capabilities of the ProClarity tools are unmatched by any other tool. The capabilities of Excel 2007 are arguably better at dealing with grid data, but the charts in ProClarity are extremely powerful and flexible.

A complete discussion of the ProClarity applications could be a book unto itself, but I discuss the basics of performing analysis with ProClarity in Chapter 6. Figure 2-3 shows an example of some of the graphical capabilities of ProClarity.

Planning with PerformancePoint Server

The planning functionality of PerformancePoint Server is completely new functionality from Microsoft. This module was developed from the ground up to meet the needs of business in performing their planning, budgeting, and forecasting.

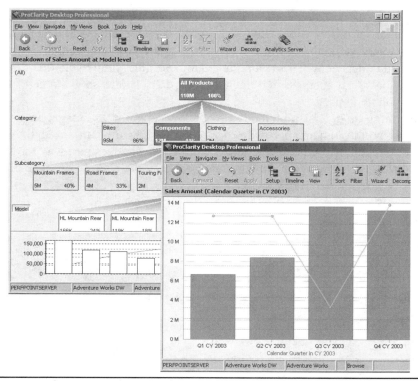

Figure 2-3   *ProClarity provides rich graphical capabilities while allowing users virtually unlimited power to analyze data in cubes.*

While many examples mentioned in any BI book are financial in nature, monitoring and analytics are not necessarily focused on financials. The planning module, on the other hand, does focus on financials. As such, the primary tool for end users to work with the planning application is Excel. Another tool, called the Planning Business Modeler, will be used by some in the organization to create financial models representing the ways the organization handles its financials. Once these models are created, users will be able to use Excel to add and update data for forecasts.

One of the primary reasons for the creation of the planning module was to ease the burden of creating strategic plans, budgets, and sales forecasts. The planning module allows companies to import data from multiple, disparate systems, and consolidate that data in a central storage location. Models can then be built which encapsulate business logic and processes. Security plays a big part in the planning module, with users only allowed to see data they are granted permission to see.

All changes are tracked automatically in order to comply with laws requiring audit trails for financial information. Having a central store for data and business rules means that everyone in the business has a single source for data, which ensures accuracy and consistency. This is a great example of the "single version of the truth," which is a goal of all business intelligence. Figure 2-4 shows an example of the planning module in use.

The planning module also includes a workflow capability, so that changes made by users can go through an approval process before they are committed to the forecast or budget. This ensures that users can't make changes part way through the year that are designed to make them look better at the end of year. The planning module is covered in detail in Chapter 7.

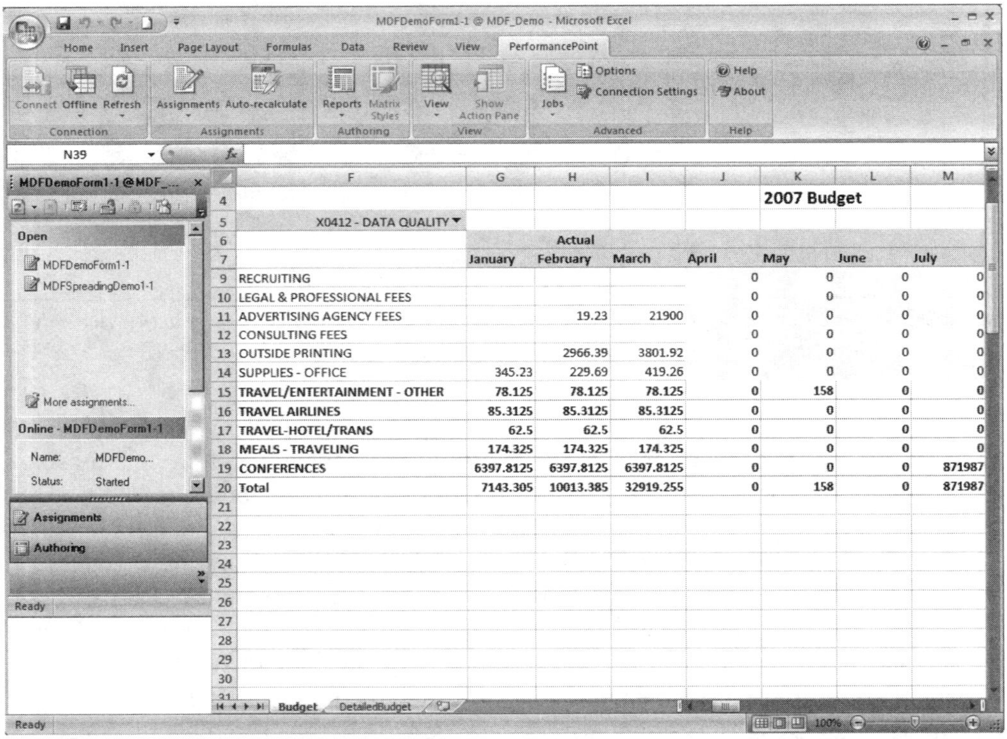

Figure 2-4 *Users can work with planning and budgets through a familiar interface: Excel.*

Summary

PerformancePoint Server includes three primary applications: monitoring, analysis, and planning. Monitoring is a way of viewing the primary drivers of the business in a way that immediately communicates the health of the organization. This is accomplished through scorecards, which are a means for viewing data at a high level and getting an immediate sense for the strength or weakness of the various metrics.

The analysis functionality is covered by reports in PerformancePoint Server and analytics tools in the ProClarity applications. This use of multiple applications to achieve true analytics is necessary in this first release of PerformancePoint Server, but should be gone in future versions.

The planning module is designed to help organizations speed the process of budgeting and forecasting, while enforcing business rules across the enterprise. Security is an important component of the planning module, tracking all changes and ensuring that users only see data to that they have permissions to.

Overall, PerformancePoint Server 2007 provides a way for companies to monitor their business performance against plans, dive deep into data, and create new forecasts and plans easily. These plans can then be used in the monitoring process, and the circle is complete. The integration of these tools and the powerful dashboards that can be built make PerformancePoint Server 2007 a powerful tool for delivering business intelligence value to the organization.

Data Warehousing and Business Intelligence

Business intelligence covers a range of technologies, and in this book business intelligence is a generic term covering the data warehouse as well as the tools and applications used to view the data from the warehouse. While the major focus of this book is on PerformancePoint Server and ProClarity, which allows users to consume data, there would be nothing to view without first building a data warehouse or data mart.

Before diving into the process of building the data warehouse, it's important to define the difference between a *data warehouse* and a *data mart*. The difference between the two is one of scope: marts cover individual business areas, while warehouses cover the entire business. Data marts focus on a particular business function, such as finance, manufacturing, sales and marketing, and so forth. There is a raging, often religious debate about the proper method of building a warehouse: whether to build a number of marts and then roll them up into a warehouse, or build a warehouse and then split out data marts as necessary. This debate is beyond the scope of this book, and the good news is that the decision is unimportant for the purposes of this book.

The process of building a data mart is identical to the process of building a data warehouse; only the scope is different. Therefore, while most companies have one or more marts and not a true warehouse, this book will use the term "data warehouse" as a generic term to cover both warehouses and marts. Because the process is the same for building both marts and warehouses, this chapter will describe that process and cover the aspects of the business intelligence process that build the foundation for delivering value to the organization.

The process of building a warehouse involves a number of steps, each of which contains an abundance of details. While entire books are written on the various aspects, this chapter will seek to distill the most important parts of the warehouse building process into an overview that will explain the importance of the decisions made here and how they can affect the delivery of business intelligence information through PerformancePoint Server and ProClarity. It is important to realize that building a data warehouse is not an easy task and many decisions must be made, some of which involve tradeoffs.

The overall flow of building a warehouse is generally described as shown in Figure 3-1. You can see that the data is located in its source systems, migrated into a relational data warehouse, and then turned into cubes for consumption by end user tools. Each part of this process contains complexities and subtleties that can greatly affect the usability and ultimate acceptance of the warehouse by business users. It is therefore critical that these pieces be taken seriously and that proper planning be done in each phase. The first phase will encompass several aspects of the system design and will lay the foundation for all the analysis that will be performed.

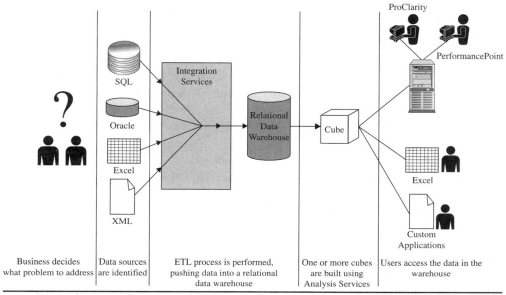

Figure 3-1   *The overall process of building a data warehouse*

Designing to Solve the Problem

An old joke in economics says that if you can teach a parrot to say, "Supply and demand," you've created an economist. The fact that economists consider this joke even remotely funny helps explain why economics is called "The Dismal Science," but it strikes close to home; if you could teach that parrot to say, "Facts and dimensions," you'd have a data warehousing guru.

Perhaps simply saying, "Facts and dimensions," isn't enough to make someone a data warehousing guru, but those two words flow through everything that is done in the data warehousing arena. Data warehousing is about solving business problems, so the first step is identifying the problem to be solved. At the very beginning, it's important to determine the business problem to be solved and the information it will take to provide a solution. In response to any problem, the question should be, "What needs to be seen, and how does it need to be analyzed?"

The *what* part of the question is usually a number of some sort. If there are quality control issues, what needs to be seen are the number of items produced, the defect rate, the cost to manufacture those items, and more. These numbers are called either *facts* or *measures* (the terms are normally used interchangeably.) Therefore, *what* the user needs to see is what is called a fact in the data warehousing sense. This is of great importance because the physical storage of information relies heavily on the facts that are identified during the analysis of a project.

After identifying what a user needs to see, the next question is *how* they need to see it. This doesn't mean how they need to view it on the screen, but how he or she needs to analyze and slice it. A single number for the defect rate is meaningless. What time period is covered by that number? What product does it represent? What assembly lines produce the most or fewest defects? What shift has higher and lower defect rates?

How an end user wants to analyze the data is a *dimension*. Time is the most common dimension; almost all data can be analyzed by time. Imagine the phrase, "I need to see defect rates by month." This sentence could be rewritten as, "I need to see <what> by <how>." The *what* portion is the fact, while the *how* is a dimension. Defect rates could be viewed by month, week, day, or even hour or minute if need be. This means that not only is time a dimension, but a dimension includes a series of values—in this case months, weeks, days, and so on.

Many facts are analyzed by more than one dimension. The phrase, "I need to see defect rates by month and assembly line" now includes two dimensions: Time and Assembly Line (or Location.) Imagine that this particular product is made in two plants, each containing multiple assembly lines. It might therefore be necessary to look at which plant has more defects, and then examine the assembly lines within that plant. It's also possible to examine all the assembly lines regardless of the plant to which they belong.

Dimensions and Dimension Tables

A dimension answers the *what* portion of a question, or how a consumer wants to analyze data. A dimension is normally stored in a single table, although this is not always the case, as will be discussed shortly.

Most dimensions are hierarchical. This means that they contain higher-level items which break down into lower-level items. Time is a perfect example: Years break down into Quarters, which break down into Months, which break down into Days, and so on. Note that there are no hard and fast rules here as to what the hierarchy should be. Some companies would use Years to Half Years to Quarters to Months to Days. Some solutions would require Weeks which might or might not roll up into Months.

Hierarchical structures occur in most dimensions. The previous example included a Location dimension in which Plants broke down into Assembly Lines. This Location dimension might actually include Country, then State/Province, then City, and finally Plant and Assembly Line. Figure 3-2 shows what the hierarchical dimensions might look like for the Time and Location dimensions for this simple example.

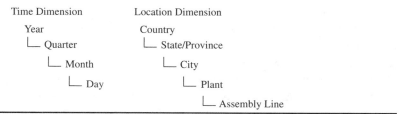

Figure 3-2 *Simple dimensions and their hierarchies*

So far only three terms have been discussed: facts, dimensions, and hierarchical dimensions. It's important to discuss two other terms: levels and members. A *level* is a position within a hierarchical dimension. In other words, the Time dimension has a Year level, a Quarter level, a Month level, and a Day level. The Location dimension has Country, State/Province, City, Plant, and Assembly Line levels. Actual data can exist at each level; for example, the data may include years 2006, 2007, and 2008. Each one of these is a *member*. Therefore, 2007 is a *member* at the year *level*. The easy way to think of this is that any actual data value is a member. Where it is located in the hierarchy is its level.

A single dimension can actually contain multiple hierarchies. One common example is a Time dimension, which may contain one hierarchy for a fiscal calendar and a different hierarchy for a Julian calendar. The hierarchies might have the same levels, but simply a different start date; the company might start its fiscal year on July 1, for example. On the other hand, the hierarchies might contain different levels. The fiscal hierarchy might contain Year, Quarter, Week, and Day, while the Julian calendar might contain Year, Quarter, Month, and Day. There is nothing wrong with either of these hierarchies; each one is simply a different way of analyzing the data.

The Structure of a Dimension Table

A dimension table is highly denormalized, which means it contains repeated data and full text descriptions, rather than key values which join to other tables. A dimension table contains columns which fully describe the item, and each row represents a unique item. For example, an individual product exists in a product hierarchy. The hierarchy consists of the levels Product Category, Product Subcategory, Product Group, and SKU. A specific computer mouse might be in the Product Category Hardware, the Product Subcategory Peripherals, the Product Group Mice, with the individual product existing at the SKU level. There are also other columns that more fully describe the product and might include information such as color, price, weight, height, width, product code, and more.

The values for such items as the Product Category and Product Subcategory are stored as text in the dimension table. This is the part of a dimension table that is denormalized; the data is repeated many times instead of minimizing storage using relational techniques. This may seem wasteful, but as will be shown later, the storage used by dimension tables is minor in the overall scheme of the warehouse.

Due to restrictions on page size, the columns of a single record are broken into multiple pieces. Table 3-1 shows several records as they would appear in the dimension table.

Note that in some cases, architects do normalize dimension tables somewhat. In this case, one separate table might be made for Product Category and another for Product Subcategory. This design is called a snowflake schema and is sometimes seen in large warehouses. There is little space savings overall because, as previously mentioned, dimension tables take up only a very small portion of the storage of a warehouse. In addition, the building of the cubes, to be described later, is slightly slower due to the need to perform joins. However, once the cube is built, there is no performance penalty from creating a snowflake schema.

Conformed Dimensions A special consideration is that of conformed dimensions. Since most companies start with data marts, they end up with a number of different structures for those different marts. One key element in bringing various marts together into a warehouse is to have the same dimension structure across those marts. The structure of the employee dimension in an HR data mart should match the structure of the employee dimension in the Sales data mart, for example. Therefore, it is important to

ProductKey	Product Category	Product Subcategory	Product Group	SKU
1	Hardware	Peripherals	Mice	759U
2	Hardware	Peripherals	Mice	A12Z
3	Hardware	Printers	Inkjet	CC84

Product Name	Weight	Color	Reorder Level	Dealer Price
FragBoy Gaming Mouse	6	Black	25	22.95
Zed Laser Mouse	8	Grey	50	11.25
Onega Color Inkjet	180	Grey	12	43.50

Table 3-1 *Three Records in a Product Dimension Table Show the Denormalization Common in a Warehouse.*

design dimensions up front not just for the current data mart, but with an eye toward handling an entire enterprise data warehouse.

This is true of any dimension that can be used across multiple data marts. Time, product, employee, and customer are just a few examples of dimensions that commonly are used across multiple data marts. Whether these tables are actually only stored once and linked to different fact tables, or whether they are physically stored multiple times, their structure should be the same. Using conformed dimensions prevent what are sometimes called "stovepipe data marts," or marts that stand alone in their own silo and cannot be integrated with other data marts.

Slowly Changing Dimensions   One of the biggest issues you'll encounter when dealing with dimensions is how to handle changes. Change is inevitable and here are two examples of this:

► A company tracks salespeople and the manager to which they report. Each salesperson is rewarded based on his or her sales, and each manager is rewarded based on the performance of the salespeople he or she manages. After a district realignment, some salespeople move from one manager to another. The salespeople need their history to go with them, but sales made under their previous manager should still be in that previous manager's numbers.

► A company wants to increase the profit on an item without increasing the price, so they decide to drop the item's size from 16 ounces to 14 ounces while maintaining the same price. Simply updating the field in the database from 16 to 14 makes it look like the product has always been 14 ounces and thus history is lost as to when the change occurred. So, is this a new item and the old one has ended, or is the size column simply changed?

As can be seen from these two simple examples, there's not necessarily an easy answer. These issues represent what are called *slowly changing dimensions*. They change slowly because people don't move from one manager to another with each transaction. Item sizes don't change with each transaction (if they do, there are other strategies, such as setting ranges of values and dropping each record into one of those buckets).

There are different strategies for dealing with slowly changing dimensions. By far the easiest way is what is called a Type I slowly changing dimension. With Type I, history is simply overwritten. In the case of the salesperson, they'd be tied to their new manager and it would look like they had always worked for this manager; all their history would now roll up to this new manager. This is great if the salesperson is a stellar performer and the manager is the one getting this person, but it's horrible for the manager losing this salesperson and having them replaced by a subpar performer.

In the case of a product, simply changing the size column in the database from 16 to 14 ounces makes it look like the size has always been 14 ounces. If sales decline because of the change, it's entirely up to an analyst looking at the data to remember when the change occurred and identify the change in size as an issue.

The advantage of Type I is clear: it's easy. No extra work is required. Data is changed and the primary key remains the same, so all history now reflects the current values as if they have never been different. The great disadvantage of Type I is also clear: history is lost. With Type I, it's impossible to credit a salesperson's sales to a previous manager, to determine when a product change was introduced, and so forth.

Another approach is the Type II slowly changing dimension. This type of dimension structure does maintain history, usually by versioning the record and then setting a start date and end date for each version. For example, a salesperson named Raju starts with a company on January 1, 2007 and works for Manager Bob. A year later, that salesperson is reassigned to Manager Maria. On the first record for salesperson Raju, the Start Date would be January 1, 2007 and the End Date would be January 1, 2008. A new record would be added for Raju that still maintained his employee ID (or some other key) but was now version 2, and had a Start Date of January 1, 2008 and no end date.

Sales would be tracked by the employee ID so that all of Raju's sales always belong to him. Raju's sales records also have the date on which they occurred, so that sales in 2007 roll up to Bob while sales in 2008 roll up to Maria. While simple on the surface, this can certainly complicate working with the data, because all queries must now look at the start and end dates for all of Raju's entries in the Employee dimension table.

The advantage of a Type II dimension is clear: history is preserved. Companies will always be able to track when the change occurred so that prior sales will still roll up to the proper manager. Product changes will be evident because a change will start a new record with a new start date.

The disadvantage of a Type II dimension is also clear: it's complicated. It makes storing, retrieving, and summing data much harder. Changes require an update to the existing record (to set the end date) and the insertion of a new record with a new version number and the start date. Taking multiple records that represent a single product or employee and making them appear as one to the end user can be a challenge.

There are other ways of handling slowly changing dimensions. There are Type III, and modifications of Type II and Type III. The actual mechanisms are beyond the scope of this book, as the goal is to show how to consume the data once the warehouse is built. Still, slowly changing dimensions are introduced here because many readers will be involved in the decision of how to store dimension data and track history, and an understanding of the tradeoffs is important.

Parent-Child Dimensions   A special type of dimension that is encountered frequently is the *parent-child dimension*, or p-c dimension for short. Product is an example of a normal, or non p-c, dimension. The Product Category level might contain members such as Hardware, Software, and so forth. The Product Subcategory level might contain members such as Peripherals, Motherboard, Video Cards, Games, Business Applications, and so on. The members at each level are unique; in other words, a Product Subcategory is not also a Category. An individual product is not also a Product Group. There is a clearly defined hierarchy and all individual products are found at the lowest level of that hierarchy, and products are found at higher levels.

Contrast that with a standard organizational chart. At the top is the President or Chief Executive Officer. Below that is a group of Vice Presidents. Next come Directors, Managers, and employees. However, one Vice President might have two Directors, another might have five, and a third Director might not have any. In addition, some parts of the business might have Managers and then Team Leaders, while other departments don't use team leaders. In other words, there's no well-defined hierarchy, so a table can't have a set number of columns to represent the levels in an organization.

In addition, everyone is an employee. The CEO is an employee and thus needs to be in the employee table. Each Vice President, Director, and Manager is also an employee. This means that there will be individual employees at each level of the hierarchy, and that the hierarchical structure is not well defined.

The classic way to handle this in a relational sense is to have an Employee ID field act as the primary key on the table. Then, in the same table, is a Manager ID field, which ties back to the Employee ID of that person's manager. The employee with either a blank Manager ID or a Manager ID that is the same as the Employee ID is the top of the hierarchy. Everyone else falls below that.

As an example, take a look at Figure 3-3. This shows a simple organization chart for a very small company. Note that some Vice Presidents don't have any Directors and that different chains contain a different number of levels.

Table 3-2 shows the relational structure that supports the organization chart from Figure 3-3. Note that a hierarchy of any level can be represented in a self-referencing table, which is a table in which one field is tied to another (usually the primary key).

Fact Tables

While dimension tables represent *how* users want to see data, fact tables represent the data users want to see. Facts are almost always numeric values such as dollar sales, unit sales, employee turnover, inventory levels, portfolio churn rate, and so forth. Often these values are fully additive, meaning that a value such as dollar sales

EmployeeID	Name	Title	ManagerID
1	Torrey	CEO	<null>
2	Hailey	Admin Assistant	1
3	Molly	VP Sales	1
4	Donald	VP Human Resources	1
5	Hannah	Director	3
6	Yoshi	Director	3
7	Raghu	Director	4
8	Mario	Team Leader	7
9	Benny	Benefits Admin	8
10	Patty	Payroll Clerk	8

Table 3-2 *The Organizational Chart in a Relational Table, Showing that the ManagerID Is Tied to the EmployeeID.*

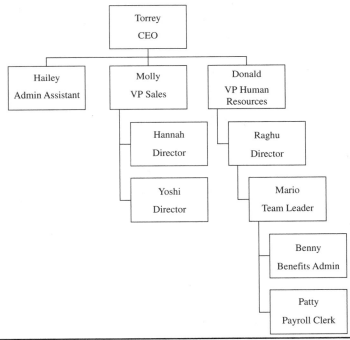

Figure 3-3 *A simplified organizational chart shows that the hierarchical structure of a parent-child dimension is not predictable as far as the number or consistency of levels.*

can be summed by any dimension and provide a valid value. Other facts, such as inventory levels, are semi-additive, meaning they cannot simply be summed across all dimensions. The ending inventory for the first quarter cannot be added to the ending inventory for the second quarter to give a valid inventory level for the first half of the year. Instead, an average can be used, or simply the ending inventory for the second quarter.

Facts, also called measures, reside in a fact table. The fact table is actually fully normalized by nature, unlike the denormalized dimension tables. Typically, dimension tables have single-field primary keys, often of an integer data type. Each fact represents a unique combination of items for the lowest level of detail for each dimension.

As an example, assume three simple dimensions: Time, Product, and Customer. The Time dimension goes to the Day level, the Product dimension goes to the SKU level, and the Customer dimension goes to the Customer level. This means that the level of detail, or *granularity*, of the fact table is by customer, day, and product. Therefore, a single record contains a particular item sold to a particular customer on a particular day. If the customer ordered the same item on the same day in two or more different orders, the products will be summed to a single record.

Each fact record will contain a foreign key back to the dimension tables, and these foreign keys make up the primary key of the fact table; after the key fields are the measures themselves. Thus, the fact table is often made up entirely, or nearly so, of numeric fields. This means that the fact table is relatively narrow, since storing numbers requires less space than storing descriptive strings. While the fact table may be narrow, it is often extremely large as far as the number of records being held. In many cases, the fact table makes up ninety eight percent or more of the total storage used by the relational warehouse.

To illustrate the sizing of a warehouse, consider the same three dimension tables: Time, Product, and Customer. If tracking 10 years of data with a daily grain, this means that the Time table will hold approximately 3652 records. The company might have 10,000 products and sell to 100,000 customers. While not every customer will buy every product every day, imagine that they did: the fact table will hold 3652 × 10,000 × 100,000 records, or 3,652,000,000,000, or 3.65 trillion records. Even at one tenth of one percent of this value, the fact table would still hold almost four billion records. These are indeed impressive numbers.

Because fact tables are often so large, most organizations estimate the storage requirements for their relational data warehouse simply by estimating the number of rows in the fact table, multiplying it by the size of the record, and then adding a percentage for the indexes. This typically works well, because the dimension tables are relatively small compared to the fact table, and most warehouse architects tend to overestimate the number of records in order to build in a cushion. Strategies for backing up and restoring large fact tables are critical, but are beyond the scope of this book.

A relational warehouse is often called a star schema, simply because of the look of the schema. In the middle sits a fact table with one or more measures. The fact table has a join back to each dimension table, which often surround the fact table in diagrams. The practice of placing the fact table at the center of the schema diagram is merely tradition, but it helps those familiar with relational warehousing quickly grasp the structure of the warehouse. In some cases a dimension table is normalized somewhat, so that a Product dimension is broken into Product, Product Category, and Product Subcategory tables. This structure is called a snowflake schema because the dimension tables branch out, much like the ice crystals of a snowflake. Figure 3-4 shows a simple star schema.

In many data warehouses, there are multiple fact tables. This may be due to several factors, two of which are relatively common. First, different fact tables may contain different dimensions. A fact table that supports manufacturing will have a product dimension and an assembly line dimension. A fact table that supports sales will have a product dimension and a customer dimension. Assembly line has nothing to do with

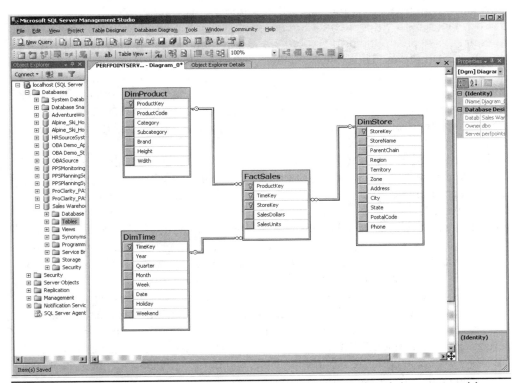

Figure 3-4 *A simple star schema showing the fact table and related dimension tables*

sales, and the customer has nothing to do with manufacturing. Note that these fact tables should, however, have a conformed product dimension table joined to them.

Second, fact tables may be at differently levels of granularity. Fact tables that contain actual data are typically at lower levels of detail, such as Day. Fact tables designed to hold forecast or budget values are often at higher levels of detail, such as Month or Quarter. Therefore, while both the sales and forecast fact tables contain a Time dimension, they have a different grain and therefore cannot be a single fact table.

One aspect of fact tables that breaks with traditional normalization techniques is that calculated fields are often included as some of the measures. Typically, calculated fields are not stored in a relational table, but there is nothing wrong with storing calculated fields in a fact table. In some cases this can improve performance by calculating the values ahead of time instead of requiring the cube engine to calculate the values on the fly. Calculations in the cube engine will be mentioned later in this chapter.

Extracting, Transforming, and Loading Data

After designing the relational data warehouse to support the needs of the business, the next step is to identify the data sources, extract the data, transform data as needed, and then load the data into the relational warehouse. This process is generically called extraction, transformation, and loading, or ETL. There are many ETL tools available and while most can connect to all the common data sources, the real differences lie in their abilities to control the flow of data and provide transformations to the data.

Data transformation is required because data stored in disparate source systems may be stored in different formats, with different codes, or using different data types. For example, one system might store a Yes as 1 and a No as 0, while another system may store the strings 'Y' and 'N.' If data is pulled from two systems and a Yes/No field is needed, then the data must be transformed so that it is consistent in the warehouse. Data consistency is one of the cornerstones of a data warehouse; all data must be in the same format for analysis to be effective.

Other issues arise when considering items such as currencies. In a global business, there are often source systems in each country recording receivables, and normally the business systems store these receivables in the local currency. If a business has branches in London, Paris, Tokyo, and New York, it's likely that data is stored in Pounds, Euros, Yen, and US Dollars. In building the warehouse, sales measured in Yen cannot simply be added to sales in US Dollars in order to get non-European sales. Instead, the data must be transformed by applying some form of currency conversion to the data before storing it in the warehouse. Whether this is done by using a day-to-day exchange rate table, the average exchange rate over a period of time, or any other method, is strictly up to the business. Therefore, business requirements often come into play during the design phase of the ETL process.

While this section on ETL will be relatively brief, there is one point that is absolutely essential: ETL often consumes the majority of the effort in building a data mart or warehouse. Some projects spend up to 80 percent of the total time in the ETL phase. This is due to a number of factors, including the complexity of identifying and extracting back end data, applying complex transformations to data to meet business rules, handling data for slowly changing dimensions, and working with dirty data. Most warehousing projects continue to tweak and maintain their ETL process long after the warehouse is in production; be sure to include ongoing maintenance in any project and budget projections.

ETL Using SQL Server Integration Services

Microsoft SQL Server 2005 ships with a robust, enterprise-scale ETL tool called SQL Server Integration Services, or SSIS. SSIS creates what are called *packages*, and each package contains some piece of the ETL process. Imagine writing a book; an author could open up a word processor and type the entire book in a single document. Instead, most often, the author creates a separate file for each chapter because it is easier to maintain and edit. Similarly, a single SSIS package could contain the entire ETL process, but typically it does not. Instead, the developers creating the ETL process create numerous packages, each providing a few steps of the entire process. This makes the entire ETL flow easier to maintain and allows for much better reuse. The flow can be changed as necessary and the different packages can be run in different orders depending on the needs of the incoming data.

Each package is broken up into to major areas: *control flow* and *data flow*. Control flow is what it sounds like: it controls the overall flow of this particular package. In the control flow area, there are containers and task which can be added to the flow; tasks do something specific while containers group together multiple tasks. For example, there are tasks that send emails (possibly due to completion or an error condition), run other packages, execute SQL statements, FTP files, and more. There are containers for looping through the tasks placed in them and containers that ensure tasks are run in a particular sequence. As one task is completed, it can then flow to other tasks, and it may flow differently based on whether the task succeeded or failed.

One of the tasks used most often in the Control Flow is the Data Flow Task, which opens another editor window. Once again, the developer is presented with many controls. There are controls to connect to both source and destination data sources, whether those sources are relational databases, XML files, Excel spreadsheets, text documents, and so forth. In addition to the data sources and destinations, there are many controls for data transformations. These include such items as conditional splits, fuzzy lookups, merging, sorting, handling slowly changing dimensions, and so forth.

A simple example of an SSIS package for a warehouse refresh might be one in which the first part of the flow executes SQL tasks to empty the star schema tables. After this step, data flow tasks are called. One task might grab data from a particular dimension table and load that data. Another data flow might pull data from multiple sources, convert some columns to a standard format, and place that data in a dimension table. Another data flow task might handle a slowly changing product dimension. Finally, a data flow task might load the fact table, looking for any records with key violations. Any bad records might be placed in a temporary table and the control flow could email the data warehouse administrator that some records failed to load properly. An example of a simple flow can be seen in Figure 3-5.

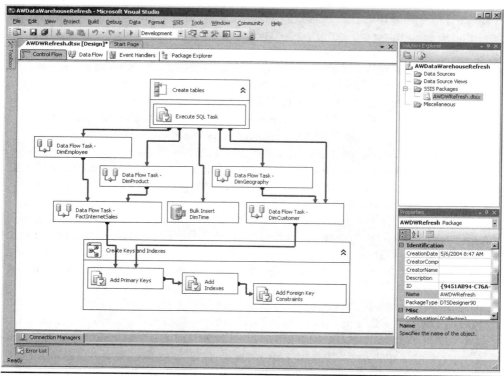

Figure 3-5   *A simple SSIS package that empties the warehouse and reloads it from scratch.*

Data Quality

Unfortunately, no company has completely clean data. The old saying is that as soon as you make something idiot proof, the universe creates a bigger idiot. While this is likely true, it's also a fact that many applications allow bad data into the system in the first place. Having bad data then makes analysis much more difficult.

Here is a real world example: A company had a large presence in the city of Ann Arbor, Michigan. One of the systems asked customers for their address and the input box for the city was a free-form text field. People living in the city of Ann Arbor found (at last count) fourteen different ways to spell Ann Arbor. These included Anne Arbor, AnnArbor, AnneArbor, Ann Arbour, and so forth. The easy solution going forward would be to fix the application so that the city was chosen from a drop-down box. Unfortunately, the owners of that application were busy and didn't see it as a priority. Even if it had been fixed, however, this did nothing to handle the existing data that was incorrect.

At this point, the business could have gone in and cleaned up all the source data. Instead, they chose to do the cleanup in their ETL process. The source system could continue to hold misspellings of Ann Arbor, but the data in the warehouse would be consistent. This was important because they wanted to analyze sales by city and when someone chose Ann Arbor, they wanted all sales for that area to come up without having to know to add in many misspellings of the city name.

The ETL process was written to handle all known misspellings of Ann Arbor. Periodically, a new one would appear and the ETL would have to be updated. Note that today, this would have been much easier thanks to the Fuzzy Lookup transformation in SSIS, but at the time the customer had to do everything manually.

Given that there are such data quality issues inside any organization, it's important for the business to come up with the rules for handling such issues. It's appealing to be able to say that everything will be fixed in the warehouse, but sometimes the effort to do so outweighs the benefits. Imagine a system in which bad records are flagged as unknown. If the estimate to truly fix the data is 2000 man hours, and less than one-tenth of one percent of the data is bad, is it worth the cost to fix? On the other hand, if 40 percent of the data is bad, fixing the data probably has a much higher priority.

Articles, whitepapers, and books can be written about data quality and the issues around it. The fact is that most organizations have bad data and still allow bad data to flow into the system. There are ways to ameliorate this but eliminating it entirely is often more costly than just living with some level of dirty data. It's important for business users to understand why bad data is in the system and what options exist to fix it, and why it might be necessary to see some percentage of data listed as unknown.

Building Cubes

When data warehousing was originally born, the star schema *was* the data warehouse. In fact, it's still often called the relational data warehouse. There's nothing wrong with this at all, and many companies query directly against the relational warehouse. The star schema is designed for the speed of retrieval, so running reports against it is certainly acceptable.

One thing that star schemas may not have, however, are summary levels. Imagine that a particular schema has a daily grain, and that there are two billion fact records in the fact table, representing 4 years of sales. If a customer wants to see yearly sales totals, this requires performing a Sum across all two billion records, summing approximately 500 million records at a time in order to get the values for each year. This can be an expensive operation on large warehouses, especially when there are many users of the system.

One solution was to preaggregate the data in the relational system. Remember that in a star schema the concern with normalization is gone, so adding calculated data is acceptable. Adding preaggregated data could be accomplished by setting some dummy values. For example, if the Year was 2007 but the Quarter was 5, the Month was 'Z' and the Day was 99, that record represented the year total for 2007. If the Year was 2007, the Quarter was 1, the Month was 'Z' and the Day was 99, that record represented the first quarter totals for 2007.

This magic number approach could get messy quickly, so many people opted to build summary tables. There was a year table, a quarter table, a month table, and then the "real" fact table at the daily grain. This had the advantage of not having messy codes, but queries had to be much smarter and know when to get different values from different tables. In addition, if there were monthly totals for each individual product and customer, even the summary tables could be quite large and require a significant amount of extra disk space.

This is where cube building engines come in. Cubes are simply a different way of storing data. Different engines work differently, but the focus here is on SQL Server Analysis Services, also called just Analysis Services, SSAS, or AS. Analysis Services does several things when creating a cube. First, it reads the data from the dimension tables and the fact table. It stores the dimension and fact records in a binary format, completely independent of the relational database engine. As it stores records, it compresses them so that less disk storage is required. How much it compresses them depends on many factors, but a general rule of thumb is that a cube will normally take up about 30–40 percent of the size of the relational warehouse. Therefore, a 1TB relational data warehouse would translate to a cube of approximately 300–400GB.

The reason a cube is stored in a binary format, at least with Analysis Services 2005, is so the data can be retrieved extremely quickly. The binary format is designed for extremely fast retrieval of data. Not only is the format designed to be read quickly and return data as fast as possible, the compression means that reads need to access less disk, so that actual reading off the drive is faster than for uncompressed data.

Part of what the cube can do as well is preaggregate the data. Cubes can store higher level summarizations of data, meaning that requests for summarized data can be returned very quickly. A cube that stores sales data at a daily level may contain aggregated data that stores sales at the month, quarter, and year level, for example. Being able to retrieve these aggregations means that the engine does not have to spend time calculating the values on the fly.

This means that cubes have two major advantages over storing the same information in a relational database: first, they are built for extremely fast retrieval of data and second, the inclusion of preaggregated data means that queries for higher-level values is extremely fast. Cubes have other benefits as well, including the ability to perform complex queries that contain a variety of dimensions, also known as multidimensional queries. Cubes can also contain other features such as:

- ▶ Key Performance Indicators (KPIs), which will be discussed in detail in Chapter 4

- ▶ Perspectives, a feature which helps narrow the scope of the cube for particular users

- ▶ Translations, so that a single cube can support multiple languages

- ▶ Actions, one feature of which allows a cube to tie to external programs or web sites

- ▶ Mining models, which support a wide variety of data mining techniques

Cubes are clearly very powerful tools for performing analysis and for quickly responding to user queries. Designing and building the cube is therefore critical to the success of the overall project. Building the cube takes a number of steps and requires a number of decisions to be made. An overview of the process is described in the following section.

Steps to Cube Design

Designing a cube for Analysis Services 2005 is done using Business Intelligence Development Studio, often called BI Dev Studio or just BIDS. BIDS is actually

Visual Studio 2005 with project templates that support BI objects such as Analysis Services projects (cubes, mining models, and so forth), Reporting Services projects, and more. If a customer doesn't have Visual Studio, the installation of the SQL Server client tools installs BIDS, which is Visual Studio 2005 with just those project templates. If the customer already has Visual Studio 2005 installed, the BI project templates are added to their existing Visual Studio installation. A link will appear on the start menu to BIDS, but there is really only one copy of Visual Studio installed on the computer.

Before venturing into the actual tools and techniques of building a cube, it's important to point out that technically, a cube can be built from a full-normalized, OLTP database. Nothing in the tools prevent cubes from being built from normalized schemas, yet this chapter just spent time discussing how to create the dimension and fact tables for a star schema. There's actually a very good reason for this.

While a cube can be built from a normalized schema, there are many reasons why creating a star schema is a best practice. These reasons include, but are not limited to the following:

▶ Data for a warehouse is often pulled from multiple sources, so performing an ETL process into a single location allows for the transformations that make data consistent.

▶ Relational data warehouses can be queried using relational reporting tools and performance is often faster than querying a normalized schema.

▶ Building cubes off a product OLTP structure can dramatically slow the performance of the OLTP system.

▶ OLTP systems are real-time and cubes are usually a snapshot in time, meaning that the cube might not match the underlying data soon after it is processed.

▶ Star schemas are designed using the same concepts as cubes (measures and dimensions), so their structure easily translates to cubes, as well as being more readable by humans.

Therefore, even though a cube can be built off an OLTP database, the best practice is to perform an ETL process and populate a star schema. This book will assume that a star schema does exist and that cubes are built from this star schema.

Starting a Project

In order to start a project, a new project is created in BIDS using the Analysis Services Project template as shown in Figure 3-6. The New Project dialog box allows for three items to be entered: the Name, Location, and Solution Name.

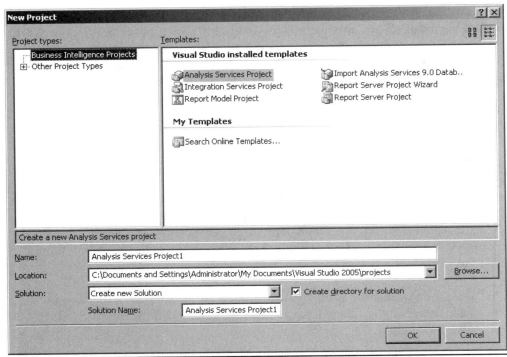

Figure 3-6 *The New Project dialog box shows the beginning of the creation of a project that will eventually hold cubes, dimensions, mining models, and other objects.*

The name is the name of the project, while the solution name is the name of the solution, where a solution holds one or more projects. In the case of cubes this could be a one-to-one relationship, but often the solution also holds the Integration Services project which contains the ETL used to populate the cube. The solution might also hold a Report Server project that contains reports that access the cube and star schema. The projects can be opened individually, but placing them all in a solution allows developers to open one file and have access to all projects and files of the warehouse. This is important because many other warehousing products view ETL, cube building and reporting as completely separate and often have completely different tools to perform those actions.

The location is simply the storage location for the files that define this project. This is often a local development machine and has nothing to do with the server on which the cubes will reside. This means that work can be done offline, without requiring a connection to the actual server that will be running the project. Later, the project will be published to a server where the cube will reside.

The next step in the process is to add one or more data sources. A data source represents a connection to one or more sources of data for the cube. Often, there is a single data source, which points to the star schema as was described in the previous section. The star schema is supposed to the single source of information for the cube, so it makes sense that this would be the only connection. In some cases, however, customers may have multiple data sources, and these sources might store their data in different formats. For example, some of the data may be in SQL Server with additional data in Microsoft Access and Oracle.

There are many options when it comes to setting up data sources, including the specific provider to use and the different types of security. These issues are beyond the scope of this particular book, although security will be revisited in Chapter 8. For the rest of this discussion, there will be a single data source that has been set up to a relational data warehouse hosted in SQL Server.

The Data Source View

One of the most powerful concepts in an Analysis Services project is that of the Data Source View, or DSV. A DSV is a logical construct that represents how the structure of the underlying database in the data source should look to Analysis Services. In its simplest form, it is merely a copy of the schema from the data source. Developers can simply add all the tables from the database in the data source and be done. The database schema is read, the joins between tables are automatically added to the DSV, and then the cube can be built.

The DSV has far greater capabilities than simply allowing a copy of the underlying database schema. First, not all the tables have to be brought in, as a subset will often suffice. This is especially true when building a data mart for a particular group. If the relational warehouse contains more than that group cares to see, the DSV would only include the tables relevant to that particular group.

Figure 3-7 shows part of the wizard that steps developers through the process of creating a DSV, using the Adventure Works DW sample database that ships with SQL Server 2005. Remember that with Analysis Services 2005, a single cube can contain multiple fact tables. This helps in situations such as recording sales at a daily level, but having a forecast or budget table at the month or quarter level. Figure 3-7 shows that there are two fact tables in this cube: FactSalesQuota and FactResellerSales. A subset of these dimensions has been added as well, in order to keep this example simple.

Note also in Figure 3-7 that there are three tables dealing with products: DimProduct, DimProductCategory, and DimProductSubcategory. This is an example of snowflaking, as described earlier in this chapter. These snowflaked tables will be addressed shortly in order to simplify the view.

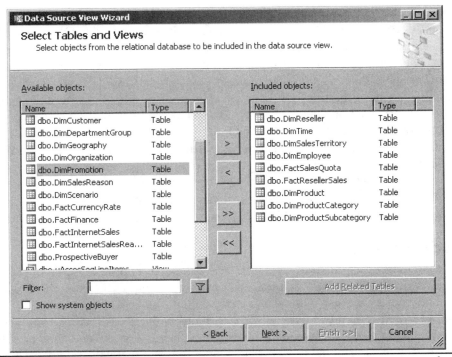

Figure 3-7   *The Data Source View Wizard steps developers through the process of creating a DSV, a logical view of the underlying physical database schema.*

After choosing the tables and views that will make up the DSV, the developer is presented with a graphical image of the DSV. This image is a schema diagram that matches the tables and views chosen in the wizard, and may look extremely complicated, depending on the number of items selected when creating the DSV. Figure 3-8 shows the DSV generated for the tables chosen in Figure 3-7.

Note that this doesn't look like a typical star schema because there are two fact tables in it. DSV diagrams become wildly more complex as tables are added, especially when there are multiple fact tables. Fortunately, there is a way to create new diagrams that show only a subset of the tables. A good practice is to create one diagram per fact table. Each of those diagrams will then show that fact table and just the dimensions upon which that fact table relies. This means that developers will have a series of easier-to-use star schemas to work with as the process unfolds.

DSVs have additional features as well, two of which are the Named Query and the Named Calculation. Named queries act like a view in a relational database; they allow for the building a query that will act as a table. The underlying schema here is

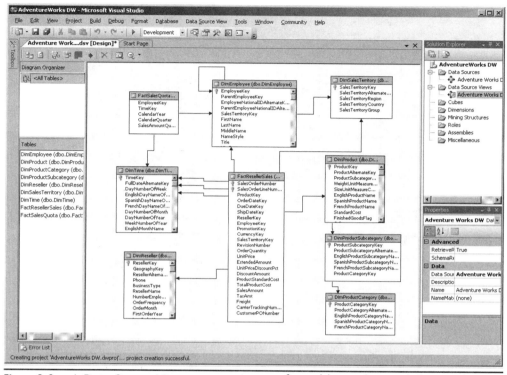

Figure 3-8   *A Data Source View representing two fact tables and several dimension tables*

a snowflake schema wherein the product dimension is made up of three tables. It is a simple matter to write a query that combines those tables into a single view or, in DSV terms, a named query. In other words, writing a standard relational query, and then naming it, makes it appear on the DSV just like any other table.

Figure 3-9 shows the same DSV as before, but the three product tables have been replaced with a single named query called DimProductStar. DimProductStar contains the columns from DimProduct, DimProductSubcategory, and DimProductCategory in a single virtual table. Creating a named query changes absolutely nothing in the underlying database; it is merely a logical construct in the DSV. Named queries are easy to identify because the symbol next to the name looks like two small tables as opposed to a single large table icon used for physical tables.

Named calculations are similar to named queries in that they are logical constructs that exist only in the DSV. However, named calculations appear as a column in an existing table. As the name suggests, these new columns may be used to perform

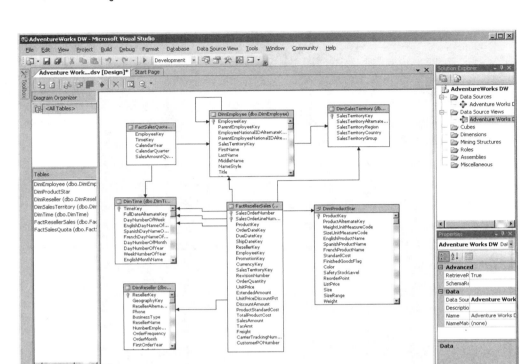

Figure 3-9 *A new view of the DSV showing a named query has been used to replace the product dimension snowflake tables, and a named calculation has been added as well.*

mathematical calculations, or they may be used to concatenate strings. For example, the fact table might store the price of the item sold as well as its cost, so a simple calculation to get the gross profit on that item could be included in the fact table in the DSV.

In the case of this example, the named calculation is being used for string concatenation. The DimEmployee table has three columns for a person's name: FirstName, MiddleName, and LastName. The named calculation shown in Figure 3-9 combines all the names into a single column called FullName. The fact that FullName is a named calculation is easy to see by the small calculator icon placed next to it.

The DSV is very powerful. Named queries can be added that, in effect, create new tables. Calculations can be added to existing tables, which can speed up cube queries later because the numbers are actually materialized in the cube itself. Tables in the

DSV can be joined or joins can be removed. Items can be renamed to friendlier names, and more. The DSV is very powerful and it is critically important because a cube can only be built from a DSV. Cubes have no knowledge of any data sources other than a DSV.

Designing the Cube and Dimensions

Once the DSV has been completed, the next step is to build the cube and dimensions. In Analysis Services 2000, there was no choice but to build the dimensions first and then build the cube. Analysis Services 2005 allows for the creation of the cube without first creating the dimensions. Instead, the cube building wizard can create the dimensions are part of the process. If it sounds tempting to simply walk through the cube building wizard and let it create the dimensions, it is. Note, however, that no matter how well the wizard does its work, it's almost a certainty that the dimensions will require some tweaks after they have been generated.

Building a new cube can be as simple as launching a wizard. Cubes only understand DSVs, so the wizard will ask what DSV to use in creating the cube. Upon examining the dimensions in the DSV, the wizard can try to build attributes and hierarchies for the dimensions. There is nothing wrong with this, but by default nearly every column in the dimension table will become an attribute, and this can lead to many attributes that may confuse end users. Secondly, the hierarchies as determined by the wizard are often incomplete or just plain silly, so fixes are often required there.

The Cube Wizard, as it is called, reads the DSV and tries to determine which tables are dimension tables and which are fact tables. Note that the wizard makes no use of the table names, so having the words "fact" and "dim" in the title does nothing to help the wizard. Instead, it looks at the relationships and tries to determine which tables belong in each category. It's also more complex than this, because a single table can act as both a fact and dimension table, but that is a discussion beyond the scope of this book.

After choosing the facts and dimensions, it is often necessary to map a Time dimension. Time or Date dimensions exist in almost every cube. There are certain functions built into Analysis Services that only work when a dimension has been identified as a Time dimension. These functions are useful for performing actions such as period over period growth calculations, moving averages, and so forth. The ability to map a Time dimension to expected time values is flexible and includes both calendar and fiscal categories.

The wizard next tries to determine the measures that exist in the fact tables. Normally the wizard does a decent job identifying the measures by looking in the fact tables for numeric columns. Sometimes it includes some of the foreign keys as measures because they are numeric fields, but key values are normally just automatically incrementing values, so making them measures doesn't make sense. Fortunately, any fields chosen as measures that shouldn't be there are easy enough to remove before continuing. The wizard also automatically adds a count to the measures for each fact table.

By default, each fact table has its measures placed into its own Measure Group. A measure group is a collection of one or more measures, and by default each fact table has its own measure group. One exception is for measures that are distinct counts; for example, a store might have 10,000 shoppers during a week, but some people come in multiple times, so the number of unique shoppers might only be 7500. Distinct counts are put in a separate measure group by default for performance reasons.

After selecting the measures the cube wizard next tries to detect hierarchies in the dimensions. As previously mentioned, this is an area in which the wizard often has problems. The good news is that the warehouse developer can modify the hierarchy design at this stage or after the wizard has completed.

The wizard not only tries to determine hierarchies, but determines attributes as well. Attributes are those items that help describe a dimension item. For example, a hierarchy for a customer might be Country, State/Province, City, and finally Customer. However, a significant amount of additional information might be stored for a customer, such as age, height, weight, income level, education level, and more. A hierarchy that goes from Country to State/Province to Height probably doesn't make sense, and neither would going from Education Level to Weight. Therefore, many of these attributes are not part of a hierarchy but are still valid for analysis.

The good news is that with these attributes, end users have the flexibility to analyze by nearly anything by simply selecting the attribute when constructing a query. The bad news is that users can be quickly overwhelmed when presented with a list of dozens of attributes from which to choose. This gets back to the discussion in Chapter 1; know the users. Most users would want to see just the hierarchies, because they provide a nice guided path through the data. Analysts would likely want to see everything and have complete flexibility to create their own queries, even if those queries involved many single attributes not included in any hierarchy.

After completing the wizard, the cube is shown in a manner similar to that in Figure 3-10. Notice that the measures are shown along the left-hand side, broken into measure groups that match the fact tables. Also note that main window with the cube diagram is labeled Data Source View at the top. This is unfortunate and leads to much confusion among those new to Analysis Services. This is not the same as the data source view itself, but is just a representation of the tables from the DSV.

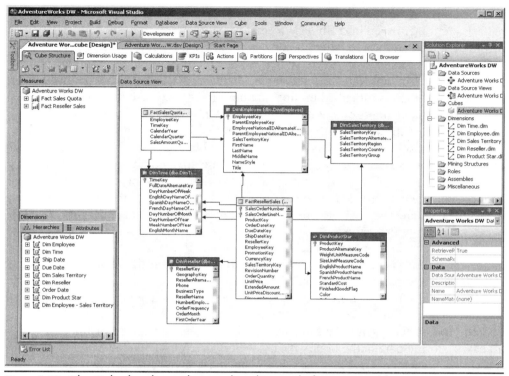

Figure 3-10 *The Cube has been designed and is ready for any modifications necessary.*

Cube Deployment and Processing

Once the cube has been designed, the files defining the cube exist only on the developer's machine. The next step is to deploy the project to a server. Whether this is a test or production server is immaterial for this discussion. The important point is that the files are transferred to a server on which Analysis Services is running. Deployment actually creates the cubes, dimensions, mining models, roles, and other objects that make up an Analysis Services project when the data is copied to the server. All of these objects are in what is called a database in Analysis Services. A single Analysis Services database may contain any number of cubes and dimensions.

Simply deploying a project from the developer's machine to a server only creates the objects, such as the dimensions and cube. It does not copy any data from the source systems and therefore, deployment by itself does not make a cube useful to others. After deployment, there is a step called processing. Processing a cube means that the cube performs a series of queries to read dimension and fact data. Data records are transformed into a binary format for storage by Analysis Services. After records are read and stored, aggregations and indexes are built.

The time it takes to process a cube depends on many factors, the main one being the size of the fact tables in the star schema database. Microsoft is often considered to have one of the fastest cube building engines on the market, but extremely large cubes can still take hours and hours to process. Don't forget, too, that processing copies data from the star schema and stores it in a new format; this means that the data is a snapshot in time and updates to the star schema will not be reflected until the cube is reprocessed. The good news is that there are a number of processing techniques. One is a full process, in which all existing data is removed from the cube and it is completely reloaded. Another only adds new records to the cube. There are others as well, and they exist to cover different needs in different situations. There is also a technology in Analysis Services 2005 called Proactive Caching, which allows a cube to update an in-memory cache instead of having to physically reprocess the cube. This feature is designed to allow cubes to be more real-time than those that are processed in the traditional, scheduled fashion.

There are also several different storage formats, such as leaving all data in the relational engine. The specifics of these are beyond the scope of the book, but the overall process is basically the same as described here. Understand that in almost all cases, storing data in the binary Analysis Services format, called MOLAP for Multidimensional OLAP, is the fastest way to retrieve data for reporting and analysis.

Delivering Data to Consumers

After the cube is built, the final step is to deliver data to the consumers. This is where, oddly enough, many companies fall down. They build a warehouse and then wonder why no one uses it. Most companies make one, or both, of the following two mistakes:

► They provide inadequate or suboptimal tools for working with the data in a cube.

► They overcomplicate the cube so much that few people can use it.

Most organizations have the Information Technology (IT) department run their data warehousing projects. While IT departments know technology, they often think differently from others in the business. What would appear to be a rather logical cube design to an IT person may appear wildly confusing to end users in human resources, finance, manufacturing, and so on. Therefore, it is critical to understand the end users, their technical skills, and most importantly, the data that they want and how they want to work with it.

The analytics portion of PerformancePoint Server, covered in version 1.0 mainly by ProClarity, is extremely powerful and perfect for analysts. However, without a set of precanned reports, many end users are bewildered by the prospect of navigating a cube, and they often don't have time to perform their own detailed analysis anyway.

Therefore, before starting a BI project, it is critical to identify the users, their need for the data, and the tools that can used to achieve these goals. Chapter 1 discussed the different types of users and tools that fit most of those situations, so it is important to remember those points moving forward. In addition to those points, consider creating hierarchies which guide users down a path that reflects the way they break up the world, their customers, their products, and so forth. If a group is used to looking at products by category, subcategory, brand, and SKU, then by all means create a hierarchy that contains that exact structure and create simple reports that allow them to drill down that hierarchy simply by clicking. For those users, hiding many of the individual attributes keeps them from feeling overwhelmed when they see a huge list of possible values from which to choose.

Summary

Building a data warehouse is not necessarily a simple procedure. After choosing a business problem to address and solve, the next step is to identify the sources for the data and construct a relational data warehouse to hold a consolidated, consistent version of that data. Next, an ETL process is created to move and transform the data from its source systems into the star schema. Remember that the ETL process is often the bulk of the effort, sometimes accounting for up to 80 percent of the time on the overall project. Realize too that while the entire project will likely require ongoing maintenance, it is the ETL that is often visited repeatedly as new cases of bad data are identified and addressed.

After the ETL portion is completed, the cube itself is designed. If the design on the star schema was good, the cube design is nearly done, at least from a high level. The DSV provided by Analysis Services is a powerful tool that allows even a well-designed star schema to be extended by renaming tables and columns, adding calculated columns, adding named queries to act as view, and so forth. The DSV step is necessary as cubes can only see DSVs as their data source.

Once the DSV is ready, the cube is built. The basic structure of the cube is similar or identical to the DSV, but then the cube can be greatly expanded. Dimensions can have hierarchies added to them. Cubes can contain calculations that would be difficult or impossible to do using relational tables. Cubes may have key performance indicators, actions, perspectives, and other features available only to cubes; features that are simply not available in relational databases.

Finally, a cube must be processed in order to read the data from the source system or systems and store it in a structure built for the speed of retrieval. Aggregations are often calculated at this time. Many organizations perform nightly or weekly updates, although monthly updates are not uncommon, nor is it uncommon to perform incremental updates throughout the day if the need for timely data is high.

Finally, once the cube is built, consumers are ready to begin accessing the data and reaping the benefits of the BI project. The rest of this book is dedicated to the tools that allow end users to access the data and make sense of it. The next chapter will introduce scorecards and key performance indicators, techniques often used by higher level management, but accessible to anyone.

Scorecards and Key Performance Indicators

As I discussed in the first chapter, there are many different categories of business users. These various users may need different information or they may need the same information as other users, but need it presented using different techniques. One of the most common ways to present information to users is through the use of a *scorecard*. Scorecards represent summarizations of a large amount of data, created specifically to provide a quick snapshot of the overall health of the business or an individual department. Scorecards are usually aimed at business decision makers, although they can be used at any level of the organization.

A scorecard used in business is similar to the report cards that students take home to show their parents. Parents are able to look at a single, simple piece of paper that shows the grade average in each class. Parents do not have to pour through a stack of individual assignments, checking the grade for each one and calculating the averages on their own. Instead, in a single glance, a parent can see the scores in all of their child's classes and get an immediate feel for how well their son or daughter is doing.

School report cards also might include additional information, such as the student's ability to get along with others, their attitude in class, and so forth. Similarly, business scorecards may show the health and trend for that particular metric, not just its value. This means that a quick glance gives a view of the overall business health and the ways that the various metrics are trending. These metrics that are tracked are called Key Performance Indicators (KPIs).

Key Performance Indicators

Key Performance Indicators, or KPIs, are the metrics shown in a scorecard. There are different types of scorecards, which will be discussed later in this chapter, but all the scorecards will contain KPIs. KPIs are the primary drivers of a business and are similar to the measures discussed in Chapter 3. In fact, many measures are also used as KPIs, although KPIs have additional attributes. It is important to understand the difference between KPIs and measures and how they are used.

KPIs and Measures

Many of the KPIs described so far, and in fact many KPIs in general, are the same as the measures that will likely be in the data warehouse. An easy example is sales: almost any organization wants to know its gross revenue. This is usually the most common aspect of measuring any business, to the point that companies are often talked about as a "five billion dollar company" or in some other dollar terms. The size of companies is almost always measured in terms of revenue.

Assume for a moment that a company had sales last month of $10M (where 'M' stands for million.) Here, sales is clearly a measure, because it has a value, because it's for a specific period of time, and because it is for all products, all customers, and so forth. This is a value that could easily be found in a cube. However, is $10M in sales last month *good* or *bad*? By itself, the measure provides no information about the quality of the number. And it is this quality, or health, of the number that first separates a KPI from a measure.

While not technically required, almost all KPIs have an indicator as to the health of the current number. This is typically done by assigning not just a value to the KPI, but also a target. In this case, the value is the current, or actual, value of $10M. If the target was $8M, most people would find this to be a very good number. If, on the other hand, the target was $15M, this particular KPI would probably look rather bad.

When displaying the Sales KPI on a scorecard, the scorecard might show only the value or both the value and the target. In addition, the scorecard will usually show an indicator of the health of that particular KPI. These indicators vary from traffic lights with Green, Yellow, and Red indicators, to faces that smile or frown, to thermometers, and so forth. Several different indicators can be seen in Figure 4-1. Realize that it is the indicator, not the numbers, that make scorecards easy to grasp quickly, and it is therefore important to use clear, easily understandable indicators.

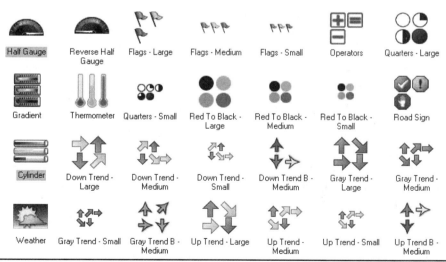

Figure 4-1 *An example of different indicators that can be used for KPIs. The goal is to create an image which clearly conveys the health of a KPI immediately.*

NOTE

In the United States, and possibly in other countries, indicators are not supposed to be based solely on color. Approximately 7 percent of men suffer from some form of color blindness and, in its most common form, may be unable to distinguish between red and green. Therefore, indicators should not only have colors but also shapes or positions which identify them.

KPIs have an indicator of their relative health against a target, but this target may be set in several different ways. It may simply be a hard-coded value, decided on ahead of time. Many companies set a revenue goal before each fiscal year and that number can be typed in as part of the KPI. Other times, the target may come from a data source such as an Analysis Services cube or Excel spreadsheet. The target may be an actual value from that data source or a calculation based on the value. For example, if a company is projecting sales for 2009, they may simply apply a formula that calculates a 10 percent increase over sales for the same time period in 2008.

Imagine that a company has set a target of having an employee turnover rate of no more than 15 percent. Each month this number is examined and for each month the value is less than 15 percent. This means that the indicator would show a good or healthy symbol. However, what if the actual values for the past three months were 7 percent, 12 percent, and 14 percent? While the number is still good, there seems to be a trend going on, and trends may be important to the business. This is another component that separates KPIs from measures: KPIs can include trends, and the calculations for determining trends can be simple or complex.

It's important to understand that KPIs that are healthy might have negative trends, as in the case with the employee turnover rate. KPIs that are unhealthy may nonetheless have positive trends, meaning that while the situation is bad, it is improving. The trend may be as simple as whether or not the current value is better than the previous value, or a complex calculation can be employed that helps factor in a longer time period. If sales decline for six straight months and in month seven are $1 higher than month six, should the trend suddenly appear as positive, or should a more complex calculation be used, such as a weighted moving average?

Trend indicators, like the health indicators, can vary, but they are usually arrows which can point up, down, or towards the middle. For each KPI, the designer of the scorecard must identify what constitutes a positive trend: an increasing value, a decreasing value, or staying within a certain range. For sales, an increasing value is clearly good. For expenses, a decreasing value should show a positive, or up, trend. For other measures, such as medical laboratory results, values might need to be in a particular range, such as between 5.2 and 8.3. Anything above or below that range is considered abnormal and therefore has a negative trend.

Deciding What KPIs to Track

Deciding on the KPIs to track can be a bit tricky because end users often get locked into a certain way of thinking. As a real world example, I worked with a business owner who paged through a monthly report that was about 400 pages long. The owner would look at each account and try to find large decreases between their current purchases and those in the past several months. He'd flag those customers and then have the salespeople check on the customers to determine if there was a problem, and if so, the company would work on correcting that problem. Naturally, this approach took quite a long time and the solution seemed simple enough. I suggested a single page report, showing all customers whose purchases in the current month had dropped by more than 20 percent over the average of their purchases in the three previous months. The business owner thought for a moment and admitted that, yes—such a report would indeed be useful and save time.

This is an example of dollar sales being used when what the business owner really wanted was the percentage growth in the account. Large drops would then be readily identifiable. This new measure would work very well as a key performance indicator, although in this case it would be more meaningful when looking at an individual customer than the entire organization, but it would still work when looking at the sum of all customers to know if overall orders were better or worse than the previous three months.

Therefore, one strategy for identifying KPIs is to examine what people do with the data they have. Looking at the data they get is simple enough, but what do they actually do with it? Do the users enter the information into a spreadsheet and perform some form or analysis? Do they calculate moving averages, lead and lag times, marginal costs, turnover ratios, and more? If so, the analysis that the end users perform is a good place to look for KPIs.

Another excellent source of KPIs is to look at business decision makers and find out what metrics factor into their bonuses. At almost all companies, upper management has targets to hit in certain areas in order to ensure their bonuses. Rest assured that those are the most important numbers to those managers and they will be tracked carefully. Providing a way for upper management to monitor those values quickly and easily will provide a tremendous win for the business intelligence project because it provides upper management with an easy and effective way to monitor their business.

Realize that there may be many KPIs and that the set of KPIs viewed may be completely different based on the user. While there is normally a set of KPIs developed for the organization as a whole, and these KPIs represent the entire business, many more KPIs can be created that focus on more narrow aspects of the business. A company-wide KPI might measure a goal to keep employee turnover to less than 15 percent a year. A narrower KPI such as the percentage of defective products produced might be of great interest to the vice president of manufacturing and the rest of the manufacturing organization, but of little interest to the sales organization. The ability to customize the scorecard for each person is one of the strengths of scorecarding. Don't think of the scorecard—think of the set of KPIs and how they can be used to build any number of scorecards.

Example KPIs

There are many example KPIs that can be tracked, and many of these depend on the functional area that will be tracking them. Remember that there are likely a set of KPIs that cover the entire business, but there can be many more of interest to only one or a few organizations within a company. With that in mind, many people generally think of KPIs as being financial in nature, so these examples will begin with some possible financial KPIs and then list a variety of KPIs for additional functional areas. Naturally there will be some overlap and this list is by no means complete. Each organization needs to determine the KPIs that make sense for their business, and this is typically done by creating a strategy map, which will be discussed later in this chapter.

Financial KPIs

Financial KPIs are often the most common because companies generally track their finances closely. Some financial KPIs might include:

▶ Sales—Both in dollars and units

▶ Expenses

▶ Gross Margin

▶ Average Sale—Both in dollars and units

▶ Cost of Goods Sold (COGS)

▶ Taxes

▶ Earnings Before Interest, Taxes, Depreciation, and Amortization (EBITDA)

Common dimensions used to examine these KPIs might include:

▶ Time

▶ Product

▶ Customer

- GL Account
- Employee

Manufacturing KPIs

Manufacturing organizations often place great importance on controls over inventory and production quality. Some common manufacturing KPIs might include:

- Units Produced
- Scrap
- Defective Units
- Defect Ratio
- Cost
- Inventory—Beginning, Ending, and Average

Some of the common dimensions used when analyzing manufacturing KPIs might include:

- Time
- Product
- Location—Plant and Assembly Line
- Defect Type
- Shift
- Employee
- Warehouse
- Shipper

Human Resources KPIs

Whether you're in a manufacturing, services, or public sector organization, managing human capital is important. Many companies find that hiring employees is extremely expensive both in time and money, and it is therefore advantageous to work to retain employees once hired. Some KPIs that might be used by a Human Resources department might include:

- Headcount
- Salary

- ► Hours
- ► Overtime—Hours and Salary
- ► Sick Days
- ► Vacation Days
- ► Length of Service
- ► Employee Turnover
- ► Continuing Education

Some of the dimensions that might be used to examine human resources KPIs might include:

- ► Time
- ► Employee
- ► Department
- ► Education
- ► Gender
- ► Race

Sales and Marketing KPIs

The sales and marketing department are often closely aligned with financial KPIs, but there are additional metrics that may be of interest to the sales and marketing organization, but which are not of interest to other organizations. Some of the sales and marketing KPIs might include:

- ► Sales—Both in dollars and units
- ► Gross Margin
- ► Click-through Percentage
- ► Web Visits
- ► Survey Response Percentage
- ► Marketing Expense

Some of the dimensions that might be used to analyze sales and marketing KPIs include:

- Time
- Product
- Customer
- Salesperson
- Promotion
- Income Level
- Education Level
- Age
- Gender

Note that the last four (income level, education level, age, and gender) are attributes of a customer. These may actually be separate dimensions or they may simply be attributes within the customer dimension. Regardless, they are analyzed as if they were separate dimensions. For example, a marketing promotion might want to target girls from ages 12 to 17, and the marketing analysts would examine the data with both age and gender working as dimensions in order to determine the effectiveness of that particular promotion.

Scorecards and Dashboards

While KPIs could be used individually, such as showing a single KPI somewhere on a web page, KPIs are usually placed on a scorecard. As mentioned in the introduction, scorecards are designed to give the consumer a set of information that is extremely easy to comprehend, providing a quick way to view the overall health of the business or individual organization within the business.

Scorecards are often a collection of KPIs, sometimes grouped into different categories. These categories are often called perspectives and will be described in more detail shortly. KPIs may also be hierarchical. Unlike measures in a cube, KPIs may break down into lower level KPIs; these higher-level KPIs are sometimes called objectives. For example, a Gross Profit KPI might break down into Revenue and Expense KPIs. The Expense KPI might then break down into a Salary, Rent,

Equipment, and other KPIs. At this level KPIs are getting quite granular and are more difficult to distinguish from measures, but companies that closely monitor their total salary expense may well provide incentives to managers to keep salaries in their departments to a minimum. Recall that if a manager finds part of his or her bonus based on a particular item, that item is an excellent candidate to be a KPI.

Given this information, scorecards are a collection of multiple KPIs, often broken down into perspectives, and sometimes the KPIs allow the users drill down to lower level KPIs. There is generally one overall scorecard for the entire business, and then many additional scorecards for different functional areas or even individual managers. Scorecards are often used by business decision makers because they provide the high level picture without the need for the person to assimilate large quantities of data, but scorecards can be useful for nearly anyone who wonders how the business is performing.

Another concept that is often mentioned along with scorecards is that of dashboards. In fact, many organizations use the terms more or less interchangeably. Technically, a dashboard is more than a scorecard because it may contain multiple scorecards or items in addition to scorecards. So while a scorecard is usually displayed as a part of a dashboard, the dashboard might also show reports, charts, company news, and so forth. In other words, a dashboard is like a personalized portal, and the terms dashboard and portal certainly do become blurred. In the case of PerformancePoint Server, scorecards are normally displayed to end users as part of a dashboard, which is hosted in SharePoint. SharePoint lets users customize their screens so that a user might be viewing a scorecard, their email inbox, some scrolling stock prices, and so on. Therefore, the term dashboard will be used throughout the book, and it will often include the viewing mechanism for scorecards, graphs, grids, and any other data presented to users.

Companies that embark upon building a scorecard often need to carefully plan what should be in the scorecard; in other words, how they'll break down their business into perspectives and then the KPIs within each perspective. These perspectives are not at all related to something called Perspectives in Analysis Services; rather, a perspective here is just a way of looking at the business. Many people are familiar with looking at a business from a financial perspective, but companies must also look at the market with the customer's perspective, asking what makes a consumer willing to spend their money on the company's products. The process of examining the perspectives and the KPIs in that perspective is often done by creating what is known as a strategy map, and the perspectives chosen can lead to what is called a Balanced Scorecard or to just a general business scorecard.

Balanced Scorecards

Scorecards have their genesis in the work of Robert Kaplan and David Norton. In 1992, they published a paper in *Harvard Business Review* about a way to monitor the health of a business using Balanced Scorecard, discussing perspectives and metrics that could be used to for companies to measure their relative success. They argued that companies could not successfully manage items they could not measure, so measurement became critical. In 1996 Kaplan and Norton published *The Balanced Scorecard: Translating Strategy into Action*, a book that more fully laid out the Balanced Scorecard concept.

Kaplan and Norton argued that companies spend far too much time focused on financials, and that financials are often a trailing indicator of the health of the business. Since it takes companies some time to close out a particular quarter, it might be mid-to-late April before a business realizes just how bad the previous quarter was, and by then some of the data is almost four months old. Kaplan and Norton argued that while examining financial data is important, it must be only one part of a broader picture. In other words, the financial perspective must be balanced against other, equally important, areas.

A Balanced Scorecard is aimed at an overall view of the entire enterprise and looks at four areas, called perspectives. These four perspectives are:

▶ Financial

▶ Customer

▶ Internal Process

▶ Learning and Growth

The financial perspective covers the standard financial goals of an organization and is of interest to those both inside and outside the organization. For most companies, the focus is on business owners or shareholders. Nonprofit organizations focus on those funding the organization through donations or other payments. KPIs often found in the financial perspective are relatively easy to identify: gross revenue, profit, earnings per share, and so forth.

The customer perspective focuses on such areas as targeting and then acquiring customers, retaining those customers, and growing business at existing customers. Businesses want to develop lifelong customers and provide comprehensive solutions. Some of the KPIs in this area might be collected through focus groups and customer surveys.

The internal process perspective focuses on internal business processes. Not only are internal management processes examined, but so are customer management processes, such as maintaining an open and ongoing dialog with existing customers. Processes such as research and development, quality control, and regulatory compliance are also covered here.

Finally, the learning and growth perspective covers the development of the people in the organization and the informational infrastructure. This may include training of employees, satisfaction surveys, and the development of technology to support people in their work. Note that training and internal systems might be designed to provide better customer service, but even systems that provide less tangible benefits may still be part of the overall strategy.

Part of the reason for the different perspectives is the belief that while financial information is often a lagging indicator, the other perspectives can be current or leading indicators. Customer surveys are especially important to some companies in helping to determine product changes and future directions. Sliding customer satisfaction in the same quarter as strong sales may foretell weaker future sales, so identifying these issues early can lead to proactive solutions to address issues. In addition, high employee turnover might indicate problems with aspects of the corporate culture that can be addressed before the loss of experienced workers begins to affect product quality.

What makes a true Balanced Scorecard is the use of the four perspectives and the KPIs in each perspective representing the metrics that are driving the business. Since Kaplan and Norton published their original Balanced Scorecard article, variations on the Balanced Scorecard theme have appeared, and the general term of "scorecards" has grown to encompass nearly anything with KPIs. These general, or business, scorecards may have KPIs from only a single perspective or may include many perspectives, which may or may not be related to the four perspectives identified by Kaplan and Norton.

Business Scorecards

A business scorecard is a general term used in this book to identify any scorecard that is not a true Balanced Scorecard. This includes an enterprise-wide scorecard that might not have Kaplan and Norton's four perspectives, or any lower-level scorecard that focuses on more narrow KPIs. The Balanced Scorecard typically only has five or six KPIs per perspective, so the KPIs are usually very general and highly aggregated. A gross revenue value in a Balanced Scorecard is for all products, while a product manager might want to analyze such a value broken down by product categories or subcategories.

Sometimes a business scorecard is even narrowly focused on a single problem, but the nature of scorecards makes them an effective way to solve the problem. Chapter 1 discussed a scorecard that was built for a nonprofit organization. Technically, there were only two true KPIs: Expenses Per Patient Day and Number of Patient Days. However, a number of KPIs were created. There was the Number of Patient Days KPI, and the overall Expenses per Patient Day. In addition, there was a Rent per Patient Day, Food per Patient Day, Utilities per Patient Day, and so on, with approximately twenty expense categories getting their own KPIs. The screen was presented with each facility showing just two KPIs and an overall score. One KPI was for the Expenses per Patient Day and the other was for the Number of Patient Days. Each facility could then be expanded to see the individual expense KPIs rolled up into the Expense per Patient Day KPI. In true scorecard fashion, some expenses were deemed more controllable than others and those expenses had higher weights when contributing to the overall score. The actual value of the score wasn't important, but it was a way to rank each facility and determine which ones were controlling costs better than others. An example of this scorecard can be seen in Figure 4-2.

Another example of a business scorecard is one employed by a company that does specialized construction. Their projects go through a series of approximately 15 phases,

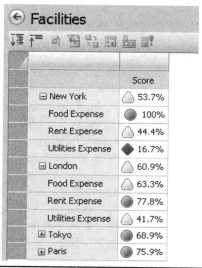

Figure 4-2 *A business scorecard ranking facilities based on their expenses, where the top level KPI could be broken down into more granular KPIs.*

including initiation, locating real estate, negotiating buy or lease contracts, and so forth. Each phase has a target for the amount of time it should take, so the time in each phase became a KPI. Each KPI is assigned a weight and then all the KPIs for the various phases are rolled up into one overall KPI that is used to sort projects. Those with the worst scores are the ones spending longer than planned in various phases, and these troublesome projects were easier to identify and examine.

One question about this scorecard might be, "Wouldn't a report have worked just as well? Couldn't the customer have just listed out the troublesome projects based on the criteria mentioned?" Certainly that's possible, but scorecards created with PerformancePoint Server have the ability to link to a strategy map (described next), analytic tools such as charts and graphs, and more. An online report could have contained some of this interactivity, but having the ability to easily identify a problem project, expand it to see the KPIs for each phase, and then assess their health proved to be an ideal way to present the information to project managers and upper level management.

It's also important to remember that some scorecards focus on a single perspective and a very narrow set of KPIs, while many others include multiple perspectives and therefore are often broader in scope and far more high level than most traditional reports, which tend to focus on details.

Strategy Maps

Strategy maps were discussed to some degree in Kaplan and Norton's first book on Balanced Scorecards, but they have since grown to become perhaps the primary tool for an organization building a Balanced Scorecard with *Strategy Maps: Converting Intangible Assets into Tangible Outcomes*, also by Kaplan and Norton. Balanced scorecards assume that something has to be measurable in order to be managed; strategy maps assume that something has to be describable in order to be measured. Strategy maps, at least for Balanced Scorecards, are broken into the same four perspectives mentioned in the scorecard, and they lay out the macro view of the organization's goals and lay out the strategy for achieving those goals.

Remember from the discussion of the Balanced Scorecard that the four perspectives are financial, customer, internal process, and growth and learning. The perspectives are in this particular order for a reason. The higher the perspective, the easier it is to measure, and the more visible it is, not just inside, but also outside the organization. Companies generally put their broad, mission statement type goals in the higher perspectives to lay out the company strategy. The lower perspectives may include more detailed strategies or lean towards tactics for achieving the goals of higher level perspectives.

The financial perspective KPIs are usually easy to identify, but what is the overall purpose of the business? Most businesses exist to make a profit, of course, but a public company generally has the primary goal of increasing shareholder value. From a financial perspective, achieving this might mean increasing profits, which in turn might come from reducing costs, becoming the leader in a particular market segment, and decreasing the debt burden of the company. There are generally only a few, very high-level goals in the financial perspective.

Next comes the customer perspective, which might include such goals as consistently meeting or exceeding expectations, being a company that it is easy to work or partner with, providing a wide array of choices, and giving back to the communities in which the company is located. All of these goals deal with better serving customers and meeting their needs, as well as being a good corporate citizen. Most of these goals will directly support such financial goals as increasing profits and becoming a leader in a particular market segment, but they probably do nothing to directly support the goal of reducing costs. Such tasks are left for the next perspective.

The internal process perspective lays out more concrete goals. It's well and good to say that the company is going to increase shareholder value, but one way it's going to do that is by being an easier company with which to work, as mentioned in the customer perspective. How it's going to achieve this goal could be one of the goals in the internal process perspective: consistently provide service that impresses customers. Other goals in the internal process perspective might include those for acquiring new customers, such as selling the appropriate products only when needed, and an operational goal might be to streamline the purchase process for new and existing customers, as well as improving workflow tools for internal use.

The final perspective is that of learning and growth. Here goals might include such things as industry expertise, effective account management, and hiring, building, and retaining excellent employees. Other goals might include providing the right tools to get the job done and having a clear growth path in the organization. Sometimes companies have goals to empower employees to handle customer issues and to effectively communicate the company goals and values to all employees.

Once these goals have been determined, they are documented in a strategy map, and lines are drawn between connected goals. Figure 4-3 shows an example of a strategy map for a Balanced Scorecard.

If the goal is to build a scorecard for a business area instead of the entire organization, it is still possible to use the same four perspectives of a balanced scorecard, or to use a simplified version of the strategy map. A strategy map for an Information Technology (IT) department might include the financial perspective goals of increasing IT effectiveness and managing IT expenditures. Customer perspective

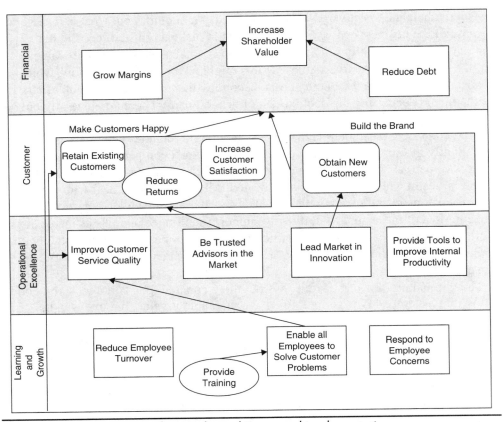

Figure 4-3 *A strategy map for a Balanced Scorecard implementation*

goals might include developing solutions and implementing changes quickly, maintaining high availability for key systems, and being a partner with the business when technological solutions are required. Internal process goals could be items such as understanding the business unit's goals and needs, providing excellent customer service, delivering projects on time and on budget, performing buy vs. build decisions, and maintaining current knowledge of technology trends. Finally, the learning and growth perspective goals might include hiring and training talented people, recognizing achievement, exposing all IT personnel to business unit strategies, and encouraging IT personnel to work for a time in the business units. Business scorecards may include strategy maps that have other perspectives—or even no perspectives at all. For example, some companies have scorecards for each employee, which might include KPIs such as attendance, training received, training delivered, productivity, and so forth. These KPIs might be shown and tracked without being placed into perspectives.

Strategy maps are often used as a way to communicate business goals at a high level. Once the goals are actually put on paper, the business has to decide what metrics it can track to achieve these goals. A goal for which no metric can be conceived is a goal that might be impossible to reach, or at least impossible to know when it has been achieved. Therefore, it is important that goals on the strategy map be broken down into KPIs that can then be tied back to those goals. Understand that some companies spend a year or more developing an overall strategy map; I sat down with an insurance company that had a huge binder covering their current strategy map and their thinking behind it, all of which had been in development for well over a year.

In PerformancePoint Server, strategy maps can be imported from those created in Visio 2007, or they can be created directly in the PerformancePoint tools using a scaled-down version of Visio. The different objects representing each goal can be tied to KPIs that are created so that people can see the scorecard as the strategy map, as a traditional scorecard, or see both side by side. This is a powerful concept because it allows people to see how well the goals are being achieved. It's important to understand that the strategy maps used by PerformancePoint Server to actually display information are usually at a much more granular level than the traditional strategy maps.

Summary

Key Performance Indicators are the basis for much of the analysis done at high levels of an organization. Far from a simple graphical display, they represent the very core metrics of the business and include both a status and a trend. Useful by themselves, KPIs become even more powerful when placed on a scorecard. Scorecards can take various KPIs, group them into different perspectives, and provide scores in each perspective as well as an overall score. KPIs at a very high level may break down into lower level KPIs to provide more detailed information. Scorecards are often part of a dashboard, which is used to display anything from a single scorecard to several scorecards, reports, and other information.

When designing the KPIs for an organization, the primary planning tool is the strategy map. With it, organizations document their goals and carefully describe the elements they will measure in order to ensure their company grows. Once the strategy map has been created, the organization seeks to identify the KPIs that will map to the goals identified. These KPIs are then created, scorecards are built, and the monitoring of the business begins.

Monitoring, Analysis, and Planning

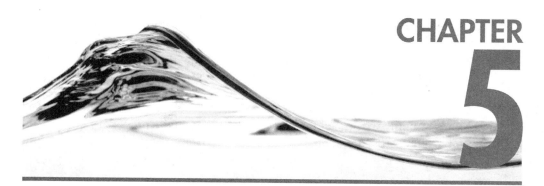

CHAPTER 5

Monitoring in PerformancePoint Server

PerformancePoint Server uses key performance indicators to create scorecards. These scorecards are then placed on dashboards, which are the objects end users will ultimately access in order to perform the monitoring piece of the monitoring, analysis, and planning triad. PerformancePoint Server uses the terminology of both dashboards and scorecards, but as mentioned in Chapter 4 the two terms are sometimes used interchangeably. In PerformancePoint Server, business intelligence developers are guided through the process of creating KPIs, building scorecards, and then placing those scorecards on dashboards. Dashboards are then published, usually to SharePoint, for consumption by others in the organization.

The scorecards and dashboards in PerformancePoint Server are built with the Dashboard Designer, which is the replacement for the Office Business Scorecard Manager 2005 Scorecard Builder. Business Scorecard Manager was used to create scorecards and dashboards using KPIs and was released prior to SQL Server 2005. While it worked with both Analysis Services 2000 and Analysis Services 2005, it failed to take advantage of some of the new features found in Analysis Services 2005, such as the KPIs built into Analysis Services 2005 cubes. Microsoft did release a converter utility that could move Analysis Services 2005 KPIs into Business Scorecard Manager and back, but the Dashboard Designer in PerformancePoint Server natively understands KPIs and all the other Analysis Services 2005 features.

Data Sources and Scorecards

The tool that will be used to create KPIs, scorecards, reports, and dashboards in this chapter is called the Dashboard Designer. The Dashboard Designer is a rich client application. It is often launched from Dashboard Central, a web page that is visible to BI developers and dashboard designers. This page is reached by typing the name of the server and then adding **/central**, or sometimes by specifying the name of the server and a port number, as shown in Figure 5-1. This page allows designers to launch the Dashboard Designer and view the Dashboard Web Preview site.

The Dashboard Designer is written in managed code and does not have to be deployed ahead of time on each developer's machine. Instead, it can be downloaded as needed. Because it is managed code, it runs inside its own protected area and therefore does not require any security verification associated with items such as ActiveX controls. And because it's a Windows Forms application, the user interface

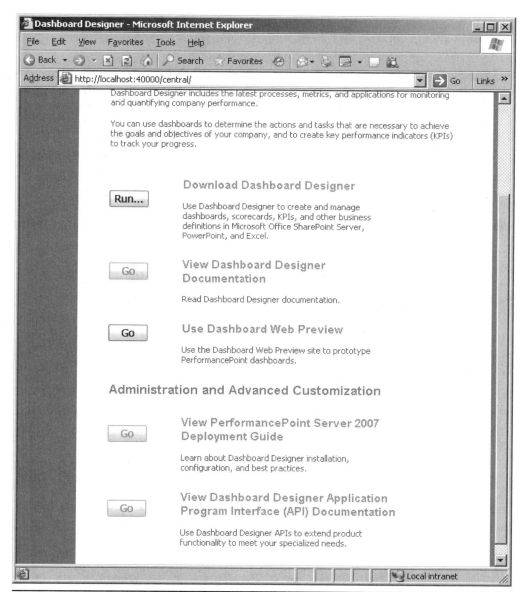

Figure 5-1 *The Dashboard Central page, from which the Dashboard Designer can be launched*

is full featured and uses the same design elements as Office 2007, which includes the use of the ribbon bar instead of a more traditional menu. Figure 5-2 shows what the Dashboard Designer looks like when first opened.

The left side of the Dashboard Designer is called the Workspace Browser and shows the objects that are currently available to be used; these objects may be newly created or they may have been retrieved from the server. The Workspace Browser shows the types of objects that can be created in the Designer: Dashboards, KPIs, Scorecards, Reports, Data Sources, and Indicators. Dashboards represent the top-level object and are therefore listed first. It's not surprising to see KPIs and Scorecards, but note that Reports are also shown as first-class objects. You should realize that whatever is listed as being in the workspace is a local copy to which changes can be made without affecting server items. No local changes reach the server until the items are published.

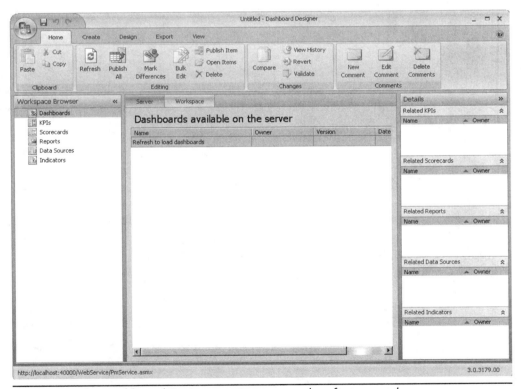

Figure 5-2   *The Dashboard Designer as it appears when first opened*

On the ribbon bar is a Refresh button that will query the server to find existing data sources, dashboards, KPIs, and so forth. Clicking this button will populate the lists that show up in the middle area, called the Workspace area, where the Server and Workspace tabs are located. If this is a new server, of course, nothing will show up in the lists. Once there are existing objects published to the server, they will show up in the lists only after the Refresh button is clicked.

Creating Data Sources

Right-clicking on the Data Sources node in the Workspace Browser brings up a context menu with the option to create a new data source. Choosing this option opens the Select a Data Source Template dialog box. This dialog breaks down the connection types into three categories: Multidimensional, Standard Queries, and Tabular Lists. There is also an All node that will show all of the different data source templates at once in the Template pane of the dialog box.

The multidimensional templates folder includes a single template for Analysis Services. The Analysis Services template can connect to both Analysis Services 2000 and Analysis Services 2005. The Standard Queries category includes just a single template to open any data source accessible via ODBC. The Tabular List category includes four templates: one for Excel Services (the web version of Excel), one to import data from an Excel 2007 workbook, one to import data from SharePoint Lists, and a final template to read directly from a SQL Server table, which includes both SQL Server 2000 and SQL Server 2005. Figure 5-3 shows all the data source types that are included with PerformancePoint Server.

Since most business intelligence applications will be based, at least partly, on Analysis Services cubes, this example will show you how to set up a data connection to Analysis Services 2005. After choosing to create a new data source and selecting Analysis Services as the template, a dialog box appears that asks for the name of the data source, the default display folder, and whether or not to grant read permissions to users who are authenticated to the PerformancePoint Monitoring Server. The name should be descriptive but is not something that will be seen by end users; it is only visible to other developers. The default display folder location is optional and will create a folder (or use an existing one) in the Workspace Browser. The folder mechanism allows for multiple items, in this case data sources, to be grouped into subfolders under the folder representing the type of object. This makes it easier to group items. For example, in companies that have many scorecards, it might help to categorize them by functional area.

Choosing to grant Read permissions to all users who are authenticated to the PerformancePoint Monitoring Server automatically adds all users to a role for that

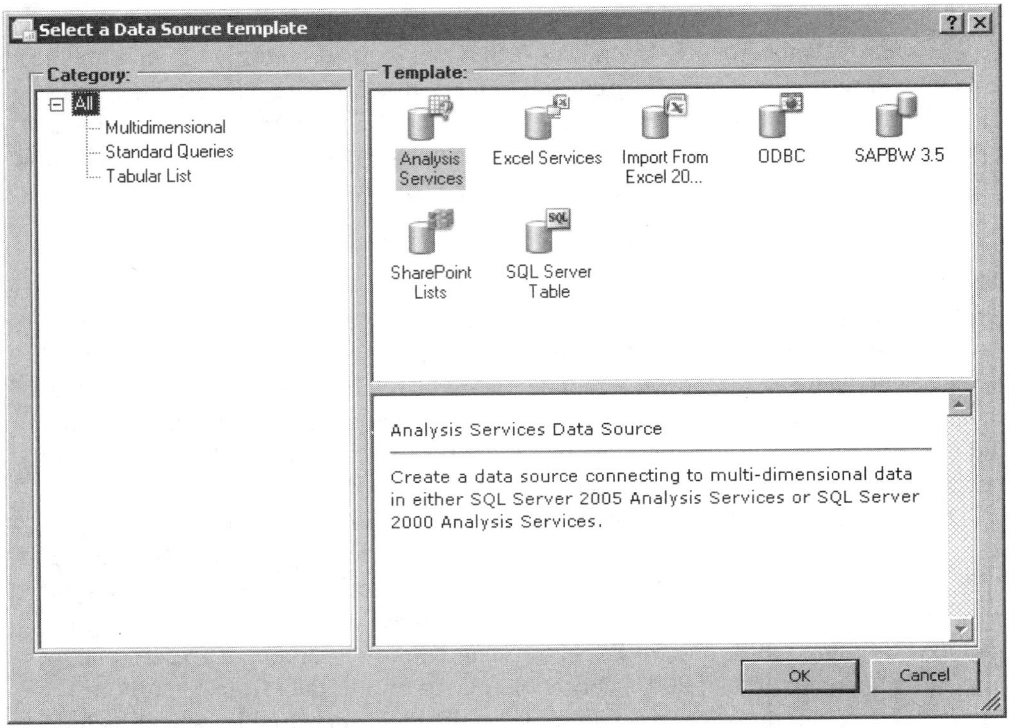

Figure 5-3 *The data source types included with PerformancePoint Server*

particular item. Without checking this, the developer will have to set up permissions as an added step later. Figure 5-4 shows the dialog box that appears when creating a new Analysis Services data source named AdvWorks.

Once the data source has been created, a settings window containing three tabs appears in the main work area: Editor, Properties, and Time. With an Analysis Services data source, there are two primary options on the Editor tab: use a standard connection or use a custom connection string. It's usually sufficient to use a standard connection, but there are some cases where custom connection string parameters are passed to Analysis Services to enable certain features. For this example, a standard connection will suffice. A standard connection requires the name of the server on which Analysis Services is running. Once the server name has been entered, dropping down the list box for Database will show the databases that are available on that particular server.

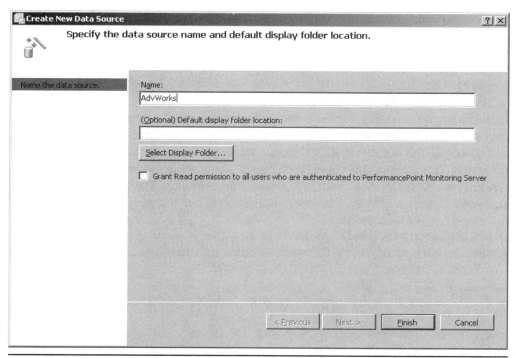

Figure 5-4 *This is the dialog box showing the creation of a new Analysis Services data source. The same three fields on this dialog box will be seen many times when working with the Dashboard Designer wizards*

NOTE

If a database exists on the server but does not appear in the list, this is due to how the PerformancePoint Monitoring Server connects to Analysis Services. PerformancePoint Monitoring Server is hosted through Internet Information Services (IIS) so it uses application pools to run in. Each application pool can be set to run under the context of an existing service, such as the network service, or an actual user name and password. Therefore, the cube must have a role that grants permissions to the user or service under which the application pool runs. Another option is to configure the server to pass the current user credentials through to Analysis Services. These options will be discussed in greater detail in Chapter 8 in the section on security.

The final option on the Summary tab is Cache Settings. By default, PerformancePoint Server will get data from Analysis Services and then cache that data for 10 minutes. After ten minutes, PerformancePoint Server will invalidate the cache and the next query will reconnect to the cube to retrieve data. If this is a cube that is updated less frequently, this time will be extended. For organizations doing real-time or near-real-time BI, shortening this cache internally might make sense. Figure 5-5 shows the Summary page filled out to connect to the Adventure Works cube in the Adventure Works DW database.

The Properties tab allows designers to set various properties of the data source. In the General Properties section there are four properties, including the name of the data source and an optional description. The Person Responsible text box is required and should be the person creating the data source, which is the value that is filled in by default. In theory this could be changed to another authorized user but it is typically left as the person creating the data source. Finally, the Display Folder text box sets an optional display folder and is a repeat of the text box shown when the data source was first created.

Next is a section entitled Custom Properties. This is useful if corporate standards require the tracking of certain information that is not already provided, such as the

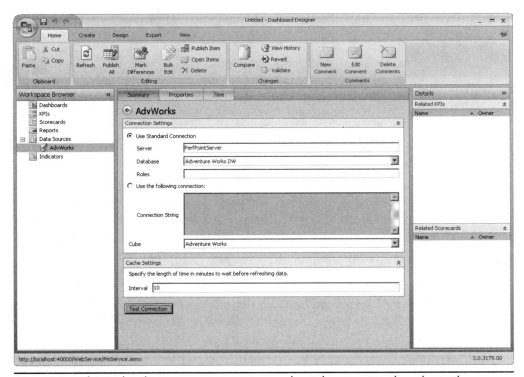

Figure 5-5   *This is the data source connecting to the Adventure Works cube in the Adventure Works DW database on a server named PerfPointServer.*

email address of the person creating the data source. When the New Property button is clicked, a dialog box appears showing that property can have one of four data types: Text, Decimal, Date, or Hyperlink. Each custom property is given a name, one of the four data types, and a value. A custom property can also have an optional description.

At the bottom of the page is a Permissions area that allows the data source author to set those that have permission to read data through the data source and those that have the authority to edit the data source. By default, the creator of the data source is added with an Editor role. Also by default, Authenticated Users are placed in the Reader role if the developer checked the box (shown in Figure 5-4) granting Read permissions to all users. If not, everyone should have Read permissions through this data source, which means that the particular role can be removed and a more restrictive one added. Also, additional roles can be added if more editors are desired. New roles need a user in the format of DOMAIN\alias, where the alias can be an individual user or an NT group. Figure 5-6 shows what this screen might look like with the addition of a custom property and a description of the data source.

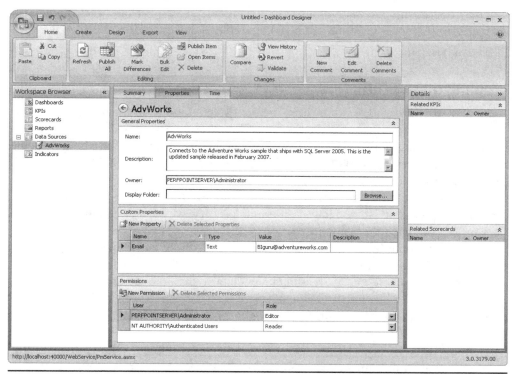

Figure 5-6   *The Properties tab of the data source sets general and custom properties, along with permissions for who can read and who can edit the data source.*

The Time tab allows users to select a member in the cube's Time dimension and map it to a date in the Dashboard Designer's Time control. Developers can assign the levels in a time hierarchy to associated levels in the Dashboard Designer, which enables the use of Time Intelligence Filters across the cube. The Time Intelligence Filters allow developers to create filter selections such as Last 6 Months, Last 4 Quarters, and more, all of which can be based on the current date. A formula might look like Year -1:Year, which would yield the previous year and the current year (meaning it would result in 2006:2007 if run in the year 2007.) A similar formula, Month-12:Month, would return the last 12 months based on the current month.

Now that the data source has been created, it's important to realize that it only exists on the machine of the developer who has created it. The Dashboard Designer application is running locally and in order for others to make use of data sources, or any other objects created in Dashboard Designer, they these objects must be published to the server. Individual objects can be published by right-clicking on them in the Workspace Browser and choosing Publish, or all changed objects can be published at once by clicking on the Publish All button on the Home ribbon. When objects are published to the server, they are automatically versioned and given a version number and a timestamp. Changes to the objects are tracked so that comparisons between versions can be compared and designers can even roll back to previous versions if necessary.

Creating a Scorecard

Generally, after creating a connection, the next step would be to create a set of KPIs. While this is certainly possible, PerformancePoint Server can actually go immediately to the creation of a scorecard and create KPIs on the fly. This is similar to the change from Analysis Services 2000 to Analysis Services 2005; in AS2000, dimensions had to be created before a cube could be built, but AS2005 allows for the creation of a cube without first building the dimensions. Likewise, Business Scorecard Manager required that KPIs be created before building a scorecard, but PerformancePoint Server does not have this same restriction.

Right-clicking on Scorecards in the Workspace Browser and choosing New Scorecard opens the Select a Scorecard Template dialog box. As with the dialog box that appears when you're creating a new data source, this dialog has two panes: Category and Template. The categories include ERP, Microsoft, Standard, and Tabular, and may grow to include other categories in the future. The list of templates included with PerformancePoint Server includes Analysis Services, Excel, SharePoint List, and more. Expect additional templates to be added by third-party vendors and as samples from Microsoft. This dialog box also has an option to use wizards to create scorecards. Certainly, using the wizards the first few times a scorecard is created helps new developers walk through the process. After developers become familiar with scorecards, some will choose to turn off the wizards and build them from scratch. Fortunately PerformancePoint Server accommodates working in either mode. These templates are extensible, and companies can create their own custom templates for both data sources and scorecards, if desired.

Choosing to build a scorecard with an Analysis Services template presents you with the Analysis Services Scorecard Wizard as shown in Figure 5-7. While the first page of the wizard is similar to that for creating a new data source, notice that a series of steps are listed down the left-hand side of this wizard. From the list, it is obvious that there are a number of steps that must be performed in order to create a scorecard. The first screen is simply asking for the name of the scorecard, an optional display folder, and whether or not all authenticated users should be given access.

The second step in the wizard is selecting a data source. This page allows for the use of data sources residing on either the workspace or the server. Recall that a newly-created data source that has not yet been published exists only on the

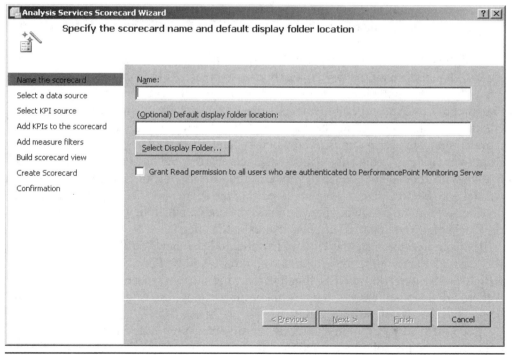

Figure 5-7   *The wizard for creating a new scorecard has the same fields as the data source wizard, but it shows a series of steps down the left-hand side.*

local machine, or workspace. Scorecard builders can choose to use local, not-yet-published data sources or those that already exist on the server. If a developer goes straight into creating a scorecard, has no local data source, and no server data sources show up, this means that the Refresh button was not clicked so the list of server data sources was not retrieved.

The third page of the wizard is where the designer selects a KPI source. There are only two options on this page: Create KPIs from SQL Server Analysis Services Measures and Import SQL Server Analysis Services KPIs. Recall that the monitoring servers' predecessor, Business Scorecard Manager, did not natively understand Analysis Services 2005 KPIs. Clearly, PerformancePoint Server can take advantage of KPIs already built into the cube, but it can also use measures in the cube to create KPIs on the fly. There are advantages to each approach, but KPIs are often best built into Analysis Services cubes. This keeps different developers from creating the same KPI with different formulas on different scorecards. Remember that one purpose of BI is to have a single version of the truth so pushing KPIs into the cube helps enforce a standard definition for that KPI. On the other hand, it's unlikely that a cube will ever have all the KPIs that will ever be needed, so PerformancePoint Server includes the capabilities to create KPIs based on the measures in the cube.

Depending on whether your choice is to use KPIs from the cube or build KPIs in Dashboard Designer from measures in the cube, the next screen of the wizard will look slightly different. Figure 5-8 shows both options; the top part of the screen shows what happens if the developer chooses to create KPIs from cube measures, while the bottom half shows the screen if the developer wants to use existing KPIs that are built into the cube. Reusing existing KPIs is relatively simple, as just clicking the Import checkbox beside each KPI will bring it into the scorecard. The more complicated approach is to now build each KPI in the Dashboard Designer from the measures in the cube. Note that a scorecard could have both kinds of KPIs but the wizard does not give designers a method for mixing and matching those. That will have to be done later by manually editing the scorecard. The approach that will be discussed in the following paragraphs is the one in which new KPIs are created in the Dashboard Designer based on measures in the cube.

If you choose to create the KPIs in Dashboard Designer, you'll see that the screen for adding KPIs to the scorecard has two buttons: Add KPI and Select KPI. Select KPI allows you to choose KPIs already created in the workspace or on the server. If there are no existing KPIs, the developer must choose the Add KPI button, which begins the process of defining a KPI.

When the Add KPI button is clicked, the first measure in the cube is added by default. The Name column is filled in with the measure name, the Actual and Targets are both set to the cube measure, and the Band Method is set to Increasing is Better.

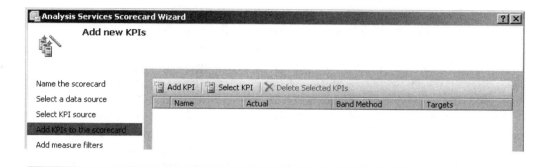

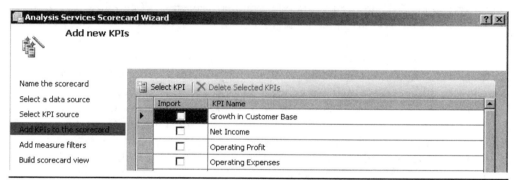

Figure 5-8   *These are the two views for adding new KPIs. The top view creates a KPI in PerformancePoint based on cube measures. The bottom view imports KPIs that are part of a cube in Analysis Services 2005.*

The Targets column contains a drop-down list of all the measures in the cube, but the developer can also type in a hardcoded value if one exists. Obviously, formulas can be placed in here as well, which will be discussed later.

The Adventure Works DW sample database is being used in the examples shown in the screenshots. Two of the measures in the Adventure Works cube are called Sales Amount and Sales Amount Quota, and these two measures will work nicely as the Actual and Targets respectively. Also, be aware that when the measures are changed, the Name field does not change, and therefore still contains the name of the first measure. It's important that developers remember to change this before moving forward.

The next step in the process is to optionally add measure filters. Measure filters are a way of selecting a member from a dimension that will limit what is seen in the value of the KPI and can be set for both the Actual and Target measures. As an example, this KPI might be for a particular product line. Therefore, selecting the checkbox to add measure filters allows the developer to choose a dimension.

In the case of the Adventure Works database, the Product dimension could be used to help filter the members. If the Product.Product Model Lines hierarchy was chosen, then both the Actual and Target could be set to Mountain to narrow the focus of this particular KPI down to the just products in the Mountain product line. While the wizard lets developers make specific selections of members from a dimension, these selections can also be made dynamic, which will be discussed later in the chapter.

The next step of the wizard allows the developer to add columns based on members from a dimension. Adding column members is optional is often used to add date values to the scorecard. For example, a company might choose to have the scorecard show the actual and target values for the sales amount for the past three years. The scorecard ends up having one column for each year, and those columns are further subdivided into actual and target columns. Once this step of the wizard is completed, the Finish button is ready to be clicked.

Clicking the Finish button shows a summary page of what has occurred, but the bottom line is that the scorecard has been created. The new scorecard is incredibly simple, assuming that no filters or column members were selected, and is shown in Figure 5-9. This scorecard shows the KPI on the row and the Actual and Target on the columns. The actual value is shown along with the target value and an indicator of the KPIs health. In the Workspace Browser a number of new items have been created including the scorecard, a KPI, and two items that appear under the Indicators folder. In the Details pane, a number of folders now appear in the Available Items window. Because this scorecard was created simply by clicking the Finish button, the health indicator is set automatically along with the layout of the entire scorecard view.

On the other hand, the developer could have chosen to set members for the columns when building the scorecard view. The dimension chosen for the columns is typically Time although this is not a requirement. If the developer did not choose dimension members when using the wizard, the dimension and members can be selected from the Dimensions folder in the Details pane, assuming that the developer has published the items to the server. Once the dimension is selected, members from that dimension can be selected. For example, if the Date.Calendar Year dimension is chosen, the members CY 2003 and CY 2004 can be selected. In order to get the data to appear, the developer can either publish the scorecard or click the Update button on the Edit ribbon. Using these settings changes the scorecard to the one shown in Figure 5-10. Note that the symbol has changed. The symbol in Figure 5-9 was a triangle and is yellow, while the circle indicator shown in Figure 5-10 is green. This makes sense in Figure 5-10, because for both 2003 and 2004, the actual values are above the targets. Whether the indicator in Figure 5-9 should have been yellow or

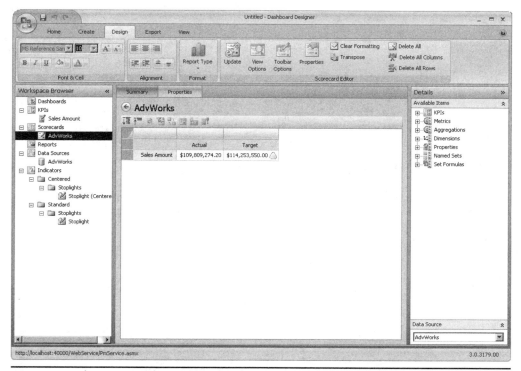

Figure 5-9 *This is a simple scorecard with a single KPI showing the actual value, the target, and a graphical indicator of the KPI's status.*

red depends on business rules and what the business decides the thresholds should be to move something into the red or bad category.

Once the scorecard is visible as shown in Figure 5-9 and Figure 5-10, it is actually interactive and can be modified. This allows designers to drag and drop elements onto the scorecard to build it graphically after the wizard has finished. Recall that Date could be placed on the columns by selecting it as part of the wizard, but it is also possible to add items to both the rows and columns in the designer window. In the Details pane on the right hand side of the Dashboard Designer is a list of available items and these include KPIs, dimensions, named sets, and so forth. By expanding these, items can be dragged from the Details pane and dropped onto the scorecard. For example, the aforementioned Product Model Lines hierarchy can be dragged from the Dimensions folder of the Details pane and dropped onto the scorecard.

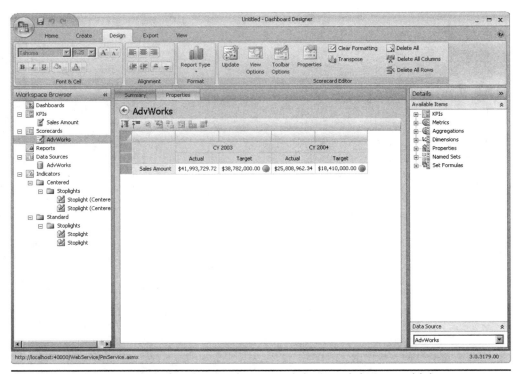

Figure 5-10 *The scorecard after the developer used drag and drop to add the Date dimension to the scorecard. The Dashboard Designer acts as a GUI design palette for scorecards.*

Visual indicators help show where it will be dropped, such as before or after the Sales Amount KPI. Once dropped, a hierarchy list appears in a dialog box that allows the developer to select which items to place on the scorecard. In Figure 5-11, items at two different levels were chosen. First, the All Products item was chosen, and then the items one level below the all level were selected as well. Clicking the Update button after this change will retrieve data from the server. The scorecard now shows those items and their actual and target numbers. Note that the measure used for the target, Sales Amount Quota, does not have detail below the All Products level, and is therefore blank in this example.

Once the scorecard has been created it is visible in the Workspace Browser. Clicking on it shows the scorecard itself in the Summary tab, but there is also a Properties tab in the main window. This is identical to the Properties page for the data source that was discussed in the previous section, with General Properties, Custom Properties, and Permissions areas on the tab.

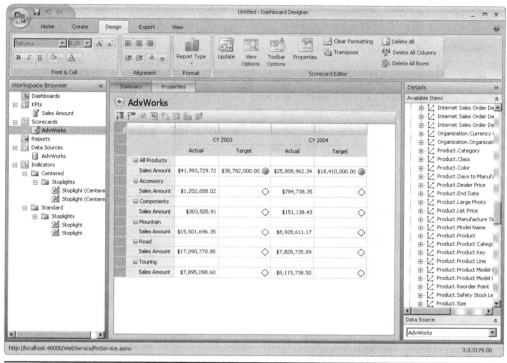

Figure 5-11   *Two different levels of the Product Model Lines hierarchy are displayed in the scorecard. Note that dimensions can be added to both the rows and columns of a scorecard and include members from various levels.*

Creating and Modifying KPIs

In the previous discussion about creating scorecards, the KPI was created as part of that process. KPIs can be created independently as well, simply by right-clicking on the KPIs folder in the Workspace Browser and choosing New KPI. Doing this opens a dialog box that gives developers the option of creating two types of objects: Objectives and Standard KPIs. An objective is basically a higher-level KPI that can have one or more child KPIs with scores that roll up into the objective. Therefore, if the objective is to Increase Profits, KPIs might include Sales, Cost Reduction, and so forth. A Standard KPI is just a KPI as was created with the scorecard in the previous section.

Choosing either an objective or standard KPI results in a screen that asks for the name, an optional display folder, and a checkbox to grant permissions to all users, just as has been seen when creating a KPI through the new scorecard wizard.

After the KPI or objective has been created, it is added to the KPIs folder in the Workspace Browser. Clicking on the new KPI in the Workspace Browser opens up the two tabs in the main work area: Editor and Properties. The Properties tab is the same as the one for both scorecards and data sources so there is nothing unique about how it works. The Editor tab, however, presents designers with the ability to modify the name, actual value, target value, how it is displayed, how the thresholds are set, and what indicator is used.

Figure 5-12 shows the dialog box that is displayed for the Number Format for a KPI. If the developer chooses to override the default display format, there are options to set a variety of parameters regarding the display. The number of decimal places to show can be set from 0 to 30. The multiplier is useful when the data is stored in the cube as a decimal but represents a percentage; for example, if a gross margin measure is stored as .12, the multiplier could be set to 100 and a percentage sign could be added in order to make it show up as 12% in the scorecard. Hard-coded symbols can be placed on the left and right sides of the value, allowing for

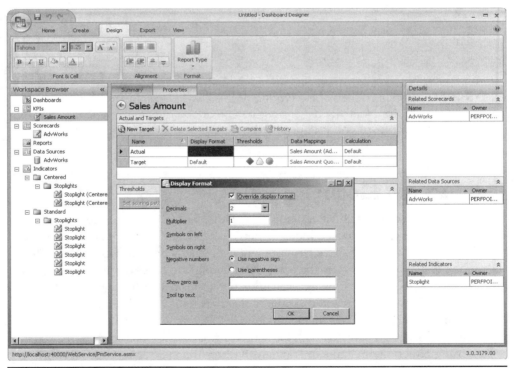

Figure 5-12   *When editing a KPI, the number format can be set manually. Otherwise, the formatting found in the data source is used.*

percent signs, currency symbols, and so forth. Negative numbers can be displayed with negative signs or in parentheses. The value of zero can be shown using any string entered, such as a dash or N/A. Finally, a tool tip can be added to the KPI so that anyone hovering their mouse over the KPI will see a tool tip pop up with additional information.

The next column is Thresholds and it is only available for the Target, not the Actual. Thresholds are the points at which indicators change from one state to another. A three-position indicator will have four values: Best, Threshold 2, Threshold 1, and Worst. Indicators with ten positions will have eleven values, and so forth. It might seem strange for Thresholds to have Best and Worst, but these come into play when creating a composite score that can be rolled up. For example, assume that the KPI is sales. If the target is $1 million, then any sales over that value are probably good, or green in a standard three position, green/yellow/red indicator. However, what is the "best" possible value for sales? Theoretically, there is no maximum. Sales could be $10 million, $100 million, or more. Therefore, at some point, a percentage of the target is usually listed as the maximum, and the default in PerformancePoint Server is normally 120%. This means that if one group hits 120% of their sales target and another group hits 140% of their sales target, both get the same "score" for that KPI; in other words, they've both achieved the best the system will consider. If this seems unfair, feel free to increase the value for best, but if it is set to a very high value such as 200%, sales for different groups that are close to each other, such as 110% and 115%, will appear to be almost identical in the grand scheme of the overall score, and in this case both will have a score of well below 100 because they are nowhere near the 200% that is defined as the best possible score.

On the flip side, the Worst is often set at 0%. However, it's unlikely for many metrics that a value of 0% will ever be achieved. Therefore, this number is often increased. If a department has a target of $1 million but only sells $500,000, is that much better than another group with the same target that sells $400,000? Therefore, this value is often placed at something like 70% and any group who sells less than 70% of their target gets a score of zero for that particular KPI. Where to set the Best and Worst are clearly business decisions and should be decided by the business leaders, not IT. Additionally, the raw score, if even shown, is far less important as a number than the scores are in comparison to each other. Most scores are used simply for ranking purposes so that the business can determine which divisions are performing better than others.

Where to set the Thresholds between Best and Worst area are business decisions. If sales reach 97% of the target, is that good enough to turn the indicator green? Or, should the indicator not turn green until sales have passed 100% of the target? And of course, at what point should a yellow indicator turn red? Figure 5-13 shows what

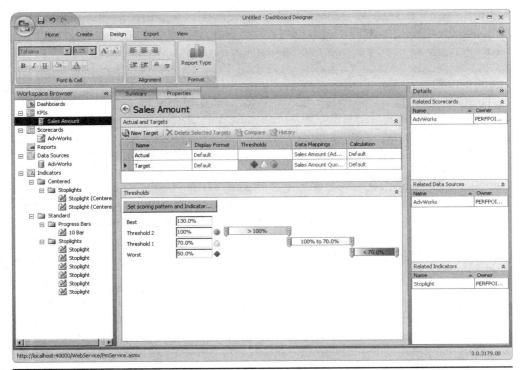

Figure 5-13 *This shows the setting of the thresholds for the current KPI. Note that the developer can type in the values or drag the sliders to adjust the values.*

the indicator might look like for the Sales Amount. In this case, the Best value is set to 130%. Therefore, any division or product group which exceeds 130% will achieve the top score in this area. Threshold 2 is set to 100% so in order to turn green, the actual must exceed the target. Anything from 100% to 70% is yellow, and anything below 70% is red. Note that the Worst is set to 50%. This means that any division or product group that sells less than 50% of its target will effectively have a score of zero for this indicator.

Note also that a button exists in the Thresholds area to set the scoring pattern and indicator. Clicking on this opens a simple wizard that contains several different methods for scoring and banding indicators. The first screen of the wizard asks what scoring pattern should be used: Increasing is Better, Decreasing is Better, or Closer to Target is Better. In addition, there are three different banding methods that control how the score is calculated. The default method is described as Band by Normalized Value of Actual/Target and works as described previously. The second method is called Band by Numeric Value of Actual, which is a much simpler formula and only calculates a score based on the value of the actual number and does not take the target into account. The final method is called Band by Stated Score (Advanced) and calculates a number between any two values chosen. As an example, imagine that the target is a calculation such as Sales Growth % from Prior Period and values of more than 10% should be green, 10% to -10% should be yellow and less than -10% should be red. All three methods are the same regardless of the scoring pattern used.

After selecting the scoring pattern and banding method, the next screen allows the designer to choose the indicator to be used. By default, if only the wizard has been used, there may be only the standard three position stoplight. It's possible to add additional indicators, and this will be discussed momentarily.

The final screen in the Edit Banding Settings wizard asks for the Worst value to be entered if the banding method is the normalized value (which is the default). This is just a hard-coded value in the wizard, but can be made into a formula later in the process. After clicking the Finish button from this page, the new indicator is created and added to the Workspace Browser.

Back on the Sales Amount summary screen, the next column in the Actual and Targets area is called Data Mappings. This is the area where both can be set to the data element to which they are tied. While both Actual and Target can be a fixed value, this makes little sense for the Actual. The Target is not a fixed value either, although it could be when companies proclaim that they want to achieve a certain percentage of gross margin or a certain maximum failure rate in quality control tests, for example. Clicking on the link for either Actual or Target in the Data Mappings column brings up the Dimension Data Source Mapping dialog box. Shown in Figure 5-14, this dialog box allows developers to choose an existing measure and optionally filter that value based on selections from different dimensions. Note that in Figure 5-14, the selections would filter the Sales Amount Quota to bikes sold in Arizona. While this is certainly possible, it's more likely that just the measure will change and will be pointed to a quota or forecasted amount, such as the Sales Quota chosen earlier. It's often better to filter the data later for the entire scorecard. This will be examined later in the chapter.

Next, the wizard allows users to add a time filter formula. This can be useful when a forecast value doesn't exist in the data source, but the developer wants to use a prior period. In such a case, a formula could be entered that would read the measure from a prior period, such as the time period in the previous year from whatever date is currently being viewed. A further and more detailed option on the screen is to use an MDX formula. Multidimensional Expressions, or MDX, is the language used to access Analysis Services, just as Structured Query Language, or SQL, is the language used to access relational data. While beyond the scope of this book, an understanding

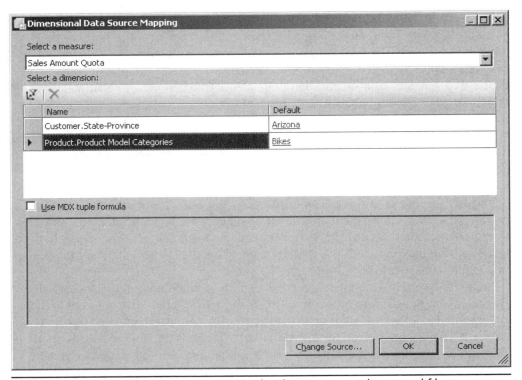

Figure 5-14 *Mapping a KPI to a measure in the data source, with optional filtering set to members in the Customer and Product dimensions*

of MDX would allow the developer to set targets such as a fixed 10% growth over the previous year and filter based on any combination of dimensions and measures.

There is also a Change Source button located at the bottom of the dialog. This allows businesses to maintain target values in something other than the cube holding the values for Actual. For example, the Target Values might be in a separate cube or even an Excel spreadsheet while the Actuals are pulled from a sales cube. This can simplify the creation of a scorecard and its KPIs by permitting the forecasting to be performed and then stored somewhere other than the Analysis Services cube.

The final column is labeled Calculation and describes how the score for this KPI should roll up if this KPI is an objective; in other words, if it has child KPIs. Clicking the link in this column brings up the Calculation dialog and presents the developer with a number of choices. These include Default, which uses the normalized weighted average score of all child KPIs. Another choice is the average of all the child KPIs, which takes each child's target and averages it to the target for this objective. Other options include the sum of child KPIs and the minimum or maximum value of child KPIs.

Returning to the Scorecard view in Figure 5-10 for a moment, notice that the Target column shows both the actual value of the target and the indicator. It is easy to change what is displayed in any Target column simply by right-clicking on the Target header and choosing Properties. This opens the Target Settings dialog shown in Figure 5-15. First, the Target column can show the target value, the actual value, or no value at all. Next, the Target column can show the score, ignore the

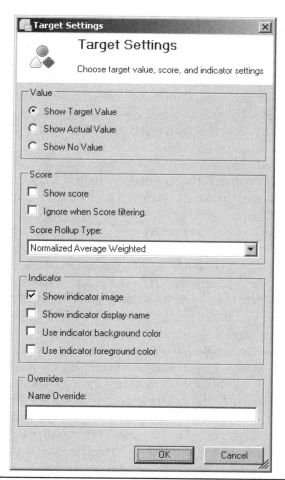

Figure 5-15 *The settings available for the target include showing the target value, actual value, or no value, as well as how the score and indicator should be displayed.*

score when filtering the scorecard, and then allow you to select both the score type and the score rollup type. There are two options for the score type: Raw and Normalized. Raw simply does a straight computation without any of the weighting that occurs in a normalized calculation. For example, if the Actual is 35 and Target is 100, the normalized score might be 23%, but the raw score is 35%. Recall that the normalized score is based on where the thresholds are set, which is why the value for a normalized score is not a straight calculation like the raw score.

The score rollup type has four options: None, Average Weighted, Indicator Count, and Worst Child. This determines how the child KPIs will roll up if this is an objective. The default is Average Weighted because each KPI can be given a different weight, so one KPI might contribute more to the score than another KPI. Indicator Count is just a count of the KPIs, while Worst Child works like a minimum function to show the lowest score of all the child KPIs as the score for the entire objective.

The next section describes what can be done with the indicator. The indicator image is shown by default, and this is often left turned on because it is the graphical images that can help people grasp information more quickly. The indicator display name varies by indicator but for the standard stoplight indicator, green appears as On Target, yellow as Slightly Off Target, and red as Off Target. The target cells can also be set to use the indicator foreground and background colors. Finally, the name override option can replace the word Target in the column header with whatever is typed into the textbox. Figure 5-16 shows an example of a scorecard in which the target column was changed to not show any value, to show the score, and the name override was set to Budget.

Note that in Figure 5-16 both indicators are circles, which means they are green. However, the score for CY 2003 is 80.5% while the score for CY 2004 is 100%. Recall from the earlier discussion that the score is based on the Best and Worst settings. In this case, the default Best of 120% was left in place. While the actual value in CY 2003 did beat the target, it was only about 108% of the target, and it needed to reach 120% in order to get a score of 100%. The CY 2004 actual, on the other hand, is approximately 140% of the target, meaning it passes the 120% Best figure and therefore gets a score of 100%. Given this, it is critical to explain to users that a score of 80.5% does *not* mean that the number is only 80.5% of the target; instead, the indicator is the only means by which the user can determine how well the value did. If the indicator does not turn green until 100% of the target is reached, this means that the actual is at least 100% of the target, even if the score is below 100%. This can be quite confusing for end users and is one reason that scores are not something that should be viewed as absolute numbers, but are a nice way to rank items and look at their relative strengths or weaknesses.

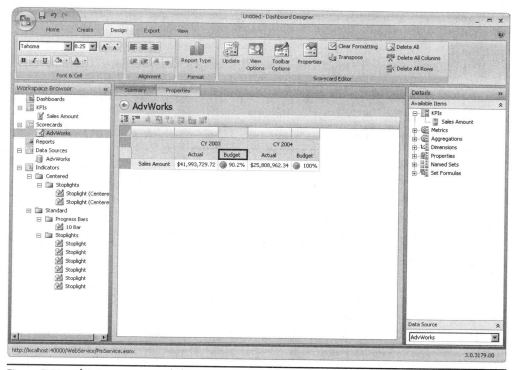

Figure 5-16 *This is a scorecard showing two targets, both in the good or On Target category, but with different scores based on how much over the target they are.*

KPIs with Multiple Targets

A single KPI can have multiple target values. As an example, a particular product line might have its own target value to sell a certain dollar amount in the next year. In addition, that same product line might have a target to be at least 20% of the total revenue for the company. This means that a single Sales Amount KPI might be filtered to that particular product group. One target would be the Sales Amount Target for that product group and the other target would be the Percentage of Total Sales.

Such a configuration can be achieved because a KPI can have any number of targets when it is being designed. Referring back to Figure 5-12, there is a button labeled New Target in the Actual and Targets area. This allows for the addition of new targets to this particular KPI, and of course each target can map to a different data source, or contain hard-coded values.

In order to set up a KPI with multiple targets, the developer clicks on the KPI in the Workspace Browser to bring up the Summary page for the KPI. For the Actual, the name can be changed to match the filtered value. As an example, imagine that this KPI will present the product category of Bikes. The designer would change the name from Actual to Bikes and then click on Data Mappings. Then a filter would be added to filter just by bikes; this is similar to what was shown in Figure 5-14 but would not also include the State-Province filter.

Next, the Target would have its data mapping changed to the target of just sales for bikes. In the Adventure Works cubes there are not sales forecasts for different product categories, so for the sake of this example a hard-coded value will be used. Again, the designer would simply click on the Data Mappings link and choose the appropriate value for the target. The name Target could be changed or left the same, depending on the needs of the business. The thresholds and indicator are set as before.

Finally, the designer would click on the New Target button to add a new target to the KPI. This target, however, will map to either the actual Sales Amount or the Sales Amount Quota without any filters. Remember that this target is all sales, and Adventure Works is mostly a company built to sell bicycles, so they determine that Bikes should be at least 90% of total sales. Therefore, the actual for bikes can be compared to either the actual sales or the quota, whichever the business determines is the better approach (typically, business would use the actual sales and not the quota in this case.) The thresholds, however, are set so that the indicator should move to the On Target position at 90% or higher.

For this new target, a name such as Total or Percentage of Total can be used. An indicator must be added as nothing comes up by default. Once the thresholds are set and the data is mapped, returning to the scorecard now reveals additional items in the Details pane. Figure 5-17 shows that while there is still just a single KPI of Sales Amount, there are three Metrics: Bikes, Target, and % of Total.

These three metrics have been placed in the grid. The column labeled Bikes is the Sales Amount measure filtered to show data for just the bikes category (which is the majority of the data). The Target column would be the sales quota set for bikes; in this case it is merely a hard-coded value of $30 million because there is not an actual forecast for bikes in the cube. The threshold is set so that the current bike sales of approximately $22.5 million are in the red, or Off Target, position. Finally, the % of Total column represents the Sales Amount measure for all products. Bikes are a significant part of this measure, but the goal is for bikes to be 90% or higher; currently bikes represent only about 87% of total revenues, so the indicator is yellow or Slightly Off Target.

Note that the % of Total column isn't actually showing the percentage, but the Sales Amount measure. If the goal was to show the actual percentage, this would be one of the times than an MDX expression would be needed. In this case, the Data

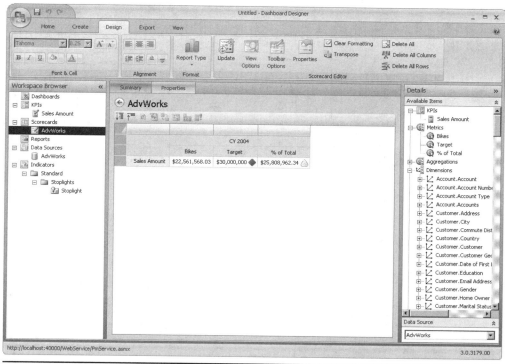

Figure 5-17 *A scorecard filtered to show data for just the product category of bikes. Note that the column header was changed from Actual to Bikes, and a second target was added.*

Mapping for the % of Total target would be the Sales Amount for Bikes divided by the Sales Amount for all products. Here is the MDX formula that accomplishes this:

```
([Product].[Product Categories].[Bikes],[Measures].[Sales Amount])/
[Measures].[Sales Amount]
```

Once this formula is added as the data mapping for the % of Total target and some formatting is applied, the actual percentage appears as shown in Figure 5-18.

Adding Multiple KPIs at Once

When adding KPIs in the Dashboard Designer, it's a relatively simple matter to click the Create ribbon and then the KPI button. Unfortunately this will only let developers add one KPI at a time and this can obviously grow tedious when there

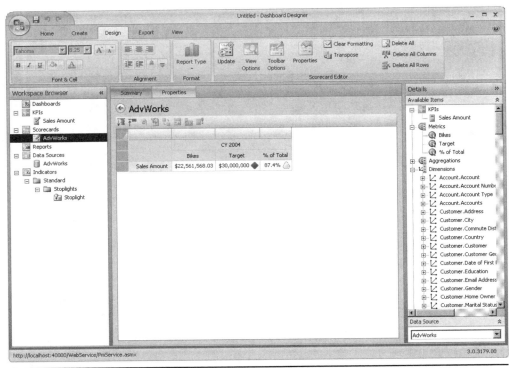

Figure 5-18 *The scorecard now shows that bikes are 87.4% of all sales, instead of showing the actual sales as before. This shows how adding an MDX calculation can enhance a scorecard.*

are dozens of KPIs that need to be added. Recall, however, that when creating a new scorecard, the wizard walks the developer through to a screen that allows for the addition of any number of KPIs at once. Technically the developer will have to click the Add KPI button once for each new KPI, but this process is still much faster than using the KPI button on the Create ribbon.

More importantly, if the KPIs are already created in the Analysis Services cube, any number can be selected for inclusion at once. Figure 5-8 showed both of these views of the wizard screen for adding new KPIs.

Therefore, one strategy for adding many KPIs at once is to simply create a new scorecard and add the KPIs there by creating many at one time; this is often faster than creating them one at a time using the KPI button on the Create ribbon. And, when the new scorecard wizard is done, the new KPIs appear in the Details pane under the KPIs folder. These KPIs can now be added to any scorecard, not just the scorecard that created them when the wizard was run.

Working with Objectives

Objectives are higher level KPIs. They are usually designed to aggregate the scores of KPIs below them. For example, a Gross Profit Margin objective might have two KPIs below it, such as in the case of the Adventure Works cube that has both an Internet Gross Profit Margin and a Reseller Gross Profit Margin. In some cases, it's even possible to have a single objective at the very top of the scorecard to get an overall score for all indicators. In fact, this is often a useful way to see a single number that represents the health of the entire business or division.

In order to create an objective, developers create a new KPI but on the first page of the wizard they select Objective instead of Blank KPI. The objective takes a name, an optional display folder, and the option to add Read permission settings to all users, and that's all there is to the wizard. The objective is added as a KPI and appears in the KPIs list.

In order to make this new objective into an actual objective, it must be added to a scorecard and then other KPIs must be placed below it. However, simply placing them below the objective is not enough. After being placed below the objective, the child KPIs are indented one level using the Decrease Level button on the Edit ribbon. As many KPIs as necessary can roll up to a single objective. Likewise, objectives can roll up into other objectives.

Figure 5-19 shows an example of a simple scorecard in which an objective has been added. The objective is named Overall Gross Profit Margin and below it are two standard KPIs: Internet Gross Profit Margin and Reseller Gross Profit Margin. These two standard KPIs are based on measures of the same names in the Adventure Works cube. The objective and the two KPIs were then placed on the scorecard in this order and the Internet Gross Profit Margin and Reseller Gross Profit Margin KPIs were selected and the Decrease Level button was clicked. Figure 5-19 shows the Decrease Level button with a circle around it so that it is easier to locate.

In addition to simply turning Overall Gross Profit Margin into an objective, the objective has an indicator and, to the right of the indicator, a score. Don't be confused by the target for the two standard KPIs showing two percentages. The first percentage, to the left of the indicator, is the target. The second percentage, to the right of the indicator, is the score. Management at the Adventure Works company has determined that their goal is for a 40% gross profit margin on sales over the Internet, and a 5% gross profit margin on sales through the reseller channel. As the indicators make plain, the goal for Internet Gross Profit Margin is being achieved; in other words, the KPI is On Target. The Reseller Gross Profit Margin, on the other hand, is well below the 5% target, registering a paltry .58%. Therefore, this indicator is Off Target and there is a correspondingly low score.

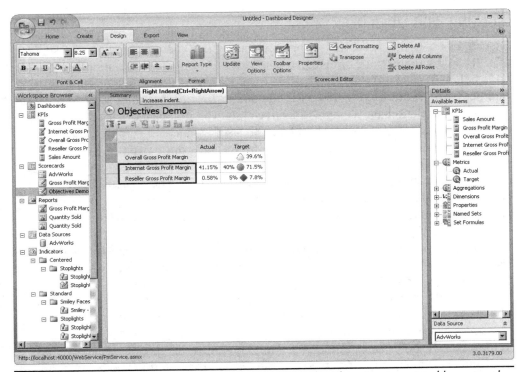

Figure 5-19 *An objective is a KPI that has child KPIs. The objective is created by using the Decrease Level button on the child KPIs.*

Taken as an overall measure of the business, however, what is the answer if an executive asks, "How is our gross profit margin?" According to this scorecard, it's slightly off target, which points to the yellow indicator. However, there can be more to it than just looking at the scores of the items below it. Not all child KPIs may be as critical as others. Scorecard developers can change the weighting of different KPIs by right-clicking on the name column of a particular KPI in the scorecard and then choosing Properties. This opens the KPI View Settings dialog box and the first option is the Score Rollup Weight, as shown in Figure 5-20. Assume that management has decided to focus mostly on Internet sales and downplay the reseller channel. Therefore, they want the Internet Gross Profit Margin to carry five times more weight than the Reseller Gross Profit Margin KPI when the score is being determined. Changing the score rollup weight from one to five while leaving the reseller score at one now results in the score for the objective moving from 39.6% to 60.8%, as can be seen in the background of Figure 5-20.

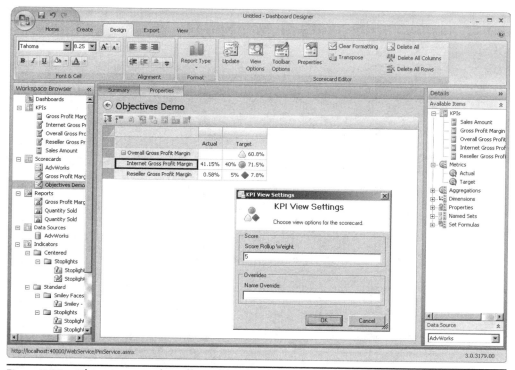

Figure 5-20 *Objectives can be affected by the Score Rollup Weight that can be set for each child KPI under an objective.*

Aggregations and Trends

Recall that one of the benefits of KPIs over measures is that they can contain a trend. So far when dealing with KPIs, no trend has been apparent. When dealing with scorecards, there is a category in the Details pane called Aggregations, and this is useful for not just trends, but also for adding sums, averages, and so forth to the scorecard.

Figure 5-21 shows a simple scorecard with a single KPI, Sales. This uses the same Sales Amount used in other examples, and the target has been set to Sales Amount Quota. Three years of data are shown and in each case, sales have exceeded the target. However, if there is a desire to also see a total for the sales for all three years, this can be achieved by dragging the Sum from the Aggregations node and dropping it on the scorecard. Notice this is simply a sum of the values shown and could just have easily been the average, maximum, or minimum.

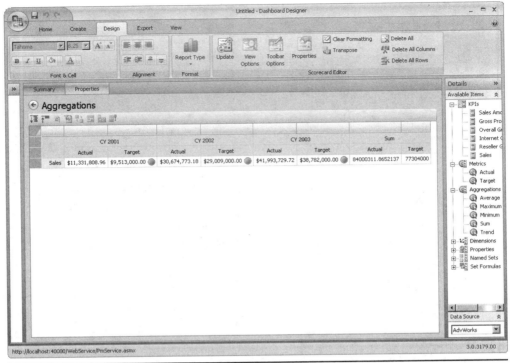

Figure 5-21 *This is a Sum Aggregation that has been added to the scorecard. Aggregations are automatically available as part of the Details pane for a scorecard.*

Trends are a little different. First, it's just as easy to drag the Trend value from the Aggregations node and drop it on the scorecard. However, exactly what is it trending? The trend that is built into the product only looks at the previous two columns and trends from those. In other words, the trend will look at the actual for 2002 and compare it to the actual for 2003, and do the same for the targets (although trends for targets are often not terribly useful.)

Figure 5-22 shows what happens when the trend is added. The sum has been removed, the trend added, and another KPI, Gross Profit Margin, has also been added. Notice that while the Actual for sales has risen from 2002 to 2003, the Actual for the gross profit margin has fallen slightly. The trend for Sales is up while the trend for Gross Profit Margin is down.

If a business decides it needs a more powerful trending algorithm than just comparing the last two periods, there are two approaches. First, a KPI can be created that includes the MDX necessary to perform the calculation. Second, a measure could be built into the Analysis Services cube that performs the trending calculation.

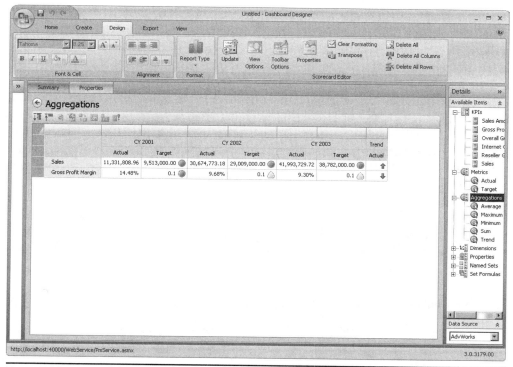

Figure 5-22 *One of the strengths of KPIs is that they can identify trends. The Trend included with the Aggregations is shown here, but it can only identify a trend over the last two periods.*

In either case, the trend indicators can be used to display the trend results to the end user, because the arrows used to show a trend are simply indicators, just like the red/yellow/green indicators seen so far.

Indicators

There are a number of indicators in PerformancePoint Server from which to choose. So far the images shown have only included a simple, three position indicator called the Stoplight. There are, however, a number of additional indicators and these include some with more than just three positions.

Currently available indicators are displayed in the Workspace Browser, but more can be added by clicking on the Indicator button on the Create ribbon. This opens the Select An Indicator template dialog box. There are two basic categories of indicators: Centered and Standard. Centered indicators are those used when the scoring pattern for a KPI is Closer to Target is Better. This is the case when a variance either direction is bad. Imagine that a company is producing cardboard boxes and the boxes have separate lids. The lids must fit snugly on the boxes but not be so small that they will not fit. Additionally, if the lid is too large, the snug fit is lost. Therefore, there is an allowable tolerance and any lids that are too large or too small are rejected as defective. Therefore, centered indicators deal with issues when variances are a problem. Standard indicators, on the other hand, are used when the scoring pattern is either Increasing is Better or Decreasing is Better.

There is actually another category of indicators listed as Blank Indicator. This allows businesses to create their own indicators. The indicators can be standard or centered and have two to ten levels. Developers can then add custom graphics files for each level as well as the text color, background color, and the display name for that level.

Under both Standard and Centered are several categories of existing indicators: Gauges, Miscellaneous, Progress Bars, Smiley Faces, Stoplights, Thermometers, and Trends. In order to add a new indicator for use with the current workspace in Dashboard Designer, simply select the desired indicator and click OK. Figure 5-23 shows the

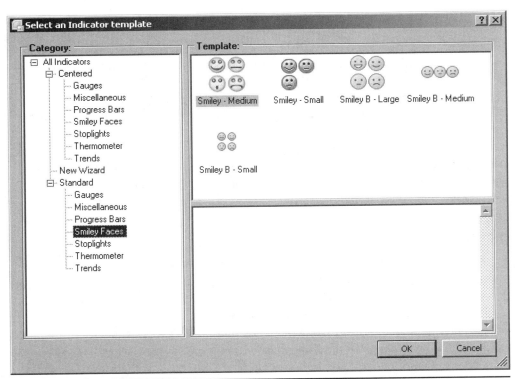

Figure 5-23   *The indicators that come with PerformancePoint Server include a variety of graphics in both standard and centered indicators.*

selection of the Smiley—Medium indicator from the Standard category. Once the OK button is clicked, the new indicator will appear in the Workspace Browser.

In order to change the indicator for an existing KPI, the developer can click on the KPI in the Workspace Browser and then click on the Thresholds cell for the target metric. In the Thresholds screen the developer can click on the Set Scoring pattern and Indicator button to bring up the Edit Banding Settings wizard. The second screen of the wizard is entitled Select Indicator and allows the developer to choose from all of the indicators currently in the workspace. Note that only the correct type of indicators will show up; if the developer chooses a scoring pattern of Closer to Target is Better, only centered indicators will appear in the list. Otherwise, only standard indicators will show up. Once the selection is made, the scorecard view can be updated to reflect the new indicator. Figure 5-24 shows the scorecard with the Smiley—Medium indicator chosen for the Target value.

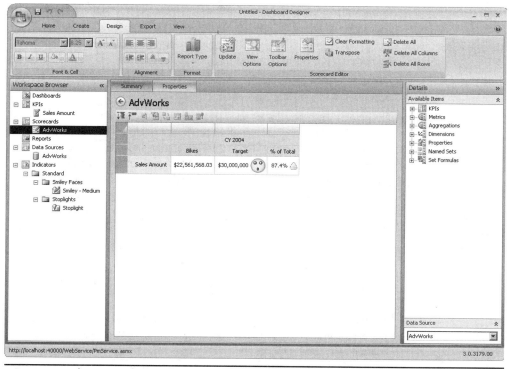

Figure 5-24 *The KPI indicator has been changed from the normal Stoplight to the Smiley.*

Reports and Strategy Maps

While scorecards are the primary focus of the monitoring piece of PerformancePoint Server, they are not the only piece. Reports also exist here, and while they blur the line with the analytics part of PerformancePoint Server, they are included here because they are part of the Dashboard Designer and can be included in dashboards, which will be discussed later in this chapter.

Right-clicking on the Reports node in the Workspace Browser and then choosing New Report opens up the Select a Report template dialog box. There are a number of different report types available, as shown in Figure 5-25. See Table 5-1 to understand what these different types of report templates do.

Report Template	Description
Analytic Chart and Analytic Grid	Analytic charts and grids are either chart or grid views of OLAP data. The charts can be either line or bar charts. Both of these chart types require Analysis Services to be the data source. These templates are preferred over the PivotChart and PivotTable templates because they are thin-client tools as opposed to the thick-client PivotChart and PivotTable controls. A caveat with the Analytic Chart and Grid is that they only work with Analysis Services 2005, so they are not backwards-compatible with Analysis Services 2000.
Excel Services	This template will pull data from Excel Services workbooks that have already been published so they can be included in a report view.
PivotChart and PivotTable	The PivotChart and PivotTable templates are included for backwards-compatibility with the Office 2003 Office Web Components. While the PivotChart includes more chart types than the Analytic Chart, the Analytic Chart and Analytic Grid are considered the successors to the PivotChart and PivotTable. This because the PivotChart and PivotTable require the download and installation of ActiveX controls on the client machine. Therefore, use of the PivotChart and PivotTable is discouraged in comparison to the Analytic Chart and Analytic Grid.
ProClarity Analytics Server Page	ProClarity Analytics Server, or PAS, is a full-featured analytics client. Eventually, the functionality available in PAS will all be moved into PerformancePoint Server. Until this, this report type will like to an existing view (or report) in PAS. This will be described in detail in Chapter 6.
Spreadsheet	This template will create an Excel workbook with the appropriate data. The workbook will be stored in PerformancePoint Monitoring Server.
SQL Server Report	This template doesn't create a report in SQL Server Reporting Services, but instead creates a reference to an existing Reporting Services report. Reporting Services reports that access BI data will be discussed in Chapter 10.
Strategy Map	This template ties KPIs to the different objectives in a strategy map that was created in Visio 2007. Strategy maps will be discussed later in this chapter.

Table 5-1 *Report Templates and Their Functions*

Report Template	Description
Trend Analysis Chart	The Trend Analysis Chart is a report that shows the history for a KPI. It has the additional (and very powerful) option to use one of the SQL Server data mining algorithms to generate a forecast for that data so that predictions can be made about future values.
Web Page	This template creates a reference to an existing web page. It does not create a new web page on its own.

Table 5-1   *Report Templates and Their Functions* (continued)

Creating an Analytic Chart Report

When you are creating a new Analytic Chart, choosing the template from the wizard (or clicking the Analytic Chart button from the Create ribbon) opens the Create an Analytic Chart Report dialog box. This box starts with the same three questions seen on most of the wizards: the name of the report, an optional display folder, and a checkbox asking whether or not all authenticated users should have Read permissions.

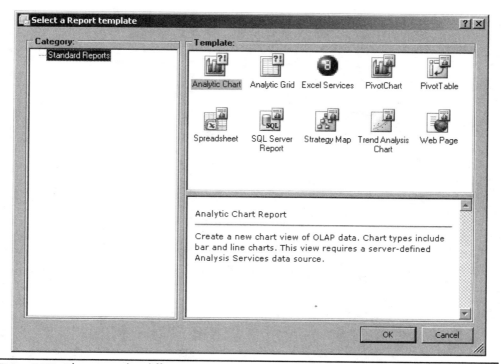

Figure 5-25   *These are the different report types provided by PerformancePoint Server. These begin to move into the analytics portion of PerformancePoint Server but are created in the Dashboard Designer.*

The second page of the wizard asks for the developer to choose a data source, and then the report is created.

Once the report has been generated, the design surface opens in the Design tab in the main work area. In the Details pane is a list of all measures, dimensions, and named sets. Developers can simply drag and drop items from the Details pane and then drop them into the three panels at the bottom of the Design tab, which includes Series, Bottom Axis, and Background. With most typical charts, the bottom axis will represent time and the series will contain one or more measures.

Figure 5-26 shows an example of an Analytic Chart showing the order quantity for eight quarters. The Order Quantity measure has been placed in the Series panel. The Date.Calendar hierarchy has been added to the Bottom Axis panel. After adding the hierarchy, the members have to be selected by the designer. Otherwise only the default member is chosen, which is usually the All member. In order to choose the individual members, developers can right-click on the dimension in the Bottom Axis panel and choose Select Members or click the drop-down indicator to the right of the hierarchy. Either will open up a dialog box which lets the developer expand the

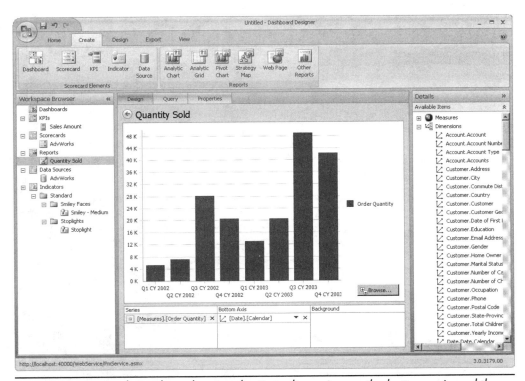

Figure 5-26 *An Analytic Chart showing the Date dimension on the bottom axis and the Order Quantity as the series*

various levels of the hierarchy and select any members desired. In this case, the four quarters from each year of 2002 and 2003 were chosen.

Notice that nothing is currently in the Background panel. By default, all dimensions are always involved in a query, but they typically are defaulted to the All level so they don't filter the data in any way by default. There are times that reports will need to be filtered by data that is not otherwise displayed as part of the chart or grid. For example, this report could have its name changed to Bikes Quantity Sold and the data could be filtered by bikes. To do this, the Product.Product Categories dimension hierarchy could be placed in the Background panel and then just the Bikes member selected. This would filter the entire report without having to actually display Bikes on the bottom axis or as part of the series.

Once the Analytic Chart has been created, it appears static in the Design pane. However, there is a Browse button that opens the report in a viewer window, and once this is rendered, the report contains some limited interactivity. Specifically, the bars of the chart are live, clickable regions. Clicking on a bar drills down one level in the hierarchy that is placed in the series. Given that in this example, a measure was placed in the Series, there's no drill down available. However, users can right-click on a bar, choose Drill Down To, and then drill down on any dimension. The user can also basically switch the report from drilling down on the dimension in the series to the one in the bottom axis by right-clicking on a bar and selecting Switch To, followed by the name of the hierarchy. For example, the chart shown in Figure 5-26 has eight bars representing the quarters of 2002 and 2003. If the user uses Switch To in order to select the Time hierarchy, then clicking on one of those bars drills down from that particular quarter to the three months that make up that quarter. Clicking on a bar for the month drills down to the individual days for that month. The drilldown path is determined by the hierarchy structure; in this case, the Date.Calendar hierarchy goes from year to quarter to month to day, so clicking on the bars follows this path of drilling down. There are other capabilities of the Analytic Chart, which will be discussed in Chapter 6 when the analysis piece of PerformancePoint Server is covered.

Creating an Analytic Grid is nearly identical to creating an Analytic Chart. One of the primary differences is that rather than a Series panel, in this case there is a Rows panel. When building charts, it is not uncommon to place both dimensions and measures on the Columns, and other dimensions on the rows. Additional hierarchies can be added to the background if they will be used to filter once this report is added to a dashboard. The Analytic Grid will be discussed in greater detail in Chapter 6.

Creating a Trend Analysis Chart

One special type of report is a Trend Analysis Chart, often just called a Trend Chart. The Trend Chart trends a KPI on a scorecard. This trend is for historical data but can also be used to create a forecast using one of the data mining algorithms built into

Analysis Services. Note that more than one KPI can be used but each KPI will get its own Trend Chart. The Trend Chart still uses the Office Web Components, but its functionality cannot be reproduced currently using the Analytic Chart.

There is a server property setting in Analysis Services that must be set in order for this feature to work. This property is named DataMining\AllowSessionMiningModels and it must be set to True, as the default value is False. In order to this, a database or data warehousing administer would open SQL Server Management Studio and connect to the server running Analysis Services. By right-clicking on the server and choosing Properties, the administrator can access the server properties and change the setting. Figure 5-27 shows both the location of the setting and the fact that it has been set to true, although it has not yet been changed. Notice also in Figure 5-27 that the Restart column does not have a Yes in it. This is good news; this means the server does not have to be restarted when this value is changed.

Once the AllowSessionMiningModels property has been set to True, the Trend Chart can be created and properly provide forecasts. To produce a forecast, there must be at least three time periods on which to build the forecast, though more values will produce better forecasts up to a point. You should realize, however, that

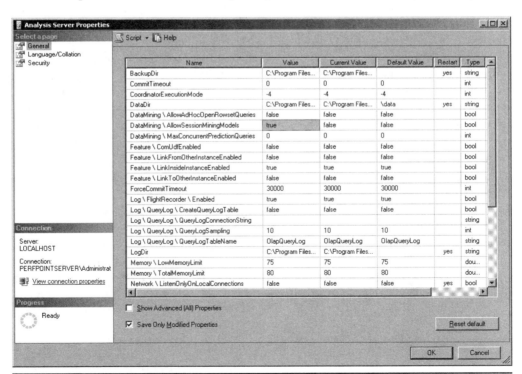

Figure 5-27 *Setting the AllowSessionMiningModel property on the Analysis Services instance in order to enable Trend Analysis Charts*

sales data for a product that occurred ten years ago probably has little bearing on sales today.

In order to create a Trend Chart, there must be a scorecard that contains the KPI of interest. For this example there is a simple scorecard that shows the Gross Profit Margin for the eight quarters covering 2002 and 2003. By right-clicking on Reports and then New Report, the Trend Analysis Chart template can be chosen. The first screen of the Create Trend Analysis Chart dialog box asks the same three questions as the others: the name, folder, and Read permission settings. The next step asks for the scorecard containing the KPIs. If a new scorecard has been created but does not show up in the list, cancel out of the wizard, publish the scorecard, and then rerun the wizard.

After selecting the scorecard, a list of KPIs appears. Remember that there is one Trend Chart per KPI, so selecting multiple KPIs on this screen will result in multiple Trend Charts. Finally, clicking the Finish button builds the report. After closing the wizard, the designer is presented with a report similar to that shown in Figure 5-28. By default, the chart shows a line graph for the actual values.

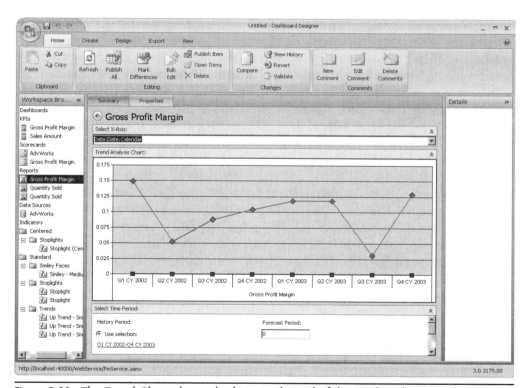

Figure 5-28   *The Trend Chart shows the historical trend of the KPI but does not show any forecast until a forecast period is set.*

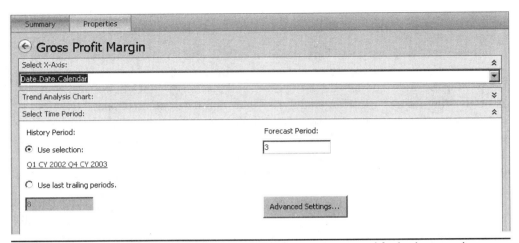

Figure 5-29 *The Select Time Period panel allows designers to modify the historical time period shown as well as forecast future periods.*

Below the chart is a panel labeled Select Time Period. This panel is shown in its entirety in Figure 5-29. This is where designers can enter the number of time periods to forecast (up to three). Designers can also choose to modify the selection of values used for input. By default this Trend Chart chose the eight quarters that were on the scorecard, but clicking on the link brings up the hierarchy where individual members can be checked or unchecked. Alternately, the developer could simply click on the radio button to enter a fixed number of trailing periods to use for the forecast. The advanced settings allow some fine tuning of the algorithm. To learn more about the algorithm, information is available on the time series algorithm in the SQL Server books online.

After choosing to forecast three periods into the future, the chart updates to that shown in Figure 5-30. In this instance, the last three periods are forecast from the data mining algorithm, while previous values are the actual values. The forecasted values actually appear in red while the historical data is in blue. In Figure 5-30, the forecast seems to be just slightly below 10% for this particular Trend Chart.

Strategy Maps

Recall from Chapter 4 that strategy maps are often used to provide a high level overview of the business. PerformancePoint Server allows for a lower-level of strategy map to be employed as a viewing tool. These strategy maps are simply Visio 2007 images that have shapes mapped directly to KPIs on a scorecard. The strategy

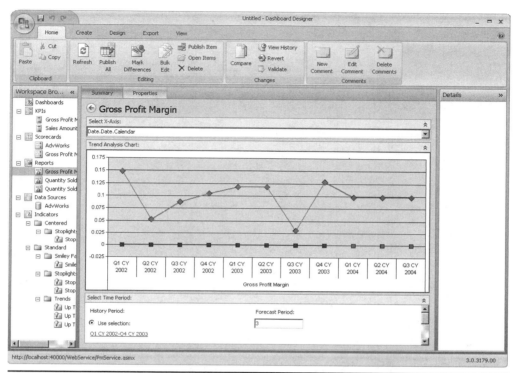

Figure 5-30 *The Trend Chart with a forecast of the gross profit margin over the next three quarters.*

maps can be created in Visio 2007 or directly within PerformancePoint Server, which basically uses a stripped down Visio editor. The shapes become live in that they can take on the name of the KPI and change color to match the color of the indicator.

In order to set up a strategy map, it will be necessary to lay out the map in Visio or the PerformancePoint Server using blank shapes. Each KPI and Objective to be represented will need its own shape on the Visio diagram. The actual shape isn't particularly important, but typically it's a rectangle or other shape that can hold text inside it.

Figure 5-31 shows a simplified strategy map that contains just a single objective and two metrics to achieve that objective. The objective is to maximize gross profit margin. The two metrics that will feed this objective are Internet Gross Profit Margin and Reseller Gross Profit Margin. These two metrics are already KPIs on a scorecard, and the strategy map objective is also an objective on the same scorecard.

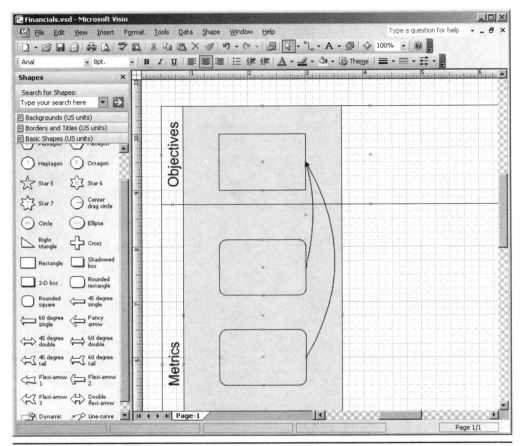

Figure 5-31   *A simplified strategy map created in Visio 2007*

In order to use this Visio file as a strategy map, the first step is to create a new report and choose the Strategy Map template. After giving the report a name, the wizard asks what scorecard will serve as the basis for the strategy map. In this case, the same scorecard that was used to demonstrate scorecard objectives will be used because it contains two KPIs that roll up into a single objective, and the strategy map was built to reflect this particular scenario. After selecting the appropriate scorecard and finishing the wizard, the report displays in the main work area of Dashboard Designer, but it is blank. The developer must click on the Edit Strategy Map button on the Edit ribbon, which launches the Strategy Map Editor dialog box. This is also initially blank, but clicking on the Open Visio File button will allow the developer to choose a Visio file to use. Figure 5-32 shows the Visio file from the previous

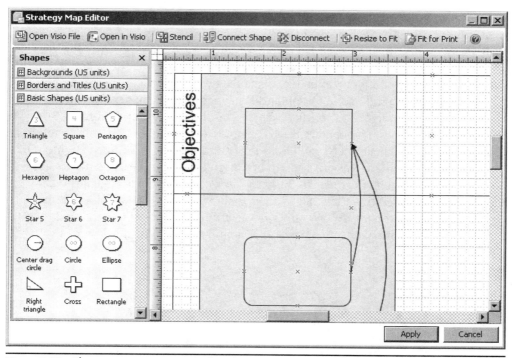

Figure 5-32 *The strategy map viewed in the Strategy Map Editor in Dashboard Designer*

figure loaded into the Strategy Map Editor. Note that it's possible to modify the strategy map here. New shapes can be added, existing shapes removed, and so forth. Note also that the Strategy Map Editor looks almost identical to full-blown Visio, including the ability to open various stencils in order to access different shapes.

Once the strategy map is laid out as desired, the most important part of the dialog is the Connect Shape button. First, the developer clicks on one of the shapes on the diagram and then clicks the Connect Shape button. This opens a dialog box that lists the KPIs on the scorecard that was chosen when the strategy map report was being created. In this example, the rectangle inside the Objectives section of the strategy map will be mapped to the KPI named Overall Gross Profit Margin, which is actually an objective in the scorecard. After selecting the KPI, it is possible to tie it to either the actual KPI or its target. (In most cases the developer will choose target.) Recall from the section on Objectives in a Scorecard that the objective doesn't have an actual—it just has a target that is an indicator of its health. Likewise, the interest here is in the overall health of the metric, which is displayed by the target. Also, by default, the text in the shape becomes that of the KPI name. This can be changed later if desired.

In this example, the two rounded rectangles are tied to Internet Gross Profit Margin and Reseller Gross Profit Margin respectively. The order does not matter, because both roll up into the objective. Once the developer clicks the Apply button, the strategy map is rendered in Dashboard Designer and the shapes take on the colors of the indicators for the KPIs or Objectives they represent. Figure 5-33 shows that the shapes now contain the KPI names and while it is difficult to tell in a black and white image, the Overall Gross Profit Margin box is yellow (Slightly Off Target), the Internet Gross Profit Margin box is green (On Target) and the Reseller Gross Profit Margin box is red (Off Target.) The text in the boxes matches that of the KPI names but editing the strategy map again will allow the developer to type anything into those boxes, so Overall Gross Profit Margin could be modified to a more business-oriented objective, such as Maximize Gross Profit Margin.

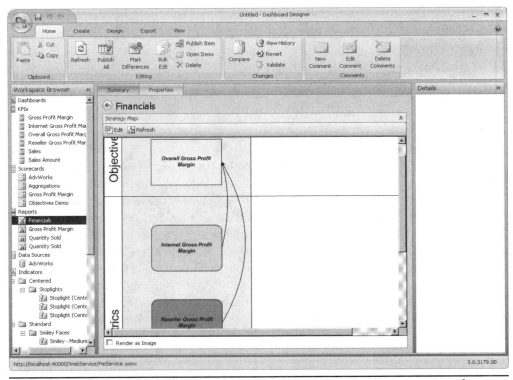

Figure 5-33 *The strategy map shapes change colors and take on the KPI names after being connected to KPIs on a scorecard.*

Dashboards—Putting it All Together

Remember that the tool used throughout this chapter is the Dashboard Designer, not the Scorecard Designer. The reason for this is that scorecards are one of several possible elements that can be placed on a dashboard, and it is the dashboard that is ultimately viewable by end users. The reason the dashboard is the element visible to end users is because a single dashboard might contain multiple scorecards, reports, strategy maps, or any combination of these elements. Additionally, a dashboard might host a variety of scorecards and reports but have a single set of parameters that the user can change to modify all of the elements on the dashboard at once.

Take as an example the Product dimension. If all scorecards and reports are created without any filtering, they are actually using all products and are thus showing totals for all products combined. However, a product manager in charge of the Bikes line might want to filter out everything but bikes, while the product manager for Clothing and Accessories wants to examine those product lines. Therefore, a drop-down could be added to the dashboard that would allow users to filter the data in all the scorecards, reports, and strategy maps on the dashboard at once.

Creating a Dashboard

Creating a dashboard works like creating just about anything else; the developer can right-click on the Dashboards node or click the Dashboard button on the Create ribbon. Either one will open the Select a Dashboard template dialog box. There are several templates available including those with two and three columns, two and three rows, and so forth. Choosing a template will make it easier to place multiple items on the dashboard.

After choosing a template and giving the dashboard a name, the dashboard opens in the main work area and contains a number of elements. One thing to note is that a single dashboard can have multiple pages, each with its own layout, title, and so forth. By default the dashboard has just a single page with the layout that was chosen when the dashboard was created. Adding and deleting pages is as simple as using the New Page and Delete Page buttons at the top of the dashboard editor. Pages will appear as tabs across the top of the dashboard when it is viewed in SharePoint.

In the Dashboard Content panel of the editor are zones that can hold scorecards or reports. The developer can add new zones, delete zones, split existing zones, and so on, just by right-clicking in the design area. To get started, however, the developer merely needs to drag and drop items from the Available Items window into the different zones. In Figure 5-34, the name of the page has been changed to Financial Overview, the AdvWorks-Multiple Targets scorecard has been added to the top zone, and the AdvWorks-Objectives scorecard has been added to the center zone.

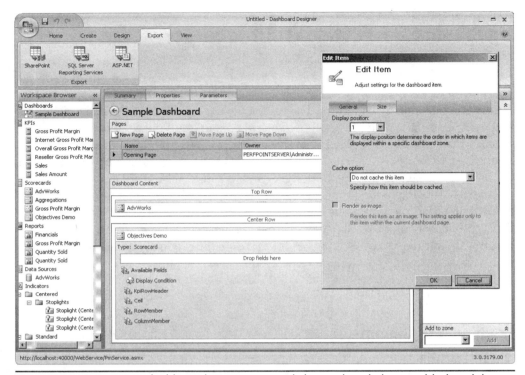

Figure 5-34   *Creating a dashboard. Two scorecards have already been added and the default page has been renamed.*

Note that each zone has properties that can be changed. The small down arrow next to the close button for each item in the dashboard will allow the developer to access the Edit Item dialog box for that particular scorecard or report. The Edit Item dialog lets users determine the order in which items in that zone are displayed. This is because a single zone can host more than one item.

The Edit Item also lets the developer decide whether or not to cache this particular item. Caching makes sense when the underlying data does not change often or when the most up-to-date information is not critical, such as when viewing fixed date, historical data. With caching turned off, it means that each time an item is rendered, PerformancePoint Server goes back to the cube to get its data.

Finally, the Edit Item dialog lets the developer set the height and width for each zone. By default, the height and width automatically adjust to fit the entire zone on the screen, but the height and width can be constrained to either a fixed number of pixels or a fixed percentage of the screen.

Zones have their own settings as well, and this dialog box is accessed by right-clicking on a zone title and choosing Zone Settings. A single zone could have two scorecards and a report, for example. These may be laid out horizontally, vertically, or stacked, in which case each item will get its own tab. The horizontal, vertical, or stacked options are in the Orientation tab of the Zone Settings.

At this point, the dashboard can be exported for viewing. Note that in Figure 5-34 the Edit ribbon is showing and one of the buttons is labeled SharePoint Site, which will be the most common choice. Before deploying the dashboard, it must be published to the server. Once the dashboard is published, clicking on the SharePoint button will first prompt the developer to select a dashboard to export, while the next screen prompts the developer to provide the name of the SharePoint server and the document library. The next screen will ask what master page to use for the display. By default, PerformancePoint Server ships with a simple set of master pages but companies are free to add their own to achieve a particular layout. Figure 5-35 shows what this particular dashboard looks like in SharePoint using the default PerformancePointDefault master page. There are buttons above each scorecard, which allows end users to slightly modify the display of roll up values, where they can see the default roll up, the "worst child" (minimum) roll up, or the number of each type of indicator, which means for the Objectives demo there would be one On Target and one Off Target.

The other way to view a dashboard is to click the Preview button on the Edit ribbon. This will show the dashboard in the browser by deploying it to a preview site.

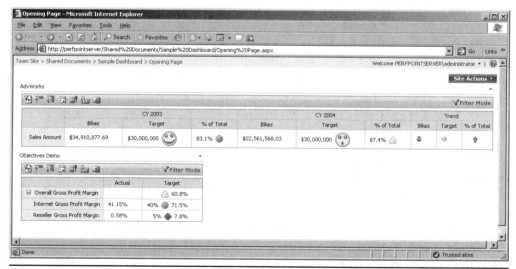

Figure 5-35 *A dashboard with two scorecards, being rendered in SharePoint*

This is useful as the dashboard under construction is not visible to others. The preview is exported as an ASP.NET page and is stored in a preview area on PerformancePoint Server, where it remains even after the preview is closed. Previewing is the preferred method while the dashboard is under construction and contains all the functionality of a fully-deployed dashboard.

Adding Filters to the Dashboard

It is possible to add filters, or parameters, to the dashboard and these filters can affect one or more of the scorecards and reports on the dashboard. Creating the filter and placing it on the dashboard is relatively easy. Hooking the filter up to the scorecards and reports is a separate process but, while still relatively easy, requires a different approach for a scorecard versus a report.

In order to create a filter, the dashboard is opened in Dashboard Designer where developer clicks on the Filters tab. In the Filters panel there is a button labeled New Filter and clicking on that opens up the Select a Dashboard Filter Template dialog box. There are a number of templates available, including MDX Query, Member Selection, Named Sets, Tabular Values, and a couple to work with time intelligence (such as the previous quarter, the same period for the previous year, and so forth.) One of the simplest ways to create a filter is to use the Member Selection template, which loads a dimension and allows the developer to select what members should appear in the list. An MDX Query is a better option if the list needs to be dynamic as in cases where values will be added or removed frequently; in this case, using the Children method or Descendants function in MDX will be useful. For this example the Member Selection template will be chosen.

After naming the filter, in this case Product Category, the data source is chosen. Since the members will come from a dimension, the AdvWorks data source will be used. The next screen asks for the dimension that contains the members and then the members themselves. The dimension will be Product.Product Categories. Be careful when selecting the members as the end users will often want to able to see the All level (the total for everything) and then individual members as well. Developers can also right-click on a member in the selector and set that member as the default member in the filter. In the example of Product Categories, the members selected are All Products, Accessories, Bikes, Clothing, and Components. Figure 5-36 shows what this dialog will look like after the selections have been made, assuming that the All member was chosen as the default value.

The next screen presents the designer with three options for how to display the members to end users: List, Tree, and Multi-Select Tree. The List is a flat list, meaning it does not show any hierarchical structure. For some lists this is fine, but users may find it confusing if there are members from different levels, such as an All level and then the children under that All level. A better choice for showing the

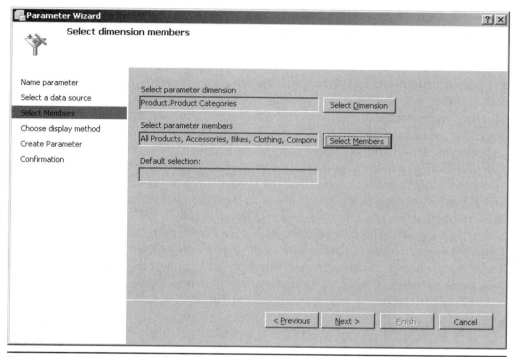

Figure 5-36 *Creating a new filter that will be placed on a dashboard. Filters are created independently of any scorecard or report.*

hierarchical structure is either the Tree or the Multi-Select Tree. As their names imply, the Tree shows a hierarchical structure of the members, but only one member may be selected. The Multi-Select Tree shows the members in a hierarchical structure and allows end users to select multiple members at once, using check boxes next to each member.

Once the filter has been created, it appears in the Available Items pane. Moving back to the Editor tab allows the developer to drag the filter and drop it on the dashboard. Typically filters are placed in a small zone at the top of the page. Simply placing the filter on the page does not tie it to anything. This is a separate process that is done for each item on the page.

Tying Filters to Scorecards

Scorecards are based on KPIs, and one of the key features of KPIs is the fact that they can include filters. If a scorecard is going to be tied to a filter on a dashboard, that KPI should not include a filter for the dimension that will be filtered on the dashboard. In other words, if the dashboard parameter is based on the Product

Categories hierarchy, the KPIs listed on the Objectives Demo scorecard should not include Product Categories as a filter in the design of the KPI itself.

Once the filter and scorecard are both placed on the dashboard, it is time to tie the filter into the scorecard. Hovering over the filter in the design view will expand it and one of the items listed is Member UniqueName. Member UniqueName is how each member in a cube is uniquely identified; in other words, values like Bikes and Clothing might not be unique across all dimensions if just the text is used, so there is a unique value that identifies each member. Clicking on Member UniqueName and dragging it will allow the designer to drag it and drop it on the scorecard. It should be dropped in the area that says Drop Fields Here to Create Links. When the Member UniqueName is dropped into the Drop fields here to create links area, the Edit Filter Link dialog box appears and is on the Link Options tab. The Dashboard item endpoint select box allows developers to select Filters, Row, or Column. Normally, this should be set to Filters, unless the Product dimension is shown on either the rows or columns. In the case of the AdvWorks—Objectives scorecard, the product is not shown anywhere so Filters should be chosen. The Edit Filter Link dialog can be seen in Figure 5-37. At this point, the setup is done. The dashboard can be published to the server and then exported to SharePoint. The end result will be shown after discussing how to also add a filter to a report.

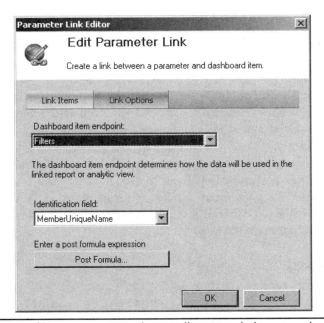

Figure 5-37 *Linking a filter to a scorecard normally means linking it to the Filters endpoint.*

Tying Filters to Reports

Connecting a filter to a scorecard is simple, because the scorecard is designed as normal and nothing special has to be done. Reports, on the other hand, require the creation of a parameter in the report. The filter on the dashboard is then linked to the parameter on the report in order to connect them.

Earlier in the chapter there was a Quantity Sold report that showed the order quantity for products across eight quarters. When this report is viewed in the designer, the Design tab shows three items at the bottom of the page: Series, Bottom Axis, and Background. Remember that the background item is often used to filter the report. In this case, because the users want to be able to filter by products, the designer would drag the Product Categories hierarchy into the Background box.

There are actually two approaches to what happens next. The first, and easiest approach, is to do almost nothing. In other words, after dragging the Product Categories into the background, the report can be published without any further changes. Once the report is placed on a dashboard, the Member UniqueName is dragged from the filter and dropped onto the report, and the Edit Filter Link dialog box appears. All of the hierarchies are shown as possible endpoints, and the developer can simply choose Product Categories and be done.

A more manual approach is for the developer to add Product Categories to the Background box and then go to the Query tab where the MDX syntax for the query is shown. Adding a dimension to the Background box adds a WHERE clause to the MDX query. In this case, the added WHERE clause is

```
WHERE ([Product].[Product Categories].DEFAULTMEMBER)
```

The default member for almost any dimension is the All level.

The developer should highlight the text between the parentheses in the WHERE clause. At the bottom, of the page is a Parameters panel. The developer should type in a name for the parameter and then click the Insert button. If the parameter is named ProdCat, for example, then

```
<<ProdCat>>
```

is inserted into the query.

Furthermore, the parameter ProdCat has a default value of

```
[Product].[Product Categories].DEFAULTMEMBER
```

which means the report will run even if no parameter value is supplied. Figure 5-38 shows what the query looks like with the parameter inserted.

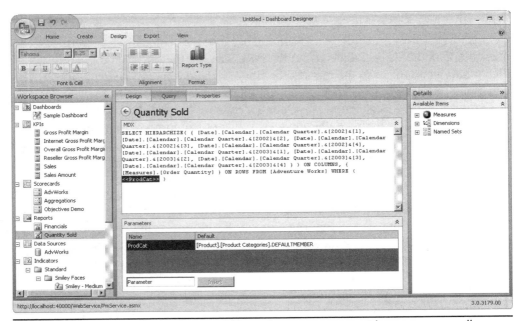

Figure 5-38   *Replacing the background filter of a report query with a parameter allows the report to be linked to a dashboard filter.*

After publishing the report to the server, the developer returns to the dashboard and drags the report from the Available Items into one of the zones. Once again, the Member UniqueName is dragged from the filter and dropped into the Drop fields here area of the report. The Edit Filter Link dialog appears. This time, however, when the developer drops down the Dashboard item endpoint list, the items that appear are the dimensions specifically added to the background, series, or bottom axis, meaning that the name of the parameter added will not show up. In this case, the developer would choose Product Categories. After clicking the OK button, the report is now tied to the parameter.

In this case, a filter, a report, and a scorecard have all been added to a dashboard, and the filter has been connected to the report and the scorecard. The process is basically the same for the scorecard and report, but the scorecard did not need any special steps. In contrast, the report may have its query modified so that the WHERE clause contains the name of a parameter created for that report, although this step is not necessary. Given that this step is optional and entails extra work, the primary reason for doing it is to make the MDX clear to anyone viewing it in the future that it is specifically designed to accept a filter when on a dashboard.

At this point, it is a simple matter of publishing the dashboard and then exporting it to SharePoint. Figure 5-39 shows the dashboard at its default, with the Product Category filter set to All Products. Notice that the AdvWorks-Objectives scorecard shows an overall score of 60.8% with a very low Internet Gross Profit Margin. Also note that the Quantity Sold report shows that the quantity of all products sold in the third quarter of 2003 was nearly 50,000.

Assume that an end user now drops down the Product Category and chooses just the Clothing category. Figure 5-40 shows the changes. First, the overall score of the Objectives Demo scorecard is now 72.7%, thanks to a much higher margin on Reseller Gross Profit Margins. Notice too that the Quantity Sold report now shows that quantity of products sold in the third quarter of 2003 was now around 14,000. This is because only 14,000 items of clothing were sold, as compared to 50,000 units of all items combined.

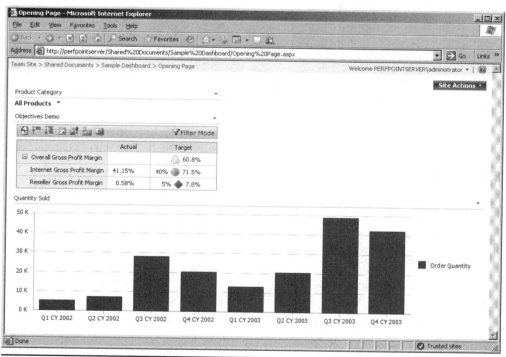

Figure 5-39 *The dashboard shows a scorecard and a report, both reporting on the totals for all products, the default value for the filter.*

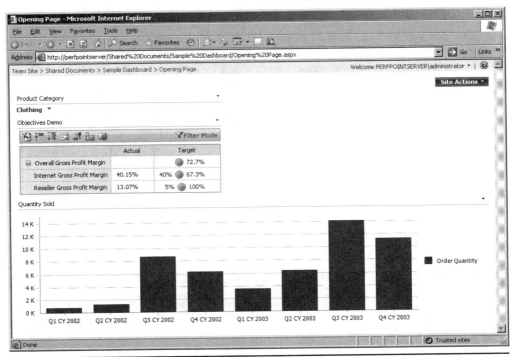

Figure 5-40   *The dashboard filter has been changed, updating both the scorecard and the report on the dashboard.*

Summary

The monitoring capabilities of PerformancePoint Server are rich and full-featured. A single tool, the Dashboard Designer, allows developers to create KPIs, scorecards, reports, indicators, filters, and dashboards. KPIs can contain an actual value and one or more target values. Aggregations can be added that include trends, averages, and more. Scorecards are built using KPIs and can include objectives that roll up KPI values. These rollups can be weighted so that some KPIs contribute more to the overall score than other KPIs.

Reports are available in addition to scorecards, and include thin client Analytic Charts and Grids as well as types based on Office Web Components. A Trend Analysis Chart is available for looking at historical trends and, through the use of a data mining algorithm, forecasting future trends.

Once scorecards and reports are created, they can be placed on dashboards which are then deployed, often to SharePoint. Filters can be added to the dashboard that update all the items on that dashboard at once.

CHAPTER
6

Analysis with PerformancePoint Server and ProClarity

One of the great strengths of building a business intelligence application is that it allows analysts and advanced data users to perform extremely detailed and complex analysis of the data. This capability, often simply called analytics, goes well beyond the relatively simple and rigidly structured scorecards and reports often available to the general business users and higher level management. Business decision makers rarely have access to the tools to perform advanced analysis on their own, simply because they lack either the time or the expertise to do so. In addition, many businesses employ analysts who are well versed in statistical methods and are therefore tasked with performing in-depth analysis of the data.

Delivering tools that provide the functionality needed for advanced analytics has always been a challenge; the more powerful the tools become, the more difficult they are to use. The good news is that many tools today, while still very powerful, are easier to use than ever. This doesn't mean that just anyone can pick them up and make them work, but it does open them up to an ever-widening audience. Today's tools also allow analysts to create complex reports or views of the data and then share these views with everyone else in the organization, greatly increasing the utility of the work done by analysts.

As discussed in Chapter 2, PerformancePoint Server has three major areas of focus: monitoring, analyzing, and planning. The analysis piece is arguably the least complete in this first version of PerformancePoint Server. While it will someday include most or all of the functionality found in ProClarity today, this first version of PerformancePoint Server will also include licenses for ProClarity, to benefit those needing truly advanced analytics. Therefore, this chapter will first cover the analytics that are built into PerformancePoint Server and then discuss ProClarity—specifically the ProClarity Standard and Professional interfaces and the ProClarity Analytics Server.

Analysis with PerformancePoint Server

As I discussed in Chapter 5, the tool for creating the monitoring components of PerformancePoint Server is the Dashboard Designer, a .NET application that runs using ClickOnce deployment available with the .NET Framework. While the Dashboard Designer includes KPIs, scorecards, dashboards, and indicators, it also includes reports as a first-class type of object that can be created. These reports represent the core of the analysis functionality built into PerformancePoint Server. There are several different types of reports available, which I will examine in detail in this section.

Table 5-1 in the previous chapter listed the types of reports that are available and what each one does. Figure 6-1 shows the screen that appears when the developer chooses to create a new report. Choosing a report type shows a simple description

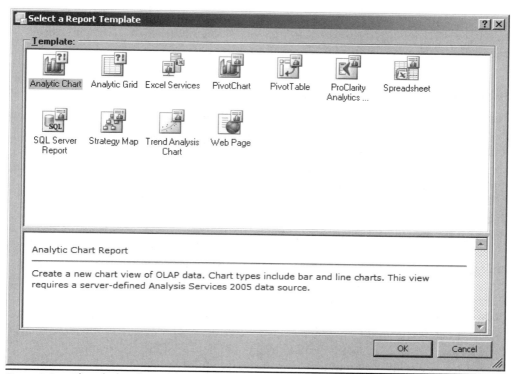

Figure 6-1   *This dialog box shows the various report types available in PerformancePoint Server.*

of each report type and explains whether there are any special conditions, such as requiring an Analysis Services data source or the presence of Excel Services.

Creating reports in PerformancePoint Server is a simple matter of either right-clicking on the Reports node in Dashboard Designer and choosing New Report, or clicking the appropriate report type on the Create ribbon in Dashboard Designer, as seen in Figure 6-2. Once the correct type of report to create is chosen, the developer

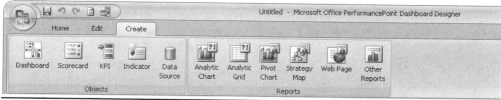

Figure 6-2   *The Create ribbon in Dashboard Designer also allows for the quick creation of many report types.*

proceeds in most cases to connect to the appropriate data source and form the query. In other cases, the reports are simply links to external items such as existing web pages, ProClarity views, or SQL Server Reporting Services reports.

Analytic Charts

Analytic Charts are the preferred way of creating chart-based reports in PerformancePoint Server. This is because the charts are completely thin client and do not require the installation of any components on the client machine, unlike some of the other report types. There are several options for the types of charts that are available: traditional bar charts, two types of stacked bar charts, and two types of line charts. Other report types include many more options, as you'll see when I discuss the PivotChart.

The Analytic Chart does include some analytic capabilities, but it's actually more of an end user tool; analysts will find that the charts provided in ProClarity are far more powerful and expose full analytical features. Still, the limited analytics capabilities of the Analytic Chart (and as discussed next, the Analytic Grid) should meet the needs of most users in an organization. This limited analytic capability includes the single most important feature, which is the ability to drill down to lower levels of detail within the chart. This one feature is enough to satisfy most users who do not have the time or background to use a complete analytic application.

One restriction of the Analytic Chart is that it requires an Analysis Services cube as a data source. This is not terribly surprising, since the chart is designed to allow users to navigate the structures of dimensional hierarchies without needing to understand how to select the appropriate items in the correct order from some set of normalized relational tables. Also, the cube source can only be Analysis Services 2005; an Analysis Services 2000 cube will not work as the source for the Analytic Chart.

When a developer chooses to create a new Analytic Chart, the Create an Analytic Chart Report wizard launches. The first screen asks the standard three questions, of course: the name, the folder, and whether or not to grant all users Read permissions. The second screen allows the developer to choose a data source for the report. Remember that if this screen is blank, the Refresh button on the Home ribbon should be clicked to pull a list of available data sources from the server. Also, a new data source should be created in the Dashboard Designer before starting the wizard.

Clicking the Finish button will generate the report and show a confirmation screen telling you that the report has been built. The Analytic Chart is then shown in the Design view in Dashboard Designer. The Design view allows the developer to create the report using a simple drag-and-drop palette. The three items at the bottom of the page are Series, Bottom Axis, and Background. Dimensions or measures placed in the Series panel will be shown on the side, or Y-axis, of the report. Dimensions or measures placed in the Bottom Axis panel will appear on the X-axis of the report. Time is often shown across the X-axis because people are used to seeing data over time, and viewing the trend over time is relatively easy this way; viewing time down the Y-axis is often an unnatural way for people to view data.

Note that either dimensions or measures can be placed in either the Series or Bottom Axis. Often a single measure is placed in the Series panel and some time hierarchy is placed in the Bottom Axis panel, although this makes it more challenging for end users to drill down, as will be discussed on a moment. The dimensions and measures for the data source are available in the Available Items pane on the right-hand side of the designer, as can be seen in Figure 6-3.

There is also a third category of items listed in the Available Items pane, known as Named Sets. Named Sets are a collection of one or more items defined by an MDX statement. As an example, imagine that a company wants to define its top ten customers as a group by which to do analysis. What makes a customer a top

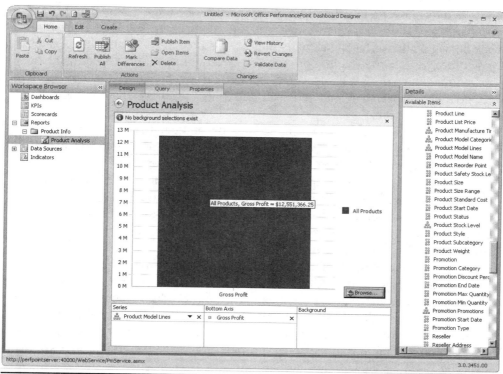

Figure 6-3   *A simple Analytic Chart showing the Big Blue Bar and items in both the Series and Bottom Axis boxes*

ten customer? This is a business decision—the definition may be as simple as the customers with the greatest purchases this year to date. Or, it could be as complex as the customers with the largest contributions to gross profit margin over the past four quarters, who have been customers for at least two years, and who have not exceeded 80% of their existing credit line. The point is that once the business defines the criteria for the top ten customers, a formula can be created that will always calculate those top ten customers with the latest data; this allows the members of the set to change frequently, depending on the criteria and the volatility of the data. The person designing the reports can then simply drag over a named set such as Top Ten Customers and the report will always show the current top ten customers. Once again, Named Sets help highlight the need for someone who understands MDX well when building a business intelligence solution based on Microsoft technology.

Figure 6-3 represents a rather boring chart on the surface. There is a single measure, Gross Profit, on the X-axis. The Y-axis contains a hierarchy of product model lines, a hierarchy that goes from the All level to the Product Line level to the Model level. There is also a tooltip shown in the screenshot because, when the mouse is moved over a bar, the value of that particular bar appears in a tooltip. In this chart, there is one large bar, sometimes referred to as the Big Blue Bar because, while boring on the surface, it actually tells users something useful: in this example Gross Profit for all products is approximately $12.6 million. Some users will question the time period that is covered, but in this case, hopefully it is obvious: since no time has been specified, this is for all time, as well as all customers, all employees, and so on.

There isn't much else that can be done with this particular chart while in Design mode, but clicking the Browse button opens a viewer that allows the developer to test how end users will be able to interact with this particular chart. Opening the chart in the Browse Analytic Report viewer is, at first, not any more exciting than viewing it in Design mode. Now, however, moving the mouse over the Big Blue Bar turns the mouse pointer into a hand, indicating a clickable region. Clicking once on the Big Blue Bar changes the view to that shown in Figure 6-4.

In Figure 6-4, it is easy to see that the Mountain Product Line is the largest contributor to Gross Profit by far (realize this is gross profit in dollars, not the gross profit margin, which is a percentage.) But why did clicking on the bar go from the All level of the Product Model Lines hierarchy to the product Line level? This is because, by default, clicking on a bar will drill the user down one level on whatever hierarchy is listed on the Y-axis (the Series). Note too that the browser window has Back and Forward buttons in the upper left-hand corner, so that users can easily go back to the previous view of the chart.

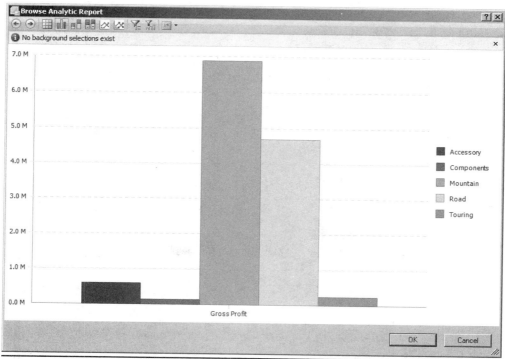

Figure 6-4   *Browsing an Analytic Chart allows a developer to preview the report and drill down on it without having to first publish it to the server.*

Clicking on the Accessory bar will show the chart as it appears in Figure 6-5. Note that in this image, the user has drilled down from the Product Line level to the Model level for accessories only. In other words, clicking the Accessory bar in the previous view only drills down on that item and excludes all others. This is an important point to understanding the term *drill down* as it is used in PerformancePoint Server and ProClarity. Drilling down means going down one level on that item only; in other words, users will see the children for that particular item only. Being able to see children for multiple higher-level items will be discussed later in this chapter.

In Figure 6-5, the user has drilled down as far as possible in the Product Model Lines hierarchy. Unfortunately, moving the mouse over a bar still shows the bar as a clickable region, but clicking on it won't actually do anything. The bar actually is right-clickable, but I'll discuss what happens when the user right-clicks in a moment.

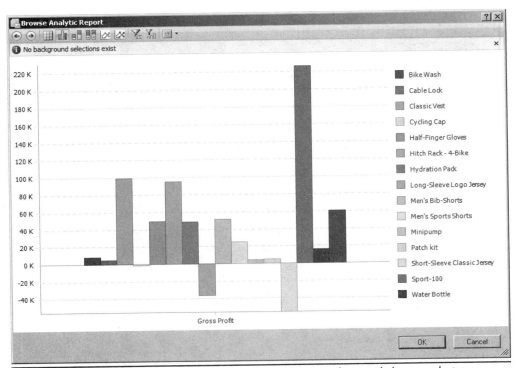

Figure 6-5 *Drilling down on a member replaces that member and shows only its children, as in this case where the user drilled down on the Accessory member.*

An alternative approach to this view would be to swap the items on the dimensions so that Gross Profit would appear on the Series and Product Model Lines would appear on the Bottom Axis. Switching the dimensions has little change at first, as the Big Blue Bar is still there. However, the first major change is that clicking on the bar when previewing with the Browse window doesn't do anything. This is because the default is to drill down on whatever is on the Series or Y-axis, and with a measure there is nothing to which a user can drill down. At this point there are two options. First, the user can right-click on a bar, choose Drill Down To, locate the dimension, and then the level to which they choose to drill down. Unfortunately, the current hierarchy on the X-axis, in this case Product Model Lines, is grayed out in the Drill Down To list, which means this will not allow someone to drill down to an item that is already on the report. Instead, the user can right-click on the Big Blue Bar and choose Switch to All Products. This switches the chart so that it will now drill down on the item on the X-axis (the Bottom Axis). Now, drilling down will work as it did before.

While using the Switch to All Products allows a user to drill down on the Product Model Lines hierarchy in this case, the display is somewhat different from the previous chart. Figure 6-6 shows the chart with Product Model Lines on the X-axis, Gross Profit on the Y-axis, and the user having drilled down once on the Big Blue Bar after choosing Switch to All Products. Note that the legend contains only the name of the measure and that the different Product Line values appear along the bottom. While it may be difficult to tell, all the bars are the same color since there is only a single value for the legend. The format users prefer to choose is up to them.

There is a simple way to switch the items on the X and Y axes if desired; first right-click on any bar and then choose Pivot. This moves all of the items from the Series to the Bottom Axis and vice versa. Therefore, any chart can easily be switched between views such as in Figure 6-5 and Figure 6-6, simply by right-clicking on a bar and selecting Pivot.

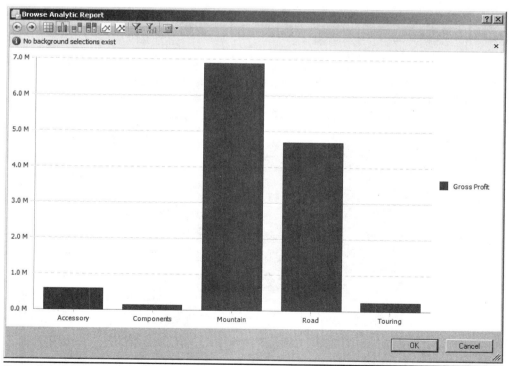

Figure 6-6   *Using a simple Pivot command switches items from the X-axis to the Y-axis and vice versa. Here, the measure has been moved to the Y-axis while Product Model Lines is on the X-axis.*

Dimensions on Both X and Y Axes

In this first example, the Bottom Axis contained a single measure, Gross Profit. However, Time was not a factor in this particular report, so the next step is to modify the report so that Time plays a role. However, where should Time go? Normally, Time goes on the X-axis, so the report is redesigned so that the Date.Date.Calendar dimension is placed on the Bottom Axis and Product.Product Model Lines is left in the Series. At this point, what about the Gross Profit measure? It can easily be moved to the Background. This keeps it active but the chart will now show a Big Blue Bar for All Product and All Time, as shown in Figure 6-7.

At this point, browsing the report and clicking on the Big Blue Bar one time displays the image shown in Figure 6-8. Why did the drill down occur on the Product Model Line hierarchy and not the Calendar hierarchy? Recall from the previous section that drilling down will occur on whatever dimension is in the Series panel. In this case, Product Model Line is on the Series, or Y-axis, so drilling down by simply clicking on a bar will drill the user down the Product Model Line dimension.

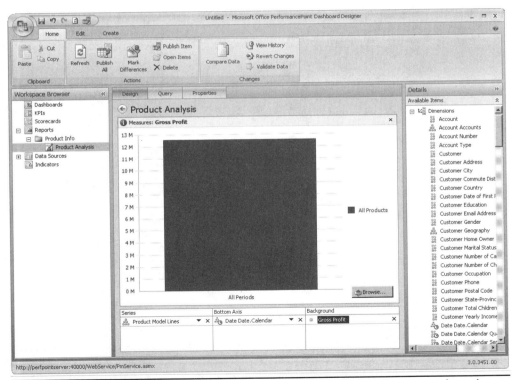

Figure 6-7 *The measure has been moved to the background and dimensions have been placed on both the series and bottom axis.*

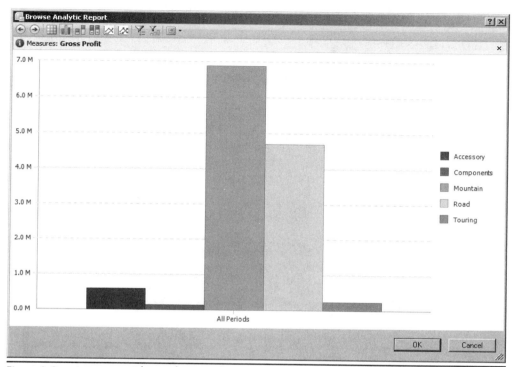

Figure 6-8   *A report with products in the series and time along the bottom axis. The measure used is placed only in the background.*

Right-clicking

There is another way to drill down, and that is by right-clicking on the bar in question. Right-clicking on a bar opens the context-sensitive menu that displays not only a drill down option, but also a number of other options. These options are displayed in Figure 6-9 and described in Table 6-1.

Table 6-1 mentions that one of the right-click options is Drill Down To. Choosing this option will give you a menu displaying all the dimensions and each dimension can then have a menu showing the levels in that particular dimension hierarchy. Take the standard report that is drilled down to the Product Line level, as shown in Figure 6-9. Each bar represents the total Gross Profit for each Product Line for all time. A simple drill down will drill down on the Product Model Lines hierarchy. The Switch To option will let the user drill down on Date.Calendar. However, what if the user instead wants to find out which sales territories contributed to the gross margin for a particular product line? Neither the Series nor the Bottom Axis have the Sales

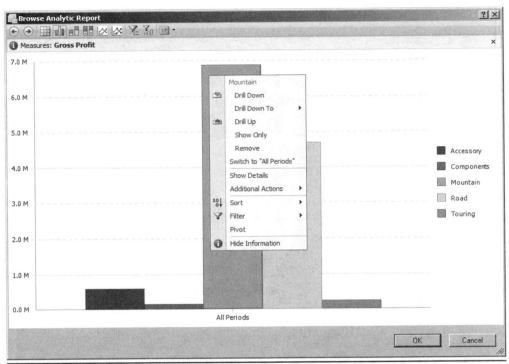

Figure 6-9 The pop-up menu shows that bars in an Analytic Chart can do more than just drill down.

Option	Functionality
Drill Down	This is the same as simply left-clicking on the bar. It takes the user down one level in the hierarchy for the chosen item.
Drill Down To	This is sometimes called *cross* drilling because it allows the user to drill down on any dimension, not just the dimensions currently in the Series and Bottom Axis. Cross drilling is explained in greater detail later on in the chapter.
Drill Up	Drill Up will take the current item and drill up to the previous level in the hierarchy. While drilling down shows only the children of the chosen item, drilling up shows the parent of the chosen items and all its siblings; in other words, it shows all items at the parent level. If the user right-clicks on the first half of 2004 and chooses to drill up, the resulting data are all the members at the Year level, not just the year 2004.

Table 6-1 The Options Available to a User when Right-Clicking on a Bar in an Analytic Report

Option	Functionality
Show Only	Show Only removes all other items and makes the current bar the only bar on the chart. If the four quarters of a particular year are shown and a user right-clicks on the first quarter and chooses Show Only, quarters two, three, and four disappear from the chart and it is redrawn with only a bar for the first quarter.
Remove	Remove is the opposite of Show Only. If a user right-clicks on a bar and chooses Remove, that one bar is removed from the graph while all others remain. This is often useful for eliminating a particularly large or small value, or perhaps all the values listed as unknown.
Switch To <Member>	The Switch To <Member> switches the dimension on which a drill down will occur. In Figure 6-9, the option is Switch To All Periods. Choosing this option and then drilling down on any bar will keep all the Product Lines on the chart, but time will now drill from the All level to the Year level for each product line. This can be seen in Figure 6-10.
Show Details	Show Details will execute a Drillthrough action in the cube, often called "drill to detail." Drillthrough will pull the actual records that make up a particular value. For example, imagine that a user is viewing the sales for a particular product on a particular day. How many individual orders were placed that day? There is no way to tell from the view as described, but using Show Details will show the individual records that contribute to that value. This is useful in many cases, but at high levels there can be millions of records contributing to a number. Fortunately, PerformancePoint will only show the first 1,000 records and give the user a message that there are more available. In addition, this feature only works if the cube designers have created a Drillthrough action. Also, Drillthrough actions only work with regular measures, not calculated measures such as Gross Profit.
Additional Actions	Additional Actions might be built into the cube, and these actions can be tied to members, levels, or an entire dimension. Take, for example, the case where a company is dealing with chemicals. On an individual chemical, an action might exist that launches an internal site that contains information about that chemical, including its safe handling procedures and what to do in the case of accidental exposure. While Show Details will call the Drillthrough action a cube, the actual will also show up here as well, along with any other actions that have been defined.
Sort	The Sort option will sort the current data either by the series or bottom axis data. The sort can be from largest to smallest or smallest to largest. In addition, users can remove the sorting here.
Filter	Filter allows users to remove empty values from the series, the bottom axis, or both, as well as turn off the filtering of empty values.
Pivot	Pivot simply swaps the dimension in the Series with the dimension in the Bottom Axis. If more than one dimension is found in either panel, it does not matter; all dimensions in the Series are swapped with all dimensions in the Bottom Axis. The chart is redrawn accordingly.
Hide/Show Information	The Hide or Show Information option will place a small information bar at the top of the graph or hide it, depending on the current state. Note that in Figure 6-10, a small bar at the top shows that the current measure is Gross Profit. This is useful because nowhere else does the chart indicate the current measure. Not only will measures show here, but if the designer has added filters to the background, such as showing data only for female customers, the information bar would show the measure and "Gender: Female."

Table 6-1   *The Options Available to a User when Right-Clicking on a Bar in an Analytic Report (Continued)*

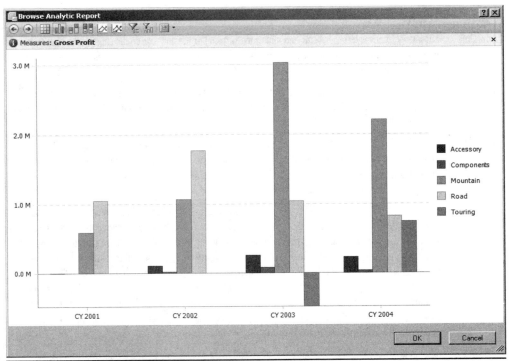

Figure 6-10 *The Show Information options places a line at the top of the chart that shows the chosen measure(s) as well as any background filtering.*

Territory in them. However, the user could right-click on a bar, choose Drill Down To, then select Sales Territory, and finally Country. This will show the gross profit by country *for that product line only.* This is an important point: the bar on which the user right-clicks acts as a filter, so the resulting data will only be for that product line. This is another case in which having the Show Information option selected is useful. As an example, assume a user right-clicks on the Road product line bar (which is approximately $14.6 million) and chooses Sales Territory and Country. The resulting chart, shown with the Show Information option on, will look like that in Figure 6-11.

Stacked Bar and Line Charts

The Dashboard Designer makes it easy to create stacked bar and line charts. Simply create a new chart which, by default, will be a bar chart. The Edit ribbon has a button labeled Report Type and clicking this shows there are six options available in this

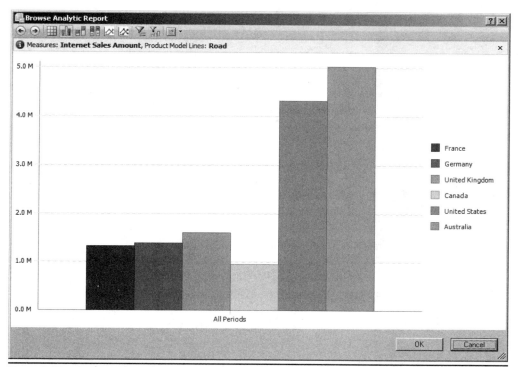

Figure 6-11   *A chart that shows a user has drilled down from a particular product line to the countries that contributed to that particular item.*

first version of PerformancePoint Server. These include Grid (which is similar to the Analytic Grid reports), Bar Chart, Stacked Bar Chart, 100% Stacked Bar Chart, Line Chart, and Line Chart with Markers. Other chart types will undoubtedly be added in future versions of PerformancePoint Server.

Choosing a line chart when the dimension on the Bottom Axis is set to the All level is quite dull; the Big Blue Bar appears as a single point. Therefore, it is useful to start at a level lower than the All level. For example, to start at the Year level, the developer can click the drop down icon next to Date.Date.Calendar in the Bottom Axis panel. This opens the Member Selector and here the developer can choose the individual years. Starting at the Year level makes the chart a bit more interesting, as shown in Figure 6-12.

Allowing the designer to select members below the All level ahead of time is useful, but imagine if someone asked that the report start at the month level for all four years. Using the Member Selector, the developer would have to expand All Periods, then each Year, each Half Year, and each Quarter just to get to the months,

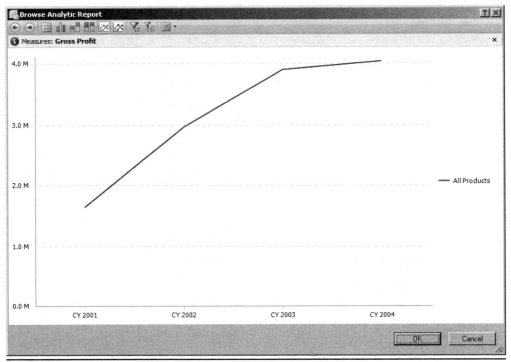

Figure 6-12 *A simple line chart created in an Analytic Chart*

and then check each individual month. This would be a tedious process. Fortunately, there is an easier way.

In the Member Selector, the developer can right-click on the All level and choose to clear all selections, check the visible items, and so forth. The first item in the list, however, allows the designer to automatically select all the members at a particular level. Note that Figure 6-13 shows that the developer is selecting Month, which really means that he or she is selecting all of the month members regardless of the year in which they are found. This is a quick way to create to select many members at a lower level of detail.

Multiple Dimensions on an Axis

So far, the examples have shown just a single dimension on the Series or Bottom Axis. In reality, there can be multiple dimensions on both the Series and the Bottom Axis, although this is done more often on Analytic Grids than on Analytic Charts.

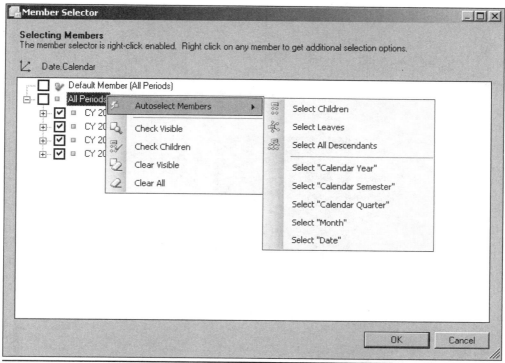

Figure 6-13   *Users can select all the members at any level without having to go and manually click on each one.*

The reason is simple: the chart quickly becomes cluttered with the additional information. Figure 6-14 shows what happens when both Products and Sales Territories are placed in the Series panel. Notice that the text for the legend doesn't fit all the text, even though the area for the chart has been expanded. Also note that the Bottom Axis now contains both the Date and Employee dimensions. The Big Blue Bar represents the All level for both Date and Employee.

If this chart is viewed in the Preview mode and the user clicks on the Big Blue Bar, what will happen? Will the bar drill down on just the Product Model Lines hierarchy, just the Sales Territory hierarchy, or both? The answer is that the chart will drill down only on the Product Model Lines hierarchy. The drill down occurs on the first dimension in the Series panel. If the user wants to drill down on another one of the dimensions, they'll have to right click on a bar and choose Switch To. There will now be three Switch To statements, each representing one of the three dimensions that are not the default for drilling down. Again, this type of view is often more useful in a grid, as will be shown later.

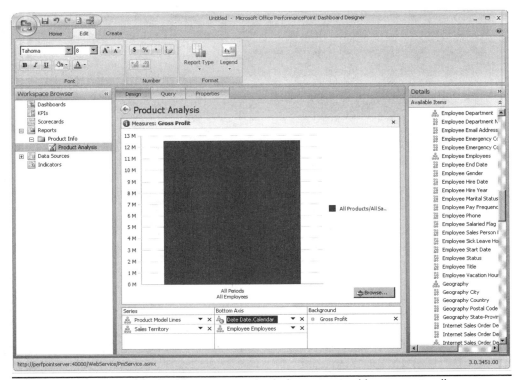

Figure 6-14   *Placing multiple dimensions on both the series and bottom axis allows a simple chart to cover more detail.*

Multiple Measures

It is certainly possible to have multiple measures on a chart at once. A developer can have multiple measures in either the Series or Bottom Axis. However, the tool will not allow for there to be measures in both the Series and Bottom Axis panels at the same time, as there would be no logical way to display the data. In addition, it is not possible to have multiple measures in the Background; the reasoning will be explained in the next section when filtering is discussed.

Placing multiple measures on either the X or Y axis may make perfect sense depending on the analysis being done. Sometimes it makes more sense to do this in a grid if the numbers vary widely. For example, Figure 6-15 shows three measures on the Y axis: Sales Amount, Gross Profit, and Gross Profit Margin. In the chart, however, only two bars are visible and, upon careful examination, there is a dot that is half obscured by one of the bars. The two bars represent the first

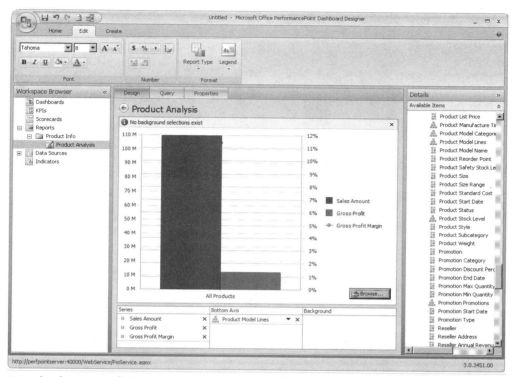

*Note that the Gross Profit Margin is automatically moved to the right-hand Y-axis but only a single point shows up because the X-axis is set to a single member (the All member).

Figure 6-15   *A report with multiple measures on the series*

two measures: Sales Amount and Gross Profit. Both are relatively large numbers, with Sales Amount showing approximately $110 million and a Gross Profit of approximately $12.5 million. Gross Profit Margin, on the other hand, is a very small number, having a value of just .1143 (11.43%). Because this chart is comparing large numbers to a percentage, it automatically moves the Gross Profit Margin to the right-hand Y-axis and makes its series type a line, while the other two measures are represented by bars. In this case, because the X-axis has only a single value, the line appears as a single point. Note that rearranging the measures to put the percentage first will show the entire point, as it will place the point in front of the bar.

Viewing this particular chart in the Browse window and drilling down on the Product Model Lines hierarchy allows the users to see the Gross Profit Margin line that appeared as a single point before. Figure 6-16 shows what this looks like.

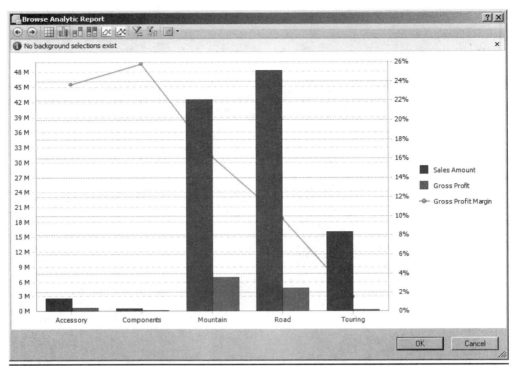

Figure 6-16 *The report has now been expanded so that the Gross Profit Margin, automatically moved to the right Y-axis, is clearly visible as a line.*

Note that in this case, the X-axis contains the Product Model Lines hierarchy, whereas many time users would expect to see Time across the bottom, especially in cases where they are examining sales figures. This also allows them to more easily spot trends in line charts.

Filtering in the Background

The Background panel has been used sparingly in the examples so far, mainly to supply the measure when the measure is not explicitly shown on the X or Y axis. In fact, when viewing a single measure, it is almost always placed in the background. However, other dimensions can be placed in the background and act as a filter for the data.

Imagine that the manager for sales to Canada requests to see the Gross Profit by time and by Product for Canada only. To do this, Product.Product Model Lines can be placed in the Series panel, Date.Date.Calendar can be placed in the Bottom Axis panel, and Gross Profit can be placed in the Background panel. However, in order to filter only to Canada, the Sales Territory. Sales Territory hierarchy can be placed in the Background panel, and the designer can use the Member Selector to expand All Sales Territories to North America; North America can in turn be expanded to show the countries in North America; and the developer can place a check next to Canada. The result of this operation is a Big Blue Bar with a value of just a bit over $1 million. If viewed in the browser, having the Show Information turned on will help show that the data has been filtered to show Gross Profit for Canada, as shown in Figure 6-17.

It would be easy to add an additional filter to this particular chart. For example, the manager for Canada might be curious about how many sales went through the Reseller channel, so the Sales Channel hierarchy could be placed in the background and the design can filter to just the Reseller channel. As you can see, the background can hold multiple dimensions at once just as the series and bottom axis can do.

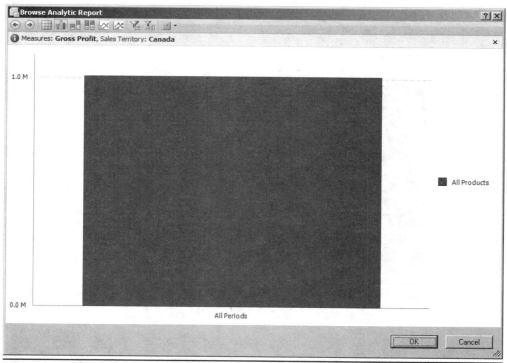

Figure 6-17 *A simple report that is actually being filtered by multiple background dimensions.*

The background can also allow another feature as well: the selection of multiple items from the same dimension. Imagine that the manager for Canada has done so well with Canada that she is also made the manager for sales to the United Kingdom. With the Sales Territory hierarchy still in the background, the developer can go into the Member Selector and choose both Canada and the United Kingdom. Viewing the chart shows the sum of the gross profit for both Canada and the United Kingdom together. Turning on Show Information is very important here, because it lists all of the members selected in the background. Figure 6-18 shows how this appears to the user, with the countries listed in the information area of the report. In order to show both countries separately in the report, the Sales Territory hierarchy would have to be moved to either the Series or Bottom Axis panels.

There is a caveat when placing multiple items from the same dimension in the background. While measures are not technically in a measures dimension, they are often treated as if Measures is a dimension (in fact, it is often referred to as the

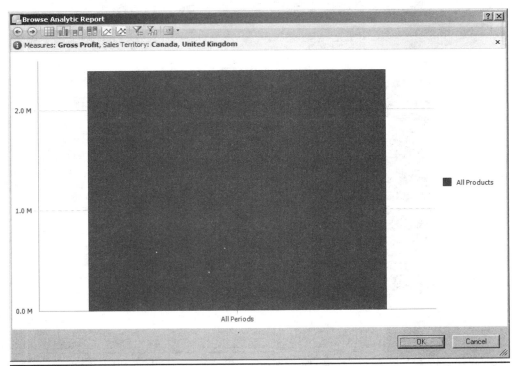

Figure 6-18   *The Sales Territory dimension now has multiple members selected for it in the background and the individual items are listed in the information area of the report.*

"Measures dimension"). However, placing more than one measure in the background is not allowed. Attempting to place two measures in the Background panel will cause the Dashboard Designer to move both measures to the Bottom Axis by default. If the developer attempts to move just one of the measures, both will move as a single unit. While it often makes sense to sum up members such as Canada and the United Kingdom for a single measure, adding up disparate measures doesn't make sense. Therefore, the Dashboard Designer will not allow multiple measures in the background.

Understanding how items work in the background is important for developers creating reports, but it is not always the best way to create reports for end users. Recall from Chapter 5 that a dashboard can have one or more filters on it. Allowing users to select items from drop-down lists is often the best way to implement the ability for users to choose the countries, products, measures, and other items they wish to see. The developer must simply remember that if measures are not to be on the rows or columns, the filter on the dashboard should not allow multiple selections to be made.

Analytic Grids

The Analytic Grid is very similar to the Analytic Chart. The wizard asks exactly the same questions for the grid as it does when the designer is creating a chart. Once the design surface is loaded up, the only difference between the grid and the chart design surface is that the grid has panels named Rows and Columns instead of Series and Bottom Axis, respectively. This makes it very easy to understand exactly how the data will look when the grid is laid out.

The grid has two features that the chart doesn't, but it also lacks many of the features found in the chart. On the positive side, the grid allows people to drill down on dimensions in either the rows or the columns. Technically the chart did this as well but the user had to right-click to do it. With the grid, drilling down on multiple dimensions is much easier. Second, the grid allows a user to either drill down (have the children of the selection replace the selection and its siblings) or expand, which means to show the children for the selection while leaving the parent and its siblings visible. In fact, expanding data is more easily discoverable than drilling down, as there is a plus sign available for expanding but the user has to know to double-click in order to drill down.

Playing off the example used to create charts, assume that the developer creates a new grid and places Product Model Lines on the Rows, Date.Date.Calendar on the Columns, and Gross Profit in the Background. Clicking the Browse button opens the report in the Browse Analytic Report viewer, and the grid is displayed. In this case, the Big Blue Bar is gone, replaced with a single value in a cell and All Periods as the column header and All Products as the row header.

Next to the items in the rows and columns are small buttons with a plus sign. Clicking on that button will expand that item; in other words, it will keep that item there but also show its children. Clicking on the plus sign next to All Periods, for example, will keep All Periods but will also add new columns, one each for CY 2001 through CY 2004. An example of this can be seen in Figure 6-19. So far, this sounds very similar to the Analytic Chart.

One difference, however, also shown in Figure 6-19, is that the user does not have to expand; instead, they can drill down by double-clicking on an item. Figure 6-19 also shows the result if a user has double-clicked on All Products. Unlike the expansion of time on the columns—which kept All Periods on the grid—double-clicking shows the children, but replaces the parents. The user is free to double-click on any member of either the rows or columns in order to drill down.

The benefits of the grid should be immediately clear: the ability to drill down or expand any dimension on either the rows or columns makes navigating the grid very simple. On the other hand, the grid lacks some of the options seen on the grid

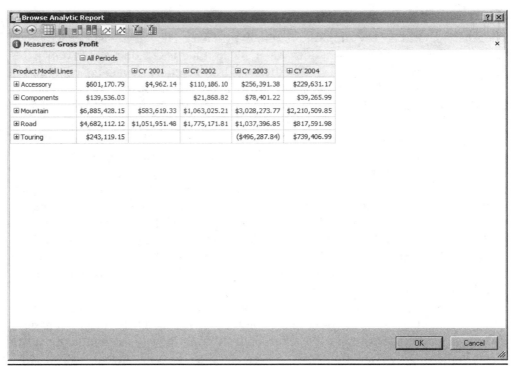

Figure 6-19 *A simple Analytic Grid report being previewed by the developer before it is published to the server. The user has expanded time but drilled down on products.*

right-click menus, so abilities such as cross drilling are gone. Therefore, realize that charts and grids each have scenarios for which one is better than the other and can make analysis easier for end users.

Multiple Measures

Showing multiple measures at once is one area where the grid can shine. Recall from the previous discussion in the section on charts that showing values in the millions compared to a small percentage forces the percentage to the right Y-axis. In a grid, however, the data is completely valid and easy to read. As with the chart, multiple measures cannot be placed in the background. If the developer attempts to do this, the Dashboard Designer will automatically move the measures to the Columns panel. This is often the desired result, however. Take Figure 6-20 as an example. In this case, products are still on the rows and time is still on the columns. The Gross Profit and Gross Profit Margin measures have also been added to the columns and some expansion of data has occurred.

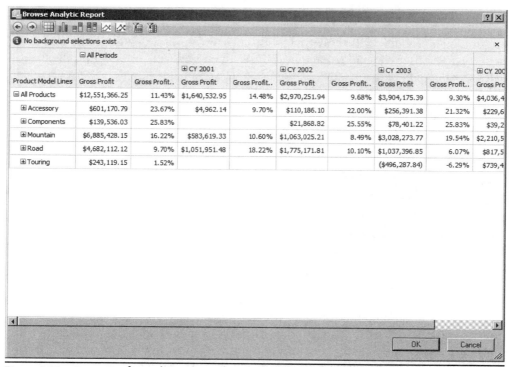

Figure 6-20 *Gross Profit and Gross Profit margin are shown side by side, but watch out for similarly named measures because of the width of the columns.*

Note one problem with the grid: the width of the column holding the measure names cuts off the word Margin for the Gross Profit Margin measure. The width of the column cannot be adjusted, and this is true for both the developer during the design phase and the user once the report is published to SharePoint. This is one reason why the ProClarity tools or Excel are sometimes better tools for some of the analysis.

Multiple Dimensions on Rows or Columns

Just as it is easy to display multiple measures on either the rows or columns, it is easy to allow for multiple dimensions to be displayed on the rows or columns. In a sense, Figure 6-20 showed this by having both the dates and measures on the columns, but imagine now that the grid should show the gross profit by products by sales territory in the rows and by time in the columns. Placing Gross Profit in the background, Date.Date.Calendar on the Columns, and both Product Model Lines and SalesTerritory on the Rows leads to such a report. When multiple dimensions are placed on either the rows or the columns, the order in which they appear in the Rows and Columns panels will determine the order in which they appear in the grid. In the example of both products and sales territories being placed on the rows, if products are first then products will show first, with sales territories indented slightly on the next row. The user can still expand or drill down on members of either products or sales territories to perform analysis. Figure 6-21 shows an example of a user having expanded both the All Products and the All Sales Territories members one time (as well as expanding All Periods.) Note that the first set of rows has the total for all products and all territories, followed by the details of the territories; the next section moves to the first product model, the repeats the territories, and so forth.

PivotChart and PivotTable Reports

The PivotChart and PivotTable are more powerful than the Analytic Chart and Analytic Grid, but the PivotChart and PivotTable reports use the Office Web Components (OWC) and this requires both an install on the client machine if they don't already exist, and it requires that each user viewing the reports have a license for the controls.

Starting either a PivotChart or PivotTable starts a wizard that asks the developer the same three questions as any other object (name, folder, and permissions). After filling in this information the design surface is rendered. PivotCharts have two buttons on the toolbar that load additional tools: Commands and Options and the Chart Wizard. Commands and Options allows for changes to the borders, toolbars, and so forth. The Chart Wizard, on the other hand, launches a dialog box that walks the developer through the process of creating a report. Unlike the Analytic Charts and

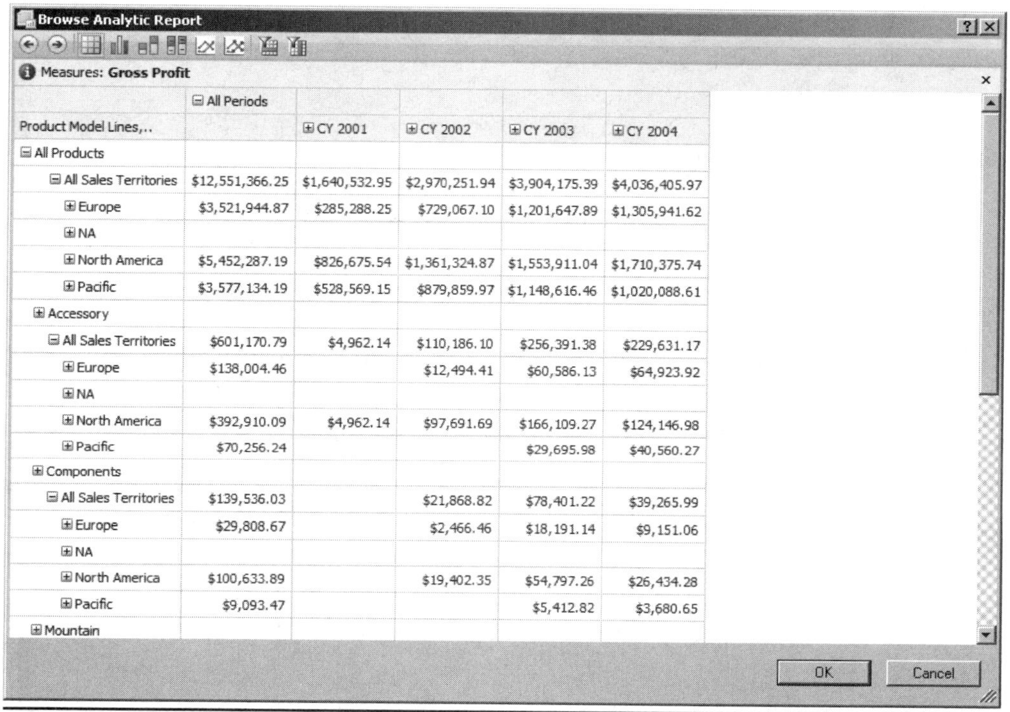

Browse Analytic Report					? X

Measures: **Gross Profit**

Product Model Lines,..	All Periods	CY 2001	CY 2002	CY 2003	CY 2004
All Products					
All Sales Territories	$12,551,366.25	$1,640,532.95	$2,970,251.94	$3,904,175.39	$4,036,405.97
Europe	$3,521,944.87	$285,288.25	$729,067.10	$1,201,647.89	$1,305,941.62
NA					
North America	$5,452,287.19	$826,675.54	$1,361,324.87	$1,553,911.04	$1,710,375.74
Pacific	$3,577,134.19	$528,569.15	$879,859.97	$1,148,616.46	$1,020,088.61
Accessory					
All Sales Territories	$601,170.79	$4,962.14	$110,186.10	$256,391.38	$229,631.17
Europe	$138,004.46		$12,494.41	$60,586.13	$64,923.92
NA					
North America	$392,910.09	$4,962.14	$97,691.69	$166,109.27	$124,146.98
Pacific	$70,256.24			$29,695.98	$40,560.27
Components					
All Sales Territories	$139,536.03		$21,868.82	$78,401.22	$39,265.99
Europe	$29,808.67		$2,466.46	$18,191.14	$9,151.06
NA					
North America	$100,633.89		$19,402.35	$54,797.26	$26,434.28
Pacific	$9,093.47			$5,412.82	$3,680.65
Mountain					

	OK	Cancel

Figure 6-21 *Multiple dimensions are placed on both the rows and columns while a single measure is in the background.*

Analytic Grids, the PivotCharts and PivotTables can report against many different data sources, including relational tables, cubes, XML, and more. PivotCharts can even be created from data entered manually at the time the chart is created.

Unlike PivotCharts, PivotTables only have one active button, Commands and Options, when first created. The Commands and Options button here is basically a conglomeration of the Commands and Options and Chart Wizard options from PivotCharts. This one button opens a dialog box that lets users connect to a data source as well as change some properties of the grid.

Once a data source is chosen, the designer can choose to either select a single table or cube, or to write a query that returns the desired records. After creating a connection for a PivotChart, a Chart Field List appears that shows all of the measures and all of the attribute hierarchies. In keeping with the previous examples, a connection to the Adventure Works cube in Analysis Services would provide a list like that shown in Figure 6-22.

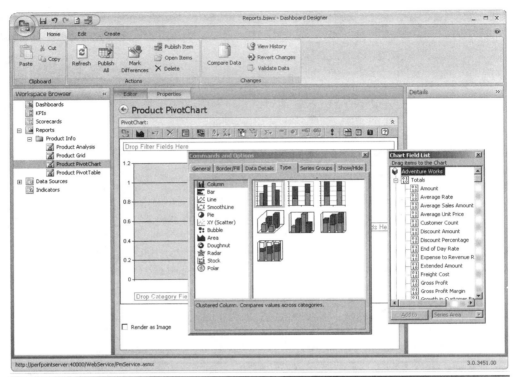

Figure 6-22 *A PivotChart showing the rich chart types and a list of the fields available in the Adventure Works cube. The downside of a PivotChart or PivotTable is the need for client-side software installation.*

Note also in Figure 6-22 that there are many different types of charts available, including bar, line, pie, area, and other chart types. Each chart type might have a variety of subtypes available as well. This makes these charts far more flexible than the Analytic Charts.

There are three areas on the chart onto which items can be dragged and dropped: the chart itself, which is the only area on which measures can be placed; an area for Series Fields (the Y-axis) 5; and an area for Category Fields (the X-axis). The hierarchies placed on the series or category areas can be expanded so that multiple selections can be made. The chart itself is interactive and double-clicking expands the data (it does not drill down) although buttons at the top of the chart allow for collapsing, expanding, drilling into, and drilling out. There are also buttons for filtering, sorting, and pivoting, and there is an area at the top of the chart for filters

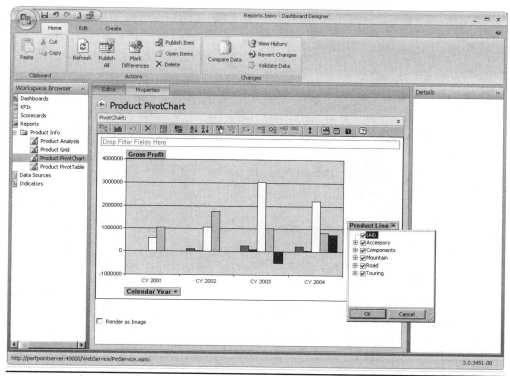

Figure 6-23 *The PivotChart showing the interactivity that can be used to make selections.*

(similar to filters on a dashboard as shown in Chapter 5.) Figure 6-23 shows a standard bar chart with Gross Profit for the four years for all products.

PivotTables are very similar. There is an area at the top that holds filters, and areas for data on the rows and columns. Multiple measures can be placed in the grid itself. Buttons allow for sorting and filtering, and there are a host of options on the Command and Options dialog box to show and hide certain items, as well as control formatting. Note that subtotals can easily be placed on the grid and developers can choose to hide or show rows and columns where all the values are empty. At both design time and runtime, columns can easily be resized to show all the data or the full text in the header. Figure 6-24 shows an example of a PivotTable with both Gross Profit and Gross Profit Margin, broken down by year and product models. Note that the formatting of the data from the cube is not honored; in other words, the Gross Profit does not show up as dollars nor does the Gross Profit Margin show up as a percentage.

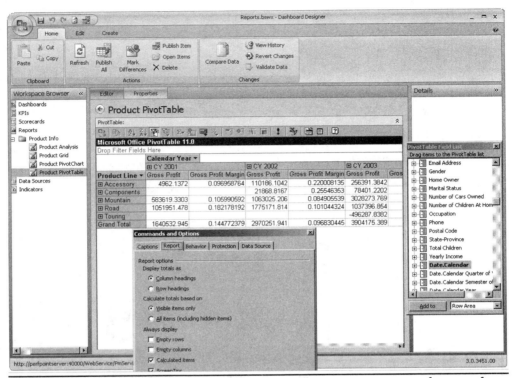

Figure 6-24   *A PivotTable showing the Field List as well as an extensive set of options for controlling how the grid is laid out.*

Excel Services Reports

Excel Services reports are simply reports that display an Excel Services spreadsheet. Excel Services is a web-based version of Excel that allows users to publish Excel spreadsheets to the server and view them in a browser. Spreadsheets may be static or contain data pulled from an external data source. If data is pulled from an external data source, users have the ability of refreshing the data in the spreadsheet.

In order to create an Excel Services report, the developer would select the Excel Services report template and then give the report a name and optional display folder. Once the report is open in the editor, the developer chooses the URL to the SharePoint site. Once the SharePoint site is selected, the Document Library is chosen; this can be a shared library or someone's personal library, although this choice will force users to enter a username and password to view a spreadsheet in someone's personal folders. Finally, the actual name of the document is selected.

In addition, an Item Name can be chosen if the page has named ranges, and the developer can also choose to show just certain rows and cells. Finally, a spreadsheet with parameters will list the parameters and those can be tied to PerformancePoint filters. Figure 6-25 shows what this page looks like after it is filled out for a simple report with no parameters.

Once the report has been set up, the developer can preview it by clicking on the View tab. This will open the report in a browser mode in the tab and let the developer confirm that it is working properly.

ProClarity Analytics Server Page

The ProClarity Analytics Server Page report will link to an existing view in a ProClarity Analytics Server briefing book. This will be covered in detail in the section on ProClarity later in this chapter.

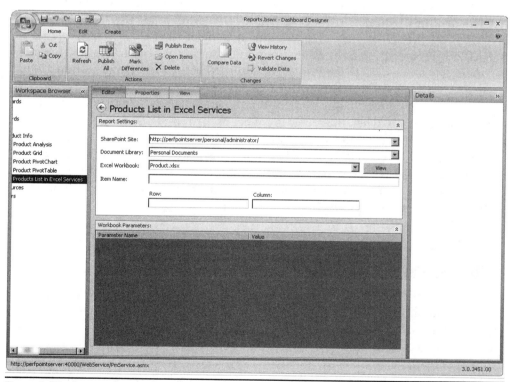

Figure 6-25 *Report Settings on the Excel Settings page*

Spreadsheet Reports

The Spreadsheet report is relatively simple. Creating one loads up the Excel grid using the Office Web Components. Note that the Office Web Components are from Office 2003, not Office 2007, so users will only have the functionality of Excel 2003 in their spreadsheet report.

More importantly, the spreadsheet control does not have direct connectivity to data sources. In other words, creating such a report will require that all the data be typed in, or at least copied from another source and pasted in. The spreadsheet control cannot directly tie to data so there are no queries available to retrieve data and fill out the spreadsheet. There is, however, a button to launch the full Excel product and users clicking that button will get a copy of the spreadsheet in Excel, as long as they have either Excel 2003 or Excel 2007 installed on their local machine.

SQL Server Reports and Web Pages

As both the Strategy Map and Trend Analysis Chart reports were covered in detail in Chapter 5, this section will conclude with a discussion of the SQL Server Reports and Web Pages. Each of these creates a link to an object that already exists. A new SQL Server report ties to an existing report in Reporting Services. The developer can choose to show or hide the Reporting Services toolbar, any parameters, and the docmap, which is a navigation tool available in Reporting Services to allow users to jump around in a report quickly. Finally, report parameters can be set so that data is passed automatically when the report is called, or the report parameters can be set to filters on a PerformancePoint Dashboard.

Web pages are extremely simple: they simply take a URL. While this may seem overly simplistic, it is an excellent way to tie non-PerformancePoint Server content into a dashboard. This is especially true when interacting with static data in other systems or with reporting tools from other vendors.

Analysis with ProClarity

There are a number of ProClarity products that are available, but the core products are thick and thin versions of an end-user analytic tool. The thick, or Windows, application is called ProClarity Desktop Professional, while the thin- or web-client version is called ProClarity Standard. Originally, all ProClarity had was the Windows client, but with the introduction of their thin client version, they renamed the Windows client to ProClarity Professional. Now, users may have the ability to choose which client they run, although administrators can control which users can see the Professional client and which are tied to just the Standard client.

Most companies today use the ProClarity Analytics Server, or PAS. PAS includes several items, including the Standard client, the Briefing Book Server, and optionally the Professional client. PAS is server based and runs with Internet Information Server (IIS) much like PerformancePoint Server. If a company chooses to install the Professional client on the server, a user can download it and install it locally. Then, when browsing content based on the server, the user can choose to open that content in either the Standard or Professional version.

The good news for users is that nearly all the functionality found in the Professional client is also in the Standard client. The main difference on which this book will focus is that developers and power users will use the Professional client to create content (called views) that will be published to the server for consumption by others. This is similar to PerformancePoint Server; most users only consume the end product of scorecards and reports, while a few people use the Dashboard Designer to create that content. In most organizations, the vast majority of ProClarity users interact only with the Standard client, but a small set of users create content for others using the Professional client.

There are other ProClarity applications as well. These include an add-in for Reporting Services and small tools such as the Selector. The following sections will focus just on the Professional client and the ProClarity Analytic Server, which includes the Standard Client.

The ProClarity Professional Client

ProClarity Professional is a Windows application that is built for one purpose: analyzing Analysis Services cubes. Unlike general purpose tools such as Excel, the single-mindedness of this approach led to ProClarity becoming the leading third-party analytics tool for accessing Analysis Services cubes. While browsing cubes may not necessarily be easy, ProClarity made it as simple as possible, while still maintaining incredibly rich functionality. The ProClarity tools are very graphical in nature, assuming that charts make data easier to grasp and comprehend quickly.

ProClarity Desktop Professional can connect to one of four sources: a ProClarity Analytics Server, an Analysis Services cube, a local Briefing Book, and a Briefing Book from ProClarity Analytics Server. These various topics will be discussed throughout the chapter, but for new users the first connection will be directly to a cube. When starting the Professional clients, users are presented with the Welcome screen shown in Figure 6-26, where they can choose between the four options.

When choosing to open a cube, there are two options: opening a cube from an Analysis Services server or opening a local cube. Local cubes are a way of storing cubes, or pieces of cubes, on machines that may not be running Analysis Services. There are many limitations with local cubes and a full discussion of local cubes

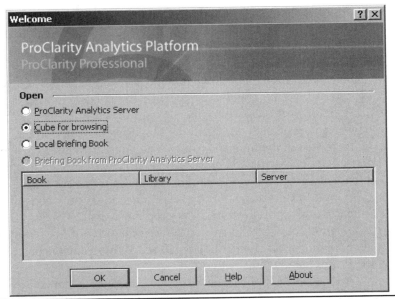

Figure 6-26 *ProClarity Desktop Professional allows users to connection directly to a cube or to use one of three other options.*

is beyond the scope of this book; see the SQL Server Books Online for more information. Figure 6-27 shows the dialog box that allows users to choose either a server or local cube; in the screenshot the Advanced button has been clicked. The Advanced button opens two additional fields on the form that allow users to enter a username and password. These options are normally used when a cube is made accessible via HTTP; this makes it easier for companies to access cubes across firewalls in some cases. The username and password can also be used when accessing cubes across domains if a trust does not exist; the user can enter credentials that allow access to the domain on which Analysis Services resides.

After selecting a server name and clicking the OK button, the user is presented with a list of the server's databases on the left, and a list of the cubes in the selected database on the right. In Figure 6-28, there is only a single database called Adventure Works DW, and on the right is a list of cubes and perspectives. A perspective in Analysis Services 2005 is much like a view in a relational database: it's a way to limit what can be seen in the cube. A perspective is not a security mechanism but a way to reduce the complexity of a cube. This means that one large cube with many dimensions can be simplified by creating different perspectives for different groups of users. As far as client tools are concerned, cubes and perspectives are treated identically.

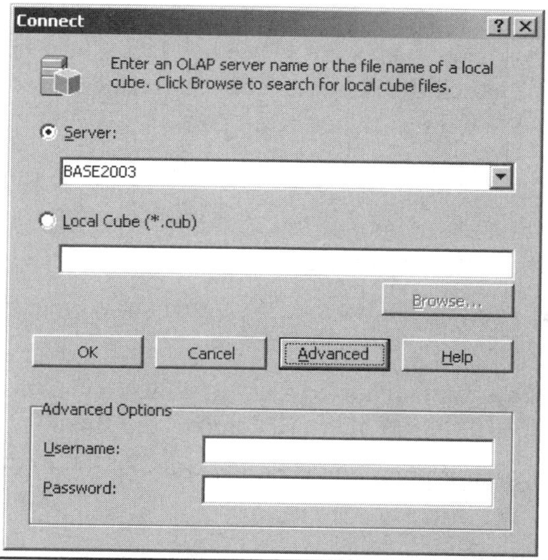

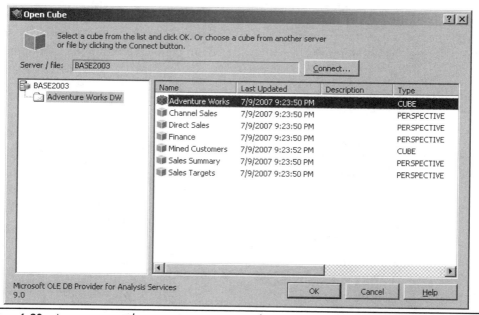

Figure 6-27 *Cubes may reside on the server or, in rare cases, locally on the user's computer. Security may require a username and password for server-based cubes.*

Figure 6-28 *A server may have one or more Analysis Services databases and each database may have multiple cubes and perspectives.*

After the user selects the cube or perspective to browse, a screen appears that allows the user to choose how they want to see the data. There are five choices on the page and a user can check the box at the bottom of the screen to make their next selection the default so that they are not again presented with this screen, which is shown in Figure 6-29. The choices available include

▶ **Chart View**   A standard bar chart by default, much like those of the Analytic Chart in PerformancePoint Server.

▶ **Decomposition Tree**   An advanced view that shows a history of the drill-down path.

▶ **Performance Map**   An advanced view in which one measure controls the size of rectangles while a second measure controls the shading.

▶ **Perspective**   A scatter point chart, good for comparing two measures at a very detailed level.

▶ **Grid**   A standard grid much like the Analytic Grid in PerformancePoint Server.

Most users will start with either a grid or a chart, although all are valid options. Starting with a chart will present users with a Big Blue Bar, just as with the Analytic Chart. This is because by default, ProClarity will select a Time dimension, if one exists, and place it on the Columns. The first dimension in the list will be placed on the Rows, and the default measure will be placed in the background. Much like the

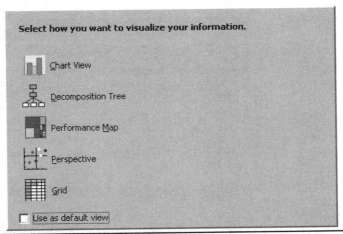

Figure 6-29   *After connecting to a cube, the user can select from five different types of view with which to start the analysis.*

Analytic Chart, the Big Blue Bar is live, and moving the mouse over it will change the cursor and a tooltip will appear that shows the actual value and may show additional information as well. Clicking on the bar will drill a user down the first hierarchy listed in the rows, just as with the Analytic Chart.

The Setup Panel

The Setup Panel can be shown or hidden by clicking the Setup button on the toolbar. Selecting the items to place on the Rows, Columns, and Background is slightly different from how it was done in PerformancePoint Server. Along the left-hand side of the Professional client is the Setup Panel, as shown in Figure 6-30. The Hierarchies tab shows all dimensions in the cube as well as an item for Measures. Expanding one of the dimensions will show all of the hierarchies under it (both the user-defined hierarchies and the attribute hierarchies). The icons are different, with multilevel, user hierarchies presented using the pyramid-type icon shown on the Accounts hierarchy in the Account dimension in Figure 6-30.

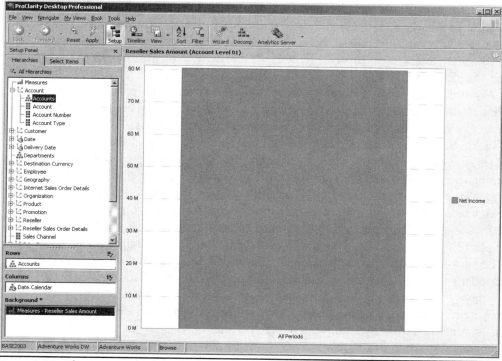

Figure 6-30   *The Setup Panel on the left-hand side of the Professional client is where users choose the dimensions and members to appear on the view.*

When a dimension is found, it can simply be dragged into the Rows, Columns, or Background. Just as with the PerformancePoint Server Analytic Charts and Grids, there can be multiple dimensions on rows and columns. Removing a dimension from the Rows, Columns, or Background can be done by right-clicking on the dimension and choosing Remove or dragging the dimension out of the Rows, Columns, or Background panes. Moving items around does not immediately change the chart by default; to update the view, the user must click the Apply button on the toolbar. Users desiring to have the chart update as they make changes can choose Auto Apply from the View menu; with this option, the chart or grid updates as soon as the mouse moves off the Setup Panel. Many users prefer the Auto Apply setting, but when making selections that may result in long-running queries, users may accidentally move off the Setup Panel before they're ready and then spend seconds or minutes waiting for the query to execute before they can finish making their changes.

The Setup Panel has two tabs: Hierarchies and Select Items. A user can click on a hierarchy or the Measures item and then click on the Select Items, or simply double-click on the choice and this will open the Select Items tab. For example, to change the measure being displayed, the user can double-click on the Measures item and the Select Items tab will appear with a list of all the measures. As explained earlier in this chapter, there cannot be multiple measures in the background at once, but selecting multiple measures here will create a drop-down for the chart, which ProClarity refers to as Slicers. Figure 6-31 shows three measures selected in the Setup Panel and the resulting Slicer that appears above the chart.

Double-clicking on a hierarchy (either user or attribute) in the Hierarchies tab opens the Select Items tab and allows users to select individual members of that hierarchy. For example, assume that the current query has Gross Profit in the Background, the Product Categories hierarchy in the Rows, and Date.Calendar hierarchy in the Columns. Now, in the Hierarchies tab, the user expands the Customer dimension and then double-clicks on the Customer Geography dimension. This opens the Select Items tab with Default (All Customers) selected. Expanding the All Customers member will reveal the members of the Country level. Selecting one of these items will automatically put the Customer Geography in the Background. Selecting two or more members will keep the Customer Geography hierarchy in the background but a Slicer will appear above the chart. In addition, an icon will appear next to the Customer Geography dimension to show that it is sliced. This symbol is shown in the illustration below left. This is fine if the desire is to keep the items separate, selecting one at a time by choosing them in a Slicer. If the goal is to combine the choices and sum them, clicking on the icon changes it to one representing combined items. This icon is shown in the illustration on the right below.

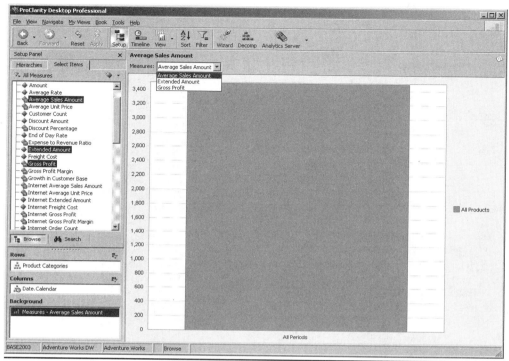

Figure 6-31 *A Slicer can be added to any view by selecting multiple members of a background dimension.*

The Select Items tab also has a very powerful tool; the ability to search through the members of a hierarchy. Clicking the Search button opens a simple textbox in which the search criteria can be entered, and clicking on Go will search all members at all levels of the hierarchy. ProClarity users will need to exercise caution as the search may lead to unexpected results. Figure 6-32 shows what happens when a user searches the Customer Geography hierarchy for the word Monica: there are customers with the first name Monica, but there is also a city, Santa Monica, that shows up in the results. As long as a match is found at any level, it is returned in the results.

To search for a term at only one level, there is an advanced search feature that can be accessed by clicking on the word Advanced just below the search textbox. The Advanced Find dialog allows users to search for members at just a single level or to search on member properties, which may include many different attributes. For example, individual customers have member properties such as gender, occupation, a home owner flag, and more.

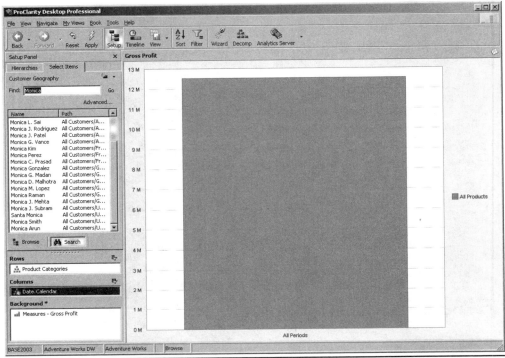

Figure 6-32 *Searching the Customer Geography dimension for the word Monica brings back customers named Monica, but also a city with the word Monica in it.*

Working with Charts

Any valid query run in ProClarity creates what is called a view. A view is a chart, grid, decomposition tree, or any other way of looking at data in ProClarity. Seeing the same data in a chart and a grid represents two completely different views. For example, the Big Blue Bar is a view. Clicking on a bar to drill down one level creates a completely different view. The important point here is that any view can be saved in what ProClarity calls a Briefing Book, which is a collection of one or more views.

Figure 6-33 shows a simple view in which the measure is gross profit, the Product Categories hierarchy is on the rows, and the Date.Calendar hierarchy is on the columns. Clicking on a bar drills down on the first hierarchy listed in the rows, and right-clicking on a bar provides a pop-up menu that allows users to drill down on other dimensions. Alternately, to drill down on the dimension on the columns, the user can click the label along the X-axis. For example, clicking on the label CY 2003 in Figure 6-33 would drill down on the year 2003.

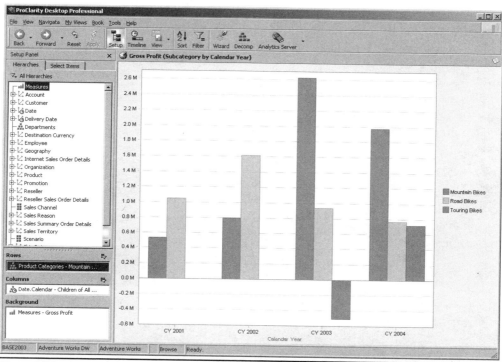

Figure 6-33 *A simple report on which the user has drilled down look at categories by year.*

Hovering over a particular bar will highlight that bar and all the matching bars on the view. For example, Figure 6-33 shows the same three product subcategories for four different years. A user who hovers the mouse over the Mountain Bikes bar will highlight the Mountain Bikes bar in all four years, dimming all other bars. A user can also hover over the text in the legend; in this example, hovering over the words Touring Bikes along the right-side of the chart will highlight all the Touring Bikes bars. Users can click on the text in the legend to drill down, which works just like clicking on one of the bars.

On the toolbar is a button labeled View. Clicking it will cycle through one of four views: Chart Only, Grid Only, a horizontal split between a grid and chart, and finally a vertical split between a grid and chart. Figure 6-34 shows miniaturized samples of these four basic views. The good news is that regardless of which format is used when the view is published, users will have an easy way to cycle through these four basic formats even if they are using the Standard client.

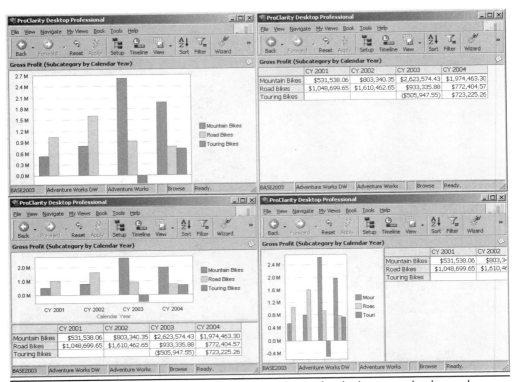

Figure 6-34 *The four basic view formats: chart only, grid only, horizontal split, and vertical split*

So far, the chart has always been a standard bar chart. However, there are three different ways of changing the chart type. First, clicking the small arrow next to the View button on the toolbar will show three options: Advanced Analysis Tools, Business Charts, and Grid. Looking at the Business Charts choice, there are six options: Area, Bar, Horizontal Bar, Line, Pie, and Point charts. The same choices can be seen by right-clicking on a blank area of the chart and highlighting Chart Type. Finally, the pop-up menu that appears when right-clicking on a blank area of the report also contains an option named Chart Toolbar, which turns on a toolbar that contains buttons for the six different chart types (as well as additional options.) Figure 6-35 shows what happens when a user has right-clicked on the chart and changed it to a line chart. The Chart Toolbar is also visible above the chart.

Changing the chart type is relatively simple, but these charts are highly configurable. There are multiple kinds of bar charts, for example, including side-by-side and stacked

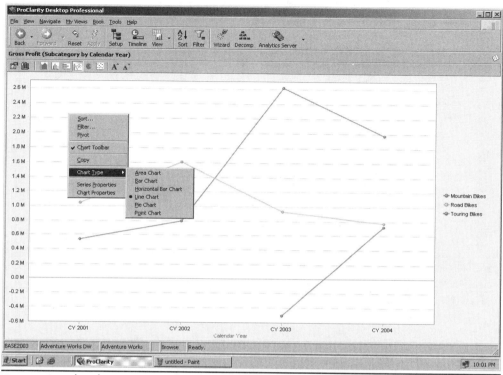

Figure 6-35 *The chart type can be changed by right-clicking on an empty part of the chart and choosing Chart Type on the menu.*

bar charts. In addition, charts can be made three dimensional (3D), the legend can be moved or hidden, fonts can be changed, a title can be added, the left axis can be scaled, and more. To access all of these options, the user should right-click in a blank part of the chart and choose Chart Properties. The Chart Properties dialog box will appear, as shown in Figure 6-36. In this figure, the user has clicked the 3D Options button and turned on the 3D Option.

Charts with a Right Axis   Recall from earlier in the chapter that trying to display two measures with very different formats, such as gross profit (measured in dollars) and gross profit margin (a percentage) forced the percentage to the right Y-axis. ProClarity charts also allow users to place a series on the right axis as well as the left. Each series can be represented differently as well; the series measured by the left axis can be a bar while the series measured on the right axis can be a line, for example. This is a common way to show actual values and percentages in the same chart.

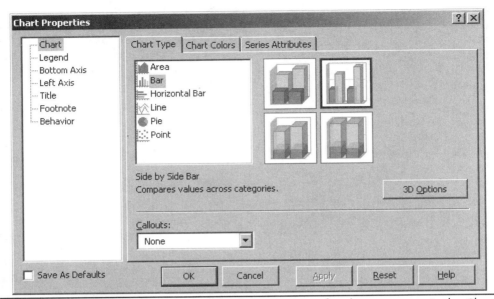

Figure 6-36 *ProClarity provides a wealth of customization for charts, as seen in the Chart Properties dialog box.*

Figure 6-37 shows two measures that have been added to the rows: Gross Profit and Gross Profit Margin. The four years of the time dimension are on the columns. Finally, a single product category, Mountain Bikes, is placed in the background. The user right-clicks on a blank area of the chart and this time chooses Series Properties. The Series Properties dialog box allows the user to select the Gross Profit Margin series, change it to a line chart, and then select the right axis. As can be seen in Figure 6-37, the Series Properties dialog shows these selections, but the chart in the background already shows the results. The left axis ranges from zero to 2.6 million, which represents the gross profit for mountain bikes. The right axis ranges from zero to 26% which covers the range for the gross profit margin. This chart easily shows two very different measures in a way that makes sense.

Working with the Grid

The ProClarity grid has already been shown because it is part of three of the four basic views. The grid is powerful and allows for both drilling down and expanding dimensions on either the rows or columns. In addition, the grid supports font and color changes, subtotals, exception highlighting, and more.

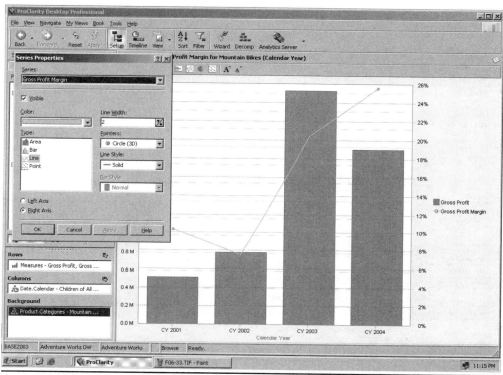

Figure 6-37 *A chart with both a left and right axis, allowing for two very different measures to be displayed on the same grid. While similar to the Analytics Chart shown in Figure 6-14, ProClarity's charts offer more customization.*

Drilling down is the same in ProClarity as it is with the PerformancePoint Server Analytic Grid: simply clicking on a member in either the rows or columns drills down on that member to its children. The children replace the parent. Figure 6-38 shows an example of drilling down on Date.Calendar where the user clicked on the All Periods member and drilled down to the four years available in the dimension.

Expanding keeps the parent on the screen while showing the children. This can be achieved by right-clicking on the member and choosing Expand, or holding down the Ctrl key while clicking on the member. In Figure 6-38, the Product Categories hierarchy has been expanded so that the All Products member is visible, as well as its children at the Category level.

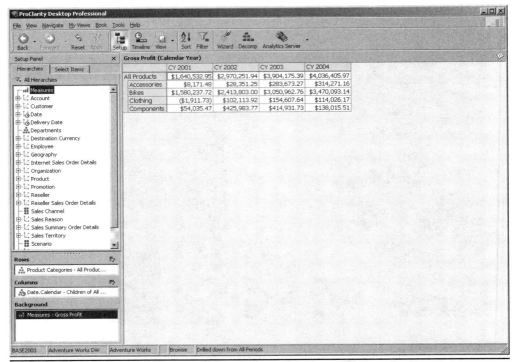

Figure 6-38 *A simple ProClarity grid with All Products expanded to show its children without replacing the parent, while Calendar has been drilled down to the Year level*

The grid has a large number of properties. Right-clicking on the grid and choosing Grid Properties opens the Grid Properties as shown in Figure 6-39. The dialog box contains a number of tabs that allow users to change how the values are actually displayed, change the column, row, and grid colors, and change the grid font. Along the left-hand side of the dialog box are options to modify the grid, add a title, or modify the drill to detail behavior. Figure 6-39 further shows that the developer has chosen to display the percent of total next to the actual values (which are on by default.) The change has been applied and the results are visible on the grid in the background. From this example it is easy to see that bikes accounted for 78% of total sales in 2003, but so far in 2004 they are accounting for 86% of sales. The grid has a grand total at the bottom added automatically when the percentage is being displayed. Percentages can be turned on for the columns, rows, or both.

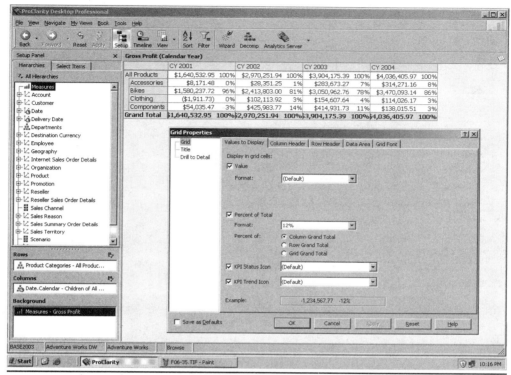

Figure 6-39 The Grid Properties dialog box allows users to heavily customize the grid, such as by adding totals and displaying the value and percent of total.

NOTE

It's important to understand that right-clicking on different parts of the grid can bring up slightly different menus. Figure 6-40 shows three different menus that can be brought up by right-clicking. The one on the top left appears when a user right-clicks on a member in the rows or columns. The menu on the top right appears when a user right-clicks on a data cell in the grid. The menu at the bottom shows what appears when a user right-clicks outside of the grid. Notice, for example, that the option for Exception Highlighting only appears if the user right-clicks on the data cells or outside of the grid, but is not on the menu if a user right-clicks on the row or column headers.

Totals   Figure 6-39 showed that subtotals are turned on automatically when the percent of total is added to the grid. However, subtotals can be added to the grid even without showing the percent of total. Right-clicking anywhere on or off the grid contains a Totals option that allows users to add column subtotals or grand totals,

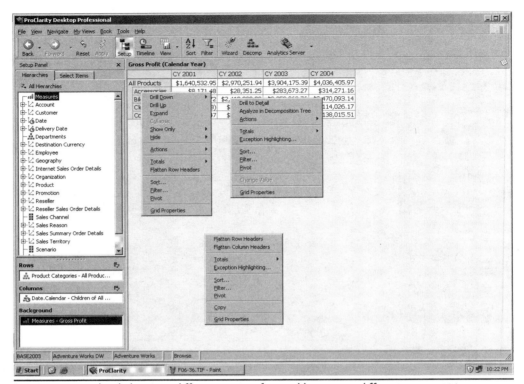

Figure 6-40   *Right-clicking on different parts of a grid brings up different menus. It's important to know what's available and where to click to get the desired options.*

as well as row subtotals or grand totals. Figure 6-41 shows that column subtotals and column grand totals have been turned on for a view that shows products and promotions on the rows. The subtotals appear as the totals of promotions for each product category, while the grand total is the total of all the product categories. By default, subtotals would also appear for the product categories, which would be the total of each promotion regardless of the product categories, but this was turned off using the Totals Options dialog, as shown in Figure 6-41. Note too that totals can be placed at either the top or bottom of the grid.

Hiding Empty Rows and Columns   Notice that in Figure 6-41 there are no values for the Customer promotion for any of the product categories or any of the years. The Customer member still shows up because it is one of the product categories, but seeing an empty entry like this can be confusing and can waste valuable screen

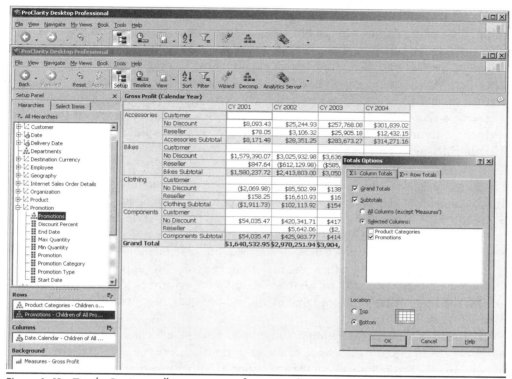

Figure 6-41 *Totals Options allow a user to fine tune the totals being displayed, including when to show subtotals and when to turn them off.*

real estate. Some views will be very sparsely populated, containing more empty cells than ones with values. In order to get rid of members that no values exist for, developers can choose to hide empty rows, hide empty columns, or both. This changes the underlying MDX query and tells it not to render any members for which no values are returned. In the Professional client, there are two small buttons at the right-hand side of the Rows and Columns areas of the Setup Panel.

Clicking the button next to the rows will hide any member for which all cells in that row are empty. For example, notice in Figure 6-41 that all four years of the Customer promotion for Accessories are blank. Clicking the button to filter out empty rows will cause this row to disappear in the grid. However, if even a single cell in that row had a value, the row would stay with three blank cells and one cell with a value. Similarly, the hiding empty columns means that all the cells in that column must be blank before it will be filtered out and not appear.

It is important to note that while many people prefer to see charts and grids with empty rows and columns filtered out, this can lead to a couple of issues. First, empty cells still have meaning, and that meaning may range from the fact that there were no values, to the fact that there might be a data problem. Second, the MDX statement that filters out the empty rows or cells can, in some situations, drastically decrease performance. This is not typical but has been seen in some cases in dealing with large cubes (200GB or larger) or very complex cube designs. Therefore, if these options are turned on and performance is an issue, try running the same queries without filtering out the empty rows and columns.

Exception Highlighting   Exception highlighting is one of the useful features that can allow standard, boring cells to jump out at the user. Good and bad values can be highlighted by changing the background colors and the font style and color so that they are immediately obvious. Up to three conditions can be added to the grid on which exception highlighting can be performed, but note that this is only a limit of the Professional user interface; the underlying engine can support a virtually unlimited number of conditions, so those wishing to perform custom programming against the ProClarity engine are free to allow more than three conditions for exception highlighting.

In order to start with exception highlighting, the designer can right-click on the data cells in the grid or outside of the grid; right-clicking on either the row or column headers will not show the Exception Highlighting option. After right-clicking in one of the two proper areas and selecting Exception Highlighting, the Exception Highlighting dialog box appears, as shown in Figure 6-42. Note that the first dropdown box lists the measures that are available in this view. The second dropdown box contains a list of conditions, including equal to, not equal to, between, and so forth. Finally, there is a box to hold the actual value.

In Figure 6-42, the view has been changed so that the measure Gross Profit Margin, and both the filter empty rows and filter empty columns buttons have been selected. In addition, the business has decided that any gross profit margin over 40% should be highlighted with a green background, while any gross profit margin of less than zero should have a red background.

In order to set this up, a designer would set the first condition to have a measure of Gross Profit Margin (the only one available in this case), the condition to "greater than," and the value to 40. In order to set the background as green, the developer would click the Configure Highlight Format button causing a new dialog box to appear that allows for the background color, font color, font type, font size, and font styles to be set. After setting up the first condition, the developer would click the Add button to add the second condition. Figure 6-42 shows the final settings for the Exception Highlighting option, and the background shows the cells with their highlights.

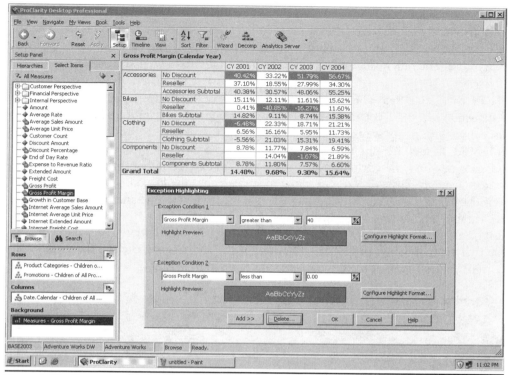

Figure 6-42 *Exception highlighting helps numbers that meet certain criteria immediately jump out by changing the background color, foreground color, and/or font.*

In order to turn off Exception Highlighting, the developer will open the Exception Highlighting dialog box and click the Delete button. A new dialog box will appear that asks which of the three exceptions should be removed. The developer is free to choose one, two, or all three.

Advanced Views

ProClarity also contains several advanced views. They're considered advanced because they go beyond the standard chart types to show data in a variety of ways that can aid analysis. These views can be seen by clicking the small down arrow next to the View button on the toolbar. The menu item Advanced Analysis Tools expands to show four options: Decomposition Tree, Internet Explorer, Performance Map, and Perspective. Of these four options, the Internet Explorer view is not really a data analysis view in the same vein as the other three. The Internet Explorer view simply opens a browser window and the developer can enter any URL, including ones that point to documents, images, and so forth. This allows for a view that doesn't point to a cube; instead, it can point to a web site, a document, or similar. Later in this chapter, various views will be saved into what is called a briefing book, and some customers use the Internet Explorer to link to documents that explain the views the user is about to explore. The other three views are explained in the following sections.

The Decomposition Tree   The Decomposition Tree, or "decomp" for short, is an advanced view that ProClarity developed and patented early in their history. It is a useful view in many ways because it shows a history of the drilling path a person has followed. In fact, it is the only view that can keep a full history of the viewing path unless a person is in a grid and always chooses to expand rather than drill down.

Choosing to start a decomp from the menu launches the Decomposition Tree Wizard. The decomp can break down a single measure at a time and breaks it down by a single hierarchy to start, although the user is free to change the hierarchy being drilled at any point while working with the decomp. Note that there is a section on the first page of the wizard labeled "Starting with" and that this section shows the current values for all of the dimensions, as shown in Figure 6-43. The values shown

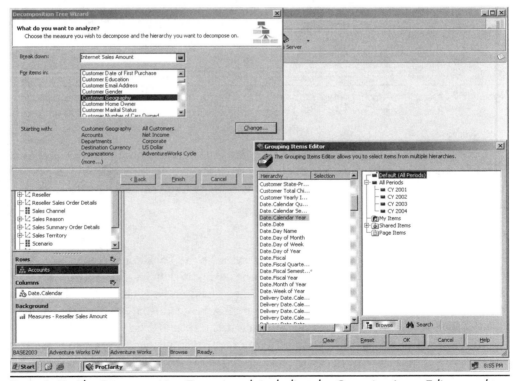

Figure 6-43 *The Decomposition Tree wizard, including the Grouping Items Editor used to make background selections*

are—in this particular cube—the default values for each dimension. This is because the developer, before starting the Decomposition Tree Wizard, reset everything in the view to the defaults. This is accomplished by clicking on the Reset button on the toolbar.

The reason why the developer would choose to reset everything to the defaults is simple yet important: the wizard will take the values of the current view as the starting point. In other words, if the year had been set to 2001 instead of the All level, the decomp would contain data for only the year 2001. Some developers and analysts jump into the decomp without realizing that they have inadvertently filtered the data based on selections made on a view. They assume, incorrectly, that the wizard will always start with default values of the All levels for all the dimensions. In order to ensure this, it is important to reset the current view using the Reset button. There are times, of course, that developers and users choose to start with values other than the All members, and this will be discussed in a moment.

In order to filter any particular background dimension, the developer or user can click on the Change button. This opens the Grouping Items Editor, also shown in Figure 6-43. From here, the user can choose a member from any dimension to use as a filter. You should understand that this means a single member. Unlike the background for a chart or grid, the decomp doesn't allow multiple selections and sum them together, nor does it add a slicer to the top of the screen. Therefore, background selections must be single members of the dimension.

Figure 6-43 showed that the selections made in the wizard were a measure of Internet Sales Amount and a hierarchy called Customer Geography. Leaving all other values set to the defaults and completing the wizard takes the user to a relatively barren screen containing just a single box at the top, along with a small chart at the bottom containing just a single bar. The box at the top is labeled All Customers and shows a value of 29M and a percentage of 100. Hovering the mouse over this box reveals additional details, such as the exact value. Clicking once on this box is roughly analogous to expanding on a grid; the parent remains while the children are now shown. In this case, the first level below the All level is Country, and there are six countries that appear. The first country listed is the United States because it has the largest value. The values are always shown sorted from highest to lowest. While both the United States and Australia boxes show amounts of 9M, hovering over them will display the actual values. In addition, the United States has a 32% in its box while Australia has 31%. That means that the United States accounts for 32% of all the sales of its parent, or in this case the All level.

Clicking on the box labeled Germany opens up the State-Province level, showing the provinces of Germany. Hessen is the largest province in terms of the measure called Internet Sales Amount. Hovering the mouse over Hessen displays a pop-up window as shown in Figure 6-44. This pop-up displays the actual value of $794,876.08, as well as some additional information. The first piece of information is that Hessen represents 27% of the group. This means that of all the provinces in Germany, Hessen accounts for 27%. Another way to look at this is that the group percentage is the percentage of the parent; Hessen accounts for 27% of all the sales in the parent, Germany. The next value is the percentage of the total, and that means the percentage of the top box of the decomp tree. In this case, Hessen accounts for 3% of the grand total, or all sales. Each member shown in a decomp tree will report the same two values: the percentage of the group and the percentage of the total. This can be very helpful when the user is far down a decomp chain and sees a value that is a large percentage of the group, but discovers it is but a tiny percentage of the total.

Figure 6-44 also shows that the user has clicked on Hessen and drilled down to the City level. München is the largest city in Hessen in terms of Internet Sales Amount and is therefore listed first. Following München are four more cities, and then a stack representing the bottom four cities. This is the only level shown in the figure that cannot fit all the members on a line at once, and shows what happens

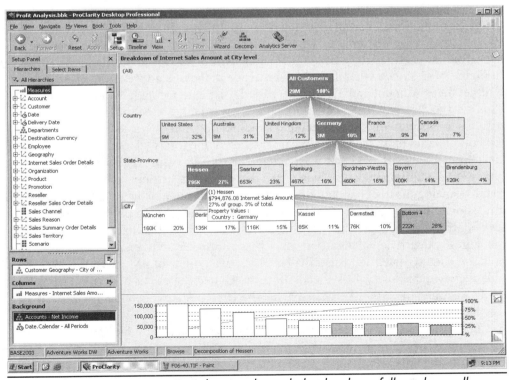

Figure 6-44 *A Decomposition Tree showing the path that has been followed as well as a pop-up showing the actual values in a particular box*

when there are too many members to fit on the screen. The members at the bottom are stacked up on the right-hand side. Clicking on the stack has the effect of moving members from the stack into the visible area, and a stack now forms on the left-hand side. In this way, the members are dealt from the right-hand stack, into the middle area, and then onto the left-hand stack. This makes the decomp usable even if the user drills down to levels with thousands of members.

Figure 6-44 also shows a Pareto chart at the bottom of the decomp. One of the complaints some customers have about the decomp is that all the boxes are the same size, and thus they do not indicate the relative size of the measure for one box compared to another. The Pareto chart does this by the showing relative sizes in a bar chart, with the values for the bars being shown on the left axis. Unless there are many members, the Pareto chart shows a bar for all the members. Those that are currently displayed on the screen are shown in a lighter color than those in the stack; the bar colors match the colors of the boxes in the decomp.

There is also a thin line moving from the lower left to the upper right in the Pareto chart. This line shows the growth from zero to 100%, with the values for the line being on the right axis. This shows how quickly a level reaches a certain percentage. For example, the line crosses the 50% threshold on the third bar, which means that the first three cities in the Hessen province account for over 50% of the total for all cities in Hessen.

The bars of the Pareto chart are live, meaning that a user can hover the mouse over one and get a pop-up window that shows the actual value as well as the percentages of the group and total. In addition, clicking on one of the bars will make that box visible if it is not already. This is useful for clicking on a bar that represents a member that is stacked up on the left or right. The member for that bar is automatically dealt to the visible region, and other members are stacked up on the left or right as necessary.

The Pareto chart can be customized to some degree using the two buttons located off to the right of it. The top button will toggle just the percentage line on and off, while the bottom button will toggle the entire Pareto chart on and off. Finally, clicking on either the left or right axis will cycle through a series of turning off all the grid lines, turning on just grid lines for the axis on which the user is clicking, and turning on grid lines for both the left and right axes.

Returning to the decomp itself, the full power has not yet been demonstrated. In Figure 6-44, the user has drilled down to the City level, and if he or she clicks on München, Postal Code will be shown (and after that the individual customers). After drilling down to the lowest level in the dimension, what's next? In this case, there is a customer named José E. Saraiva who has ordered approximately $8,000 worth of products from the Adventure Works company. What products has José ordered? To find out, the developer can right-click on the José's box and choose Drill Down, then Product Categories, and then Product. This will now show all the products that relate just to this customer. This cross-drilling capability is incredibly powerful, as it allows a user to easily investigate data across multiple dimensions, all within the decomp. There is no need to return to the Setup Panel to perform this advanced analysis; in fact, changes in the Setup Panel have no affect on the decomp. Figure 6-45 shows the selection described here being made.

In the previous example, the user cross-drilled on the lowest level of the Customer Geography dimension, but a cross-drill can actually occur at any level. I have worked with customers that use the decomp almost exclusively, drilling from geography to reseller to product to customer, all the while analyzing costs and revenue. This customer finds the decomp ideally suited for their end users because it requires minimal training (the Setup Panel isn't required) and it has great impact. If, at any time, a user wants to drill down a different chain that is three levels up, they can simply click on a box on that higher level and move the drill down to that member. In this particular example, the user has chosen the largest boxes to drill down for some time. Figure 6-46 shows the end result of the cross-drill, in which it

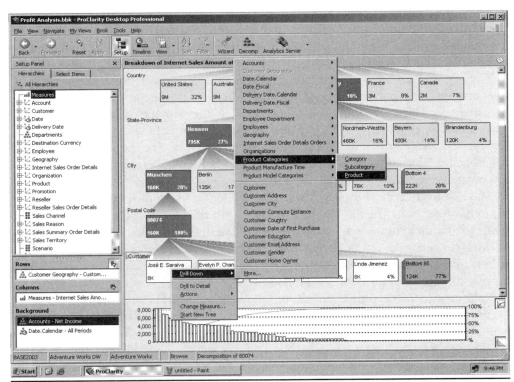

Figure 6-45 *The Decomposition Tree allows for easy cross-drilling, which allows users to drill from one dimension to another.*

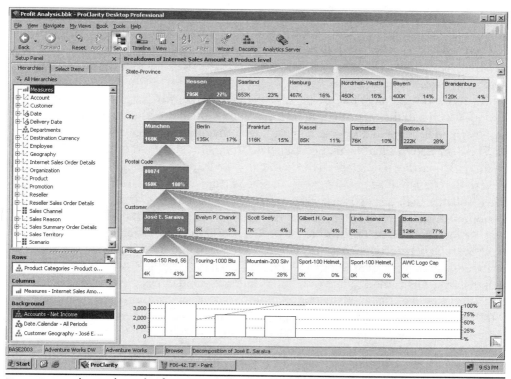

Figure 6-46   *The end result of a cross drill in which the analysis jumped from the Customer dimension to the Product dimension*

is now shown that José has purchased three rather expensive bikes, two helmets, and a hat. Note also that the Pareto chart is showing grid lines only for the left axis, a change made by the developer simply to clean up the chart a bit.

There is one last item to discuss in regards to the decomp. In this case the decomposition tree was created by launching it from the menu after resetting all values to the defaults. Sometimes, users will want to take the current value and start a decomposition tree at the point. Fortunately, this is simple. Right-clicking on a bar in a graph or a cell in a grid will bring up a menu and one of the options is Analyze in Decomposition Tree. Choosing this will create a decomposition tree with that value at the top, and the user is free to drill and cross-drill from that point forward. Note that whatever values were set in the chart or grid are still set in the decomp, so if a user has right-clicked on a cell that is for just a particular month, the decomp will only show data for that particular month regardless of which dimension the user drills or cross-drills into.

The Perspective Chart One of the advanced chart types is the Perspective Chart, sometimes called the Perspective view or just the Perspective. The Perspective Chart is a type of scatter point chart that compares two measures simultaneous. This is another excellent way to compare values that vary widely, such as the gross profit and gross profit margin. These values were compared previously using a chart with both a left and right axis, but the perspective can do it easily by placing one measure on the X axis and the other measure on the Y axis. In addition, the perspective chart shines when looking at a large amount of data, making it very easy to spot outliers.

The Perspective Chart cannot be launched from a regular chart or the grid like the decomp, so starting the Perspective Chart can only be done by clicking the down arrow next to the View button and choosing Advanced Analysis Tools and then Perspective. This launches the Perspective Wizard, the first step of which is similar to that of the Decomposition Tree Wizard. It asks what items should be analyzed, meaning the various members of the dimensions. It's often useful to have reset all the values to their defaults before launching the Perspective Wizard and making the selections there, as the selections will often be at a low level of detail. As a simple example, assume that the user selects the Product Categories hierarchy and clicks the Change Selection button to open the Change Selections dialog. From there, the user could right-click on All Products, choose Select Descendants, and then Product. In one simple operation, the user has selected all individual products. Figure 6-47 shows what the first step of the wizard would look like after the user has made their selection.

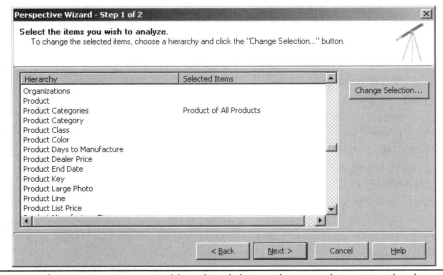

Figure 6-47 *The Perspective Wizard has the ability to change selections on background members in much the same way as the Decomposition Tree Wizard.*

The second step of the wizard asks the user to select the X-axis and Y-axis measures. In this case, Gross Profit will be placed on the Y axis and Gross Profit Margin will be placed on the X-axis. Both of these are interesting because they can have negative values as easily as having positive values. Figure 6-48 shows what this first perspective chart looks like.

There are several items to discuss when looking at the Perspective Chart. First, the dots are live, meaning that hovering the mouse over a point will create a pop-up that shows what the dot represents (which individual product, in this case) as well as the actual values for both measures. Second, the dots in Figure 6-48 are all the same shape and color. This is rather boring, but beyond that, it also fails to convey as much information as possible. This will be remedied in a moment.

Finally, there are two sliders. By default, they start out at zero, as shown here in Figure 6-48. They can be dragged up and down or right and left. As they move, the percentages they show change. For example, note that the slider on the right axis in

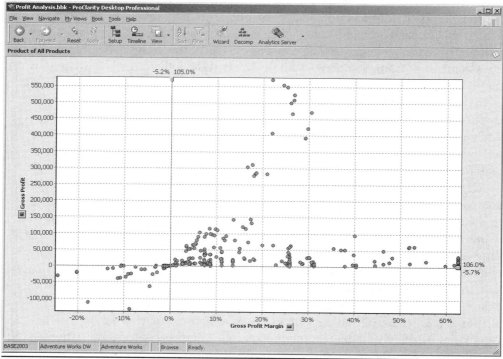

Figure 6-48 *A Perspective chart with a number of data point to compare Gross Profit and Gross Profit Margin*

Figure 6-48 shows 106% and -5.7%. This means that 106% of the total gross profit is above the line and -5.7% is below the line. The numbers don't exactly get back to 100% because so many of the points cut the line that it's hard to make it exact. However, if the user begins dragging this slider upwards, the 106% value starts to dwindle rapidly. As the slider climbs, fewer dots appear above it, representing those products that had a higher gross profit. Likewise, moving the top slider to the right narrows down the products that contribute to the gross profit margin. The ideal scenario would be to have as many products as possible in the upper right-hand corner of the perspective, but this is rarely the case. Figure 6-48 shows that the products with the highest gross profit margins tend to have smaller gross profits, which means they simply don't generate as much revenue as items with lower margin. For example, some of the highest margin items include bike stands and tire tubes, which do not generate anywhere near the same gross profits as a very expensive mountain bike.

Many of the dots tend to cluster together, forming a jumbled mess. If the user wants to see a cluttered area of the chart better, she can right-click in that area and then choose Zoom to zoom in on it. Right-clicking after zooming in will now present a Zoom Out option. In addition, a user can click and drag on the background to draw a rubber band around a certain area. Then, upon releasing the mouse, a menu will pop up with two options: Zoom and Show Only. This only works if the user clicks and drags from the upper left to the lower right. Other directions will draw the rubber band but not display the menu.

In order to provide even more information, it's possible to make the dots more useful. For example, are most of the high-margin items in the Accessories category? Are they in clothing, or bikes, or some other category? Fortunately, there's a way to change the color and shape of the dots to represent values at other levels of the hierarchy.

Right-clicking in an empty area of the perspective chart will show a menu with an option named Data Point Attributes. This will show a dialog box in which the user can select a member of a hierarchy and make any dots that belong to that member have a specific color and shape. In this case, the dots represent individual products. Custom data point attributes could be placed at either of the two levels above product, in this case the category or subcategory. Because there are so many subcategories, this example will choose just the four categories of Accessories, Bikes, Clothing, and Components. The user selects one of the categories and assigns a color and a shape to it and then clicks the Add button. Figure 6-49 shows what the Data Point Attributes dialog box might look like when the user is done. Clicking the OK button returns the user to the perspective chart.

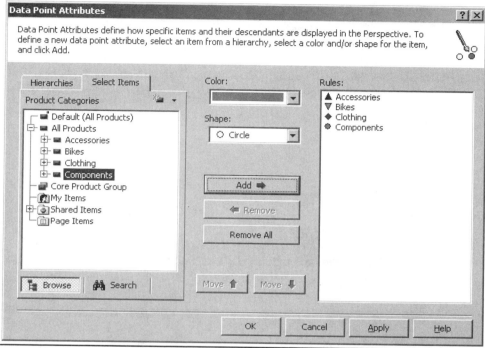

Figure 6-49 *The Data Point Attributes dialog box allows users to assign colors and shapes to various dimension members.*

Once data point attributes have been set, the perspective chart shows additional information and becomes more useful. Figure 6-50 shows the perspective chart with the data point attributes set. With these new settings, it is obvious that all the items near the top of the chart are bikes. Most of the items along the right-hand side of the chart are accessories, with one or two clothing items there as well. It should be noted that many clothing items, and a number of bikes, are also towards the lower left-hand corner, which represents the worst of the worst. Figure 6-50 also shows sliders that have been moved. The top slider shows that 82% of the gross profit margin is generated by the items to the right of the line, and the right slider shows that nearly 40% of the gross profit is generated by the few items above the line.

Changes to the Perspective can be accomplished relatively easily. Right-clicking on a blank part of the chart and selecting Perspective Properties will allow the user to change colors, fonts, and so forth. The properties window will also allow the user to change the size of the data points so that the indicators are smaller or larger depending on needs. Right-clicking also shows an option named Configure Axes

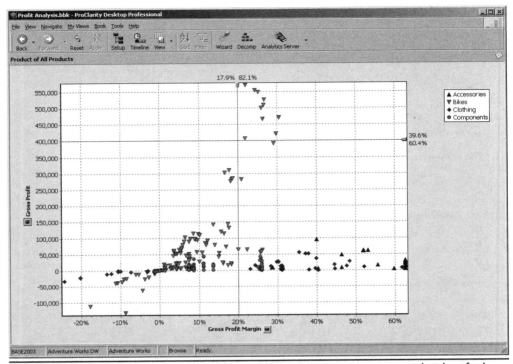

Figure 6-50   *After setting data point attributes, the user can now more easily identify the product categories with the highest profits and the highest margins.*

which lets the user change the measure on each axis, but there's an easier way as well: each Axis has a small button next to the measure name which, when pressed, will show a list of all the measures. In this way, the user can easily change measures on the fly. Finally, right-clicking also shows an option called Perspective Wizard which simply runs the wizard again, allowing for other choices to be made.

It's important to note that this example selected the individual products but all other dimensions were left at their default values. However, nothing prevents the user from selecting members from multiple dimensions. For example, the user might choose individual products in the Product dimension and individual countries in the Geography dimension. In fact, the user could do something as detailed as individual products and individual customers, but this could produce thousands of data points and might be hard to analyze even in the perspective chart. In addition, all queries so far in this chapter have taken no more than a few seconds on the my admittedly underpowered virtual machine. A query of all customers and all products, however, takes over ten minutes before the machine runs out of memory. Most users who ask for such granular detail will soon discover that just because they *can* ask for so much information doesn't mean they *should*.

The Performance Map   The Performance Map, sometimes called a heat map, is an advanced chart type that fits all of its data into a rectangle. Inside that rectangle, members are shown in rectangles, and the size of each member rectangle is determined by a measure selected by the user. Each rectangle, however, is color coded, based on another measure also selected by the user. This means that the size of the rectangle might represent sales, so larger rectangles are good. The color coding might be controlled by the margin, so those with the highest margins stand out, as do those with the lowest margins.

Starting the Performance Map is done by selecting the down arrow next to the View button and choosing Advanced Analysis Tools and then Performance Map. If the developer has reset the values and has the Big Blue Bar when the Performance Map is launched, it will be a rather uninteresting single color and just show the name of the measure. At the top of this large green box are some options that need to be set to get the full value out of the Performance Map.

The first item is a box labeled Show. This box determines what will be shown in the Performance Map. Clicking on it shows a list of the hierarchies, both attribute and navigational, so the user is free to choose the members for just about anything. Note that measures do not show up in the list, and one or more of the dimensions might be grayed out. If one or more dimensions are grayed out, it means they are in the columns for the view. This will be addressed in a moment. For this example, the user will select the Product Categories hierarchy and choose the Subcategory level.

Setting up the Performance Map to base both the size and color on different measures now requires using the Setup Panel. In this case, the user selects two measures, Gross Profit and Gross Profit Margin, and moves Measures to the columns as the *only* dimension on the columns. Other dimensions can be placed in the columns but selecting more than one value from that second columns dimension often has undesired results. It's fine to move dimensions to the background and make single selections, however.

Once the two measures are selected, the first measure selected will determine the size of the product subcategory rectangle, while the second measure selected will determine the color of the product subcategory rectangle. This is an important point, because there's no way to drag and drop the order of the measures. The order in which the user selects the measures determines which one will be used to size the rectangles and which will be used to determine the color of the rectangles. If the user first clicks on Gross Profit and then, holding down the Ctrl key, selects the Gross Profit Margin measure, the view will look like the one in Figure 6-51. In this view, the largest boxes are for those subcategories generating the highest gross profits.

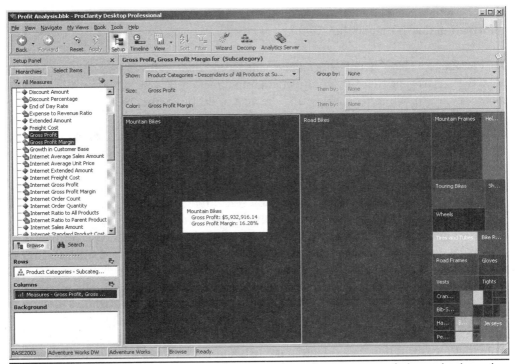

Figure 6-51 *A Performance Map that shows size based on Gross Profit but color based on Gross Profit Margin*

Mountain bikes and road bikes clearly jump out as the two top sources of gross profits. What is not as obvious in a black-and-white screenshot is that the color of Mountain Bikes is a very dark red, nearly black, and the color of Road Bikes is red. This means that at the default settings, these two measures subcategories have below average gross profit margins. The default color scheme ranges from bright green (the highest gross profit margins) to bright red (the lowest gross profit margins.) In the middle is black, representing an average gross profit margin. In color, it's easy to see that Tires and Tubes is bright green and Jerseys is bright red, while Mountain Bikes is near the middle.

Once again, these colors are based on an automatic read by the Performance Map of the range of possible values, but the user is free to adjust these ranges. Figure 6-51 shows that by hovering the mouse over a rectangle, a pop-up will appear that shows the actual underlying values. Mountain Bikes have a color of almost black, meaning they are somewhere near the middle of gross profit margins. However, the pop-up shows that mountain bikes are generating a gross profit margin of just over 16%, a figure many companies would find quite acceptable. Therefore, a user can modify the values to better suit the business conditions. Right-clicking anywhere in the Performance Map and choosing Performance Map Properties opens the dialog box shown in Figure 6-52. Using this dialog box, the user can modify the color scheme and the color range, as well as turn on or off the setup pane at the top of the map. If the stated business goal is to have items generate a margin of at least 15%, the user could change the middle value to .15 and that would turn Mountain Bikes ever so slightly green, meaning they were now above the desired gross profit margin value.

Another option for the Performance Map is to group the items being shown. In Figure 6-51 the subcategories are shown for all time. To break them down by years, the user can drop down the first Group By box, select Date.Calendar, and then Calendar Year. This has the effect of adding Date.Calendar to the Rows, but also of grouping the items in the Performance Map as shown in Figure 6-53. Realize that at this point it can be very difficult to read many of the boxes, so it might be helpful to select only a few of the larger subcategories.

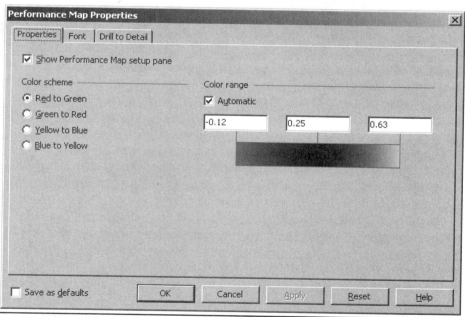

Figure 6-52 *The colors on a Performance Map can be adjusted so that good values always show up as good, regardless of the distribution of values.*

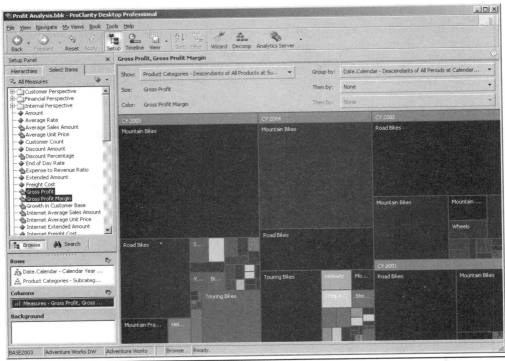

Figure 6-53 *Performance Maps can be grouped by up to three dimensions. In this case, the map is grouped by year.*

Briefings Books and Publishing to PAS

Each view in ProClarity is but a fleeting glimpse of the data. As soon as a value is changed in the Setup Panel, or someone drills up, drills down, expands, cross-drills, or does anything else, the view has changed and a new view is available. Fortunately, the Briefing Book allows for the saving of views so that they can be recalled later. A Briefing Book is merely a collection of one or more views stored in a file for later retrieval, and can be organized into folders or simply displayed in a flat list. The Briefing Book can then be saved to disk, allowing it to become the unit of distribution. (In other words, the file can be emailed to others, put on a file share, and so forth.) In addition, it is the Briefing Book that is published to the web server running the ProClarity Analytics Server, or PAS.

There are two major points to realize about Briefing Books. First, Briefing Books do not store any data. Rather, they store the query and any changed properties, such as background colors, font changes, exception highlighting, and so forth. Each time a user looks at a view in a Briefing Book, ProClarity connects to the data source and runs the query. In this way, the user is always seeing the current cube values. Second, a single Briefing Book may contain views that connect to different cubes. This means that a single Briefing Book may have views that connect to a cube storing the actual sales as well as a cube containing the forecast numbers. The user may be oblivious to the fact that views are connecting to different cubes. To the user, it is a seamless experience as they simply click from one view to the next.

Saving a view at any point in time is simple. Every time the ProClarity Desktop Professional client is started it opens a Briefing Book in much the same way that starting Microsoft Word opens with a blank page. If a user opens Word and then closes it, without doing anything to the blank page, Word closes without asking the user to save the document. ProClarity Desktop is slightly different, in that the user may create many views and perform a wealth of analysis but closing the application does not prompt the user to save anything. This is because no matter how much work the user does, unless he or she explicitly saves a view to the Briefing Book, no changes to the Briefing Book have occurred, so ProClarity doesn't have to save the book.

Adding a view to a Briefing Book is simple: the user simply gets a view designed as desired and then clicks on the Book menu and chooses Add to Briefing Book. A dialog box will appear that allows the user to give the view a name and then the view is added to the Briefing Book. If this is the first time the user has done this for a particular book, the Briefing Book pane will be added to the UI and the new view will show up in it. Future views can be added to the Briefing Book either by using the Book menu or by clicking the Add button on the Briefing Book pane. Figure 6-54 shows the Briefing Book pane open and a view from the book to the right. Whenever a view from the book is displayed, the icon next to the view name changes to that of a magnifying glass over the page. As soon as the user makes a single change to the view, such as expanding a value, the view has changed and the icon will revert to the standard icon of a page.

There is also an Organize button on the Briefing Book pane, which corresponds to an option on the Book menu, Organize Briefing Book. This opens a dialog box that allows the user to reorder pages in the Briefing Book and add folders to organize views.

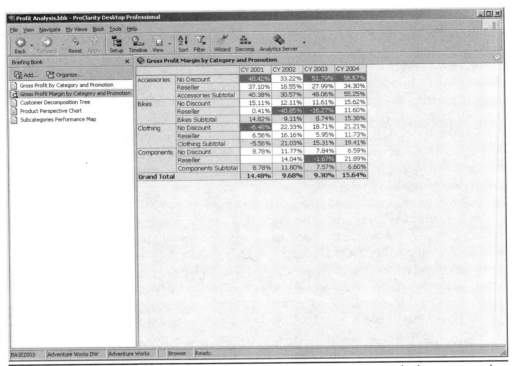

The following table shows the Gross Profit Margin by Category and Promotion view:

		CY 2001	CY 2002	CY 2003	CY 2004
Accessories	No Discount	40.42%	33.22%	51.79%	56.67%
	Reseller	37.10%	18.55%	27.99%	34.30%
	Accessories Subtotal	40.38%	30.57%	48.06%	55.25%
Bikes	No Discount	15.11%	12.11%	11.61%	15.62%
	Reseller	0.41%	-40.85%	-16.27%	11.60%
	Bikes Subtotal	14.82%	9.11%	8.74%	15.38%
Clothing	No Discount	-6.48%	22.33%	18.71%	21.21%
	Reseller	6.56%	16.16%	5.95%	11.73%
	Clothing Subtotal	-5.56%	21.03%	15.31%	19.41%
Components	No Discount	8.78%	11.77%	7.84%	6.59%
	Reseller		14.04%	-1.67%	21.89%
	Components Subtotal	8.78%	11.80%	7.57%	6.60%
Grand Total		14.48%	9.68%	9.30%	15.64%

Figure 6-54 *A Briefing Book is a file that stores one or more views. Only the query and formatting is saved; no cube data is stored in a Briefing Book.*

For example there might be a series of views that deal with Internet Sales and a different set of views that deal with Retailer Sales. Grouped into separate folders, these views will be grouped according to the data they present. The dialog box to organize views in a Briefing Book is shown in Figure 6-55.

Once a Briefing Book has one or more views, it can be saved by clicking on the File menu and clicking Save Book or Save Book As. There are two possible formats for saving the Briefing Book: a proprietary binary format with the extension .bbk, or as an XML file with a .xml extension. In most cases the choice of a format is of little consequence, as both are single files that represent all the views in the Briefing Book, and if the book is published to PAS, the format of the book is immaterial. Once a book is saved to disk, a user can reopen it at any time by clicking on the File menu and choosing Open Book or Reopen Book.

PAS is the ProClarity Analytics Server which is covered in detail in the next section. One of the surprising facts about PAS for many new users is that by itself, PAS can do nothing. A user cannot launch PAS by itself and connect to cubes and

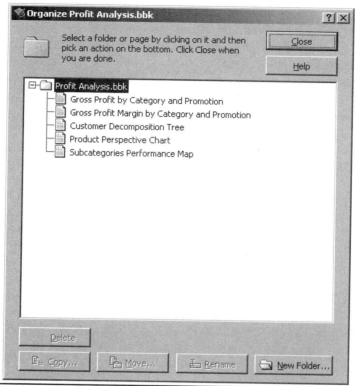

Figure 6-55 *A dialog box allows users to organize a Briefing Book by reordering views and placing them into folders.*

perform analysis. Instead, the starting point for any analysis is a view in a Briefing Book. This means that someone, often a developer or power user, must create a Briefing Book in the Professional client and then publish that book to PAS so that others will be able to use that book's views as a starting point.

Publishing a Briefing Book to PAS is relatively simple as long as the user has access to the server and has been granted publishing rights. Publishing rights are one of the many parameters that a PAS administrator can set on the server, and for now this walkthrough will assume that the user does indeed have publishing rights. On the toolbar in the Professional client is a button labeled Analytics Server. By default, clicking the large button will open a Briefing Book that is on the server. However, clicking the down arrow next to the Analytics Server button will open other options, such as Publish Book and Manage Books. These options are also found on the file menu under Analytics Server.

Choosing Publish Book will first ask the user to select the web server running PAS. Normally this is an internal server and takes the form of http://<servername>/ pas, where "pas" is the virtual directory to which PAS was installed. This name can be changed during installation. Once the user is connected, the dialog box shown in Figure 6-56 appears, although the user has already clicked the New Library button. This dialog box allows the user to select an existing library (or, in this case, create one since none exist) as well as manage books or connect to a different server. A Library is merely a collection of one or more Briefing Books. Many organizations create a library per business unit and place all the books for that business unit with that library. In this example, the user is creating a library simply called Sample Analytics.

Once a library is chosen, the user can enter the name of the book, which defaults to the name of the Briefing Book file when it was saved on the client machine. Once the user clicks OK, all the views from that Briefing Book are published to the server. There is a SQL Server database that stores the view definitions as well as the Briefing Book names, users, their permissions, and so forth.

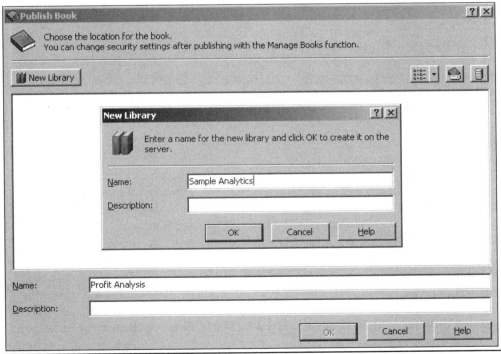

Figure 6-56 *Publishing a book to ProClarity Analytics Server provides thin-client users with a starting point from which to perform their analysis.*

Once the views are published to PAS, users are free to view the book and the views inside it, as long as they have the proper permissions. If the user publishing the book has enough authority, they can choose to manage the book and set permissions as to which roles can see the book and which cannot. For the purpose of this narrative, the user will have access to the book, so it is time to analyze the data using the thin, or Standard, client of PAS.

The ProClarity Standard Client

The ProClarity Standard client is the completely thin-client version of ProClarity that is part of the ProClarity Analytics Server. It is a series of pages that allow nearly all the same functionality as the Desktop Professional client while being completely web-based. As a web-based application, the Standard client does have significant differences in how certain actions are performed, but most of the functionality of the Professional client is available. In a few rare cases, the Standard client even includes functionality not found in the Professional client, as will be pointed out in the following sections.

Perhaps one of the most significant differences between the Standard and Professional clients is that the Standard client does not include any drag-and-drop capabilities. The Standard client is not AJAX-enabled, but instead operates like a series of traditional web pages. Users start by selecting the library they want to view, then a book in that library, and finally a view in the particular book. The view is rendered and looks as close to the view saved in the Professional client as possible; there are minor changes to the display because of limitations of a web client versus a rich Windows application.

Another major difference between the Standard and Professional clients is the lack of pop-up menus when right-clicking on a chart or grid. The menu that appears when a user right-clicks is the standard Internet Explorer menu and has nothing to do with the underlying page being viewed. Internet Explorer does not see the ProClarity view as different from any other web page it might render, so the menu does not contain any ProClarity-specific options. Instead, items are most often selected by left-clicking on them and then selecting options in one of the Standard client tabs, some of which mimic the Professional client's Setup Panel while others include sorting, filtering, and so forth. The differences between Standard and Professional and the ways to analyze data using the Standard client is discussed in the next sections.

Working with Charts and Grids

When working with charts and grids, it's important to remember that clicking on the member names does not drill down as it does in the Professional client. Clicking on a cell in the grid allows the user to drill to detail (something that may or may not be available in the cube) or analyze that value in a Decomposition Tree. Clicking on a member in the rows or columns shows a menu that drill down, drill up, expand, show only, or hide. However, note that there are small down arrows next to row and column members, as well as small up arrows above the row headers and next to the column headers. These arrows allow for one-click drilling down or drilling up. Figure 6-57 shows these arrows as well as the menu that appears if someone clicks on a member.

The down arrows actually have a couple of options: they can either expand or drill down, and this can be set by the user to perform one function or the other. This is done by clicking on the Navigation tab in PAS. There are two buttons that allow the user to choose the navigation mode: Drill Down mode and Expand mode. Clicking the Drill Down mode makes the small down arrows act like a drill down; in other words,

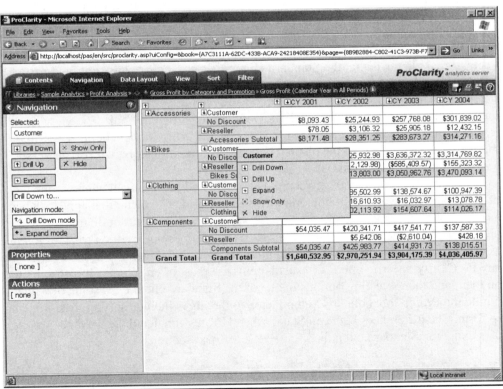

Figure 6-57 A grid in the Standard client provides almost all the same features as the Professional client, but many of the actions are performed in different ways.

the children will be shown but the parent will disappear. Clicking the Expand mode will make the down arrow keep the parent on the screen and the children will appear under that parent. Figure 6-57 shows these two buttons, along with the other buttons on the Navigation tab, which duplicate those that appear on the pop-up menu. Being able to configure the default for a click on one of the arrows is one advantage PAS has over the Professional Desktop product, which does not allow users to make Expand the default for a click.

Charts work similarly, where clicking on a bar or pie slice, members in the legend, or the members along the bottom axis cause a pop-up menu to appear. This means that PAS does not allow users to simply click on a bar to drill down; the user must click on the bar and then choose an action from the pop-up menu.

One of the great features in the Professional client is the ability to click the View button and cycle through the four base views: chart only, grid only, horizontal split, and vertical split. There is no View button in the Standard client but clicking on the View tab shows three of these options as buttons: Grid only, Grid and Chart, and Chart only. The Grid and Chart button shows a horizontal split. Also, the View tab includes buttons to change the type of chart, including bar, line, pie, and more. Figure 6-58 shows these options on the View menu, as well as the same grid from Figure 6-57 but now displayed as both a grid and chart.

Figure 6-58 also shows that there are options on the View tab for adding or removing totals, including grand totals and subtotals on both the rows and columns. A Total Options button allows users to more finely tune the totals, just as they could do in the Professional client. Finally, options exist to flatten row and column headers so that the children are not indented in relation to the parent.

The Sort and Filter tab expose the same functionality as in the Professional client, with the caveat that the ability to hide empty rows and empty columns is found only on the Filter tab. Note that after changing an option on one of these tabs, or on any other tab, the Apply button at the top of the tab becomes enabled and the user must click it to see the changes in the chart or grid.

The final tab is the Data Layout tab, which is the PAS version of the Professional client's Setup Panel. Recall that there is no drag and drop in the Standard client, however, so working with this tab is somewhat different. First, moving a dimension from the background to the rows or columns, or vice versa, requires the user to click on the dimension and then click the Up or Down buttons to move that dimension up and down. For example, clicking on a dimension in the background and clicking the Up button moves that dimension to the bottom of the Columns box. If there is already a dimension in the Columns box, clicking the Up arrow again will move the dimension to the top of the Columns box; clicking it again will move it to the bottom of the Rows box. Another click moves it up the Rows box until it eventually reaches the top and the Up button becomes disabled. Likewise, repeatedly clicking the Down

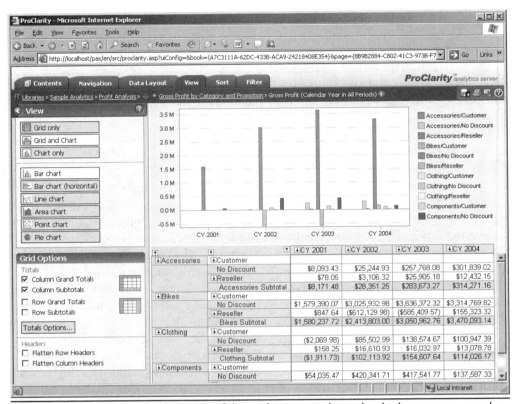

Figure 6-58 *A horizontal split is one of three chart types through which a user can cycle, thanks to the View tab. The View tab also lets users change the type of chart.*

button will move it down through the Rows and Columns until it is returned to the Background.

It is relatively easy to work with the dimensions to move them around, but there is no tab to select the members of the dimension as there is in the Professional client. Instead, double-clicking on the dimension brings up the Edit Hierarchy window. This window allows the user to browse through the hierarchy and select different members, or search using the Search tab. Alternatively, the user can click on a level and choose the Add Descendants drop-down list to add all the children, all the leaf level values, or all the descendants at all the levels under that level. The Edit Hierarchy window can be seen in Figure 6-59.

Once members have been selected, they need to be moved to the right-hand pane using the Add button. This is one case in which users need to be careful: it's often easy to add members without remembering to remove the members that are already there.

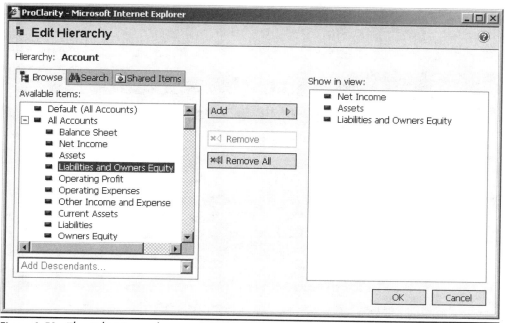

Figure 6-59 *The Edit Hierarchy screen is used to select the members of the dimensions.*

Therefore, it is important that users learn to use the Remove and Remove All buttons to get rid of existing values if the goal is to show just the new selection, especially when the All member shows up in the pane by default.

Working with Advanced Chart Types

The charts and grids in the Standard client maintain most of the functionality found in the Professional client, but this is not the case with two of the advanced chart types. The Perspective Chart and the Performance Map are relatively static. The Perspective Chart is rendered just as an image, meaning that the sliders do not move and hovering over a data point does nothing. The Performance Map is a bit more interactive: hovering over a rectangle does show the values for the two measures affecting size and color. The user even has the ability to double-click on dimensions and change the members and the Performance map will update accordingly, but there are no options for modifying the values that affect the color, or to change the color scheme.

The Decomposition Tree, on the other hand, works exceptionally well in the Standard client. Clicking on the plus sign in a box does indeed expand the children of that item. The Pareto chart at the bottom is live and, while the bars in the Pareto chart do not provide tooltips, clicking on one will make sure that value is visible

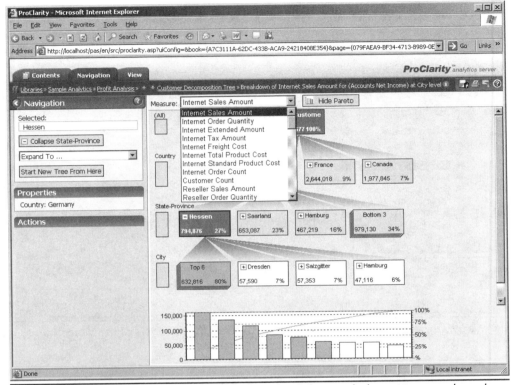

Figure 6-60   *The Decomposition Tree in the Standard client includes a Measure drop-down to speed analysis.*

even if it means reshuffling the boxes in order to make it appear. Clicking on a stack on either end will deal the boxes just as it did in the Professional client.

Finally, the Standard version of the Decomposition Tree has one advantage over the Professional client's Decomposition Tree: there is a Measure dropdown at the top of the decomposition. This allows the user to easily change the measure without rerunning the wizard (which doesn't exist in the Standard client). It is a simple feature that makes analysis just a bit easier. Figure 6-60 shows the Standard client Decomposition Tree and the Measure drop-down.

Adding PAS Views as Reports in PerformancePoint Server

ProClarity is a powerful analytics tool, and a license for PerformancePoint Server includes a license for ProClarity. However, simply having the two tools does not mean that users will have to jump back and forth between two different experiences.

Instead, it is easy to add a view from PAS to PerformancePoint Server. This is because one of the report types in PerformancePoint Server is ProClarity Analytics Server Page, and this can tie to an individual view that resides in a Briefing Book that was published to a PAS library.

Adding a report that uses a PAS view is simple. The developer would create a new report and choose the ProClarity Analytics Server Page report template. After giving the report a name, the Edit pane appears. First, the developer enters the name of the server and the virtual directory holding PAS, which is often http://<servername>/pas. Next, the developer clicks the Browse button to see a list of the libraries on that server. Expanding a library shows the books and expanding a book shows the individual pages, or views. Choosing a view and clicking OK, the developer is returned to the Edit pane. The only choice now is to disable the ability to launch into the Decomposition Tree, disable the ability to perform a Drill to Detail, disable both, or turn off all interactivity, which simply shows a static view. The Edit pane can be seen in Figure 6-61.

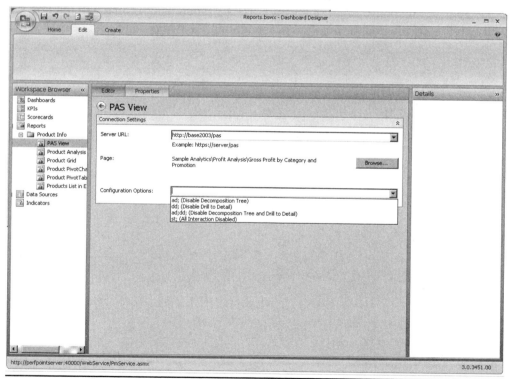

Figure 6-61 *PerformancePoint Server includes a report template for adding ProClarity Analytics Server views as a report.*

Summary

Out of the box, PerformancePoint Server has decent tools for providing simple analytics reports to end users. The Analytic Chart and Analytic Grid report types work well for very limited analysis, and the use of more powerful, but no longer thin, tools such as the Office Web Components can add to the analytic capabilities. However, for true analysts needing powerful analytics capabilities, nothing matches the power of the ProClarity tools. It is for this reason that the first version of PerformancePoint Server will include ProClarity 6.3 as well.

The ProClarity tools are often considered the most powerful tools for performing analysis against cubes. There is much more to them than mentioned in this single chapter; indeed, users can create custom sets of members and store those on the server to be shared with others. Both the Standard and Professional clients can export to Excel. And, views stored in PAS can be accessed by PerformancePoint Server using the PAS View report type, thus helping integrate PerformancePoint Server with the ProClarity tools. Future versions of PerformancePoint Server are expected to include most or all of the current PAS functionality; time will tell how well the PPS development team does at integrating the two products.

Planning Module in PerformancePoint Server

The third piece in the PerformancePoint Server triad is the Planning module. While the monitoring piece of PerformancePoint Server is an enhancement of Office Business Scorecard Manager 2005, and the analysis piece in reality is ProClarity, Microsoft built the planning module from ground-up for PerformancePoint Server 2007. The Planning module of PerformancePoint Server 2007 enables business users to interact with — and continuously contribute to — business planning, budgeting, and forecasting in real time, using the familiar and easy-to-use Microsoft Office environment. Microsoft Office Excel serves as the end-user interface for the module planning, where end users ultimately write their changes back to a central data model that may contain data on actuals side-by-side with planning data.

There are three components to the Planning module within PerformancePoint Server 2007: one server component and two client components. The server component is called the Microsoft Office PerformancePoint Server 2007 Planning Server. The client components are Microsoft Office PerformancePoint Server 2007 Planning Business Modeler and Microsoft Office PerformancePoint Server 2007 PerformancePoint Add-in for Excel. This chapter will cover all three components in detail, starting with the administration of the Planning Server.

Planning Administration Console

The initial setup and administration of the PerformancePoint Server 2007 Planning Server, or just Planning Server for short, is done through the Planning Administration Console. This is a web-based administration console that can be used to administer multiple Planning Servers. In the examples used throughout this chapter, the name of the server hosting the Planning module is PerfPointServer. To access the Planning Administration Console, the developer would open Internet Explorer and go to the web site *http://<Server Name>:46788/*. In our example, the web site would be http://perfpointserver:46788/, as shown in Figure 7-1. The port number, 46788, is the default TCP port for the Planning Administration Console. The default port number can be changed by going to the properties of the PPSPlanningAdminConsole web site within the Internet Information Services (IIS) Manager.

The left pane of the main administration console web site contains links to various aspects of server administration. The first link, Connection, provides a simple page for making a connection to the Planning Server. This link is open by default when the developer connects to the Planning Administration Console web site.

In the Location textbox, the user would enter **http://<Server Name>:46787/**, which in our case will be **http://PerfPointServer:46787/**. Please note that the TCP port number is 46787, which is the default port number for PerformancePoint ServerPlanningWebServices.

As mentioned earlier, one of the advantages of a web-based administration console is that several Planning Servers can be administered from the same web

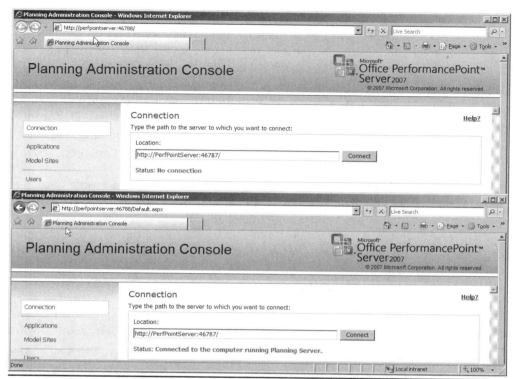

Figure 7-1   *The top half of the figure shows the Connection page within the Planning Administration Console before the connection is established. The bottom half shows the same page after the connection is established.*

site by connecting to the different servers from the Connection page. Once the server location has been entered, the developer clicks on the Connect button. Once a successful connection is established, the Status changes from No Connection to Connected to the Computer Running Planning Server.

Applications

The first step in the process is creating the Planning Server Applications. Within the planning module of PerformancePoint Server 2007, there is a predefined hierarchy for creating Business Models. The highest level of this hierarchy consists of an application. Applications logically contain all components in Planning Server. An application serves as the primary container for

▶ All information that needs to be stored for describing the business data

▶ The processes that control data access

▶ The security settings that define who can access the data definitions

A PerformancePoint Server 2007 Planning Server installation can have multiple applications. New applications can be created from the applications management page within the Planning Administration Console or from the Planning Business Modeler, which is one of the client tools that described later in this chapter. However, an existing application can be edited and managed only from the applications management page within the Planning Administration Console. There are also some advanced features of an application that can only be configured from the Applications Management page within the Planning Administration Console. Hence, it is recommended to create the initial application from the Planning Administration Console as described next.

The second link on the left pane of the Planning Administration Console page is called Applications. This link opens the Applications Management page. The only option that is enabled in the Applications Management page of a freshly installed Planning Server instance is the Create button, as shown in Figure 7-2. Clicking on this button will bring up the Create Application dialog box. The explanation of each field is given in Table 7-1.

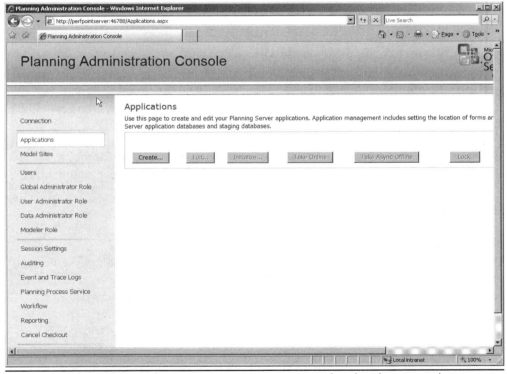

Figure 7-2   *This is the Applications Management page within the Planning Administration Console as it appears when first opened.*

Field	Explanation
Name	This is the name of the application. This is a required field as denoted by the asterisk (*) next to the field. The name of the sample application used in the example in this chapter is Budget.
Label	This is the label for the application, which is a unique internal identifier for the application. This is also a required field. This may or may not be the same as the application name.
Description	An optional description of the application.
SQL Server Computer name	The name of the server that hosts the back-end SQL Server databases.
Application Database name	This is the name of the main database used by the Planning application. The naming convention for the application database is <Application Name>_AppDB. In our example, it is named Budget_AppDB.
Staging Database name	The staging database is where the data for the actuals are stored before loading into the application database. The staging database plays an important role in a planning application, as will be described later in the chapter. The naming convention for the staging database is <Application Name>_StagingDB. In our example, it is named Budget_ StagingDB.
Form Templates location	This is the location of the templates that are the basis for the forms that are ultimately available to the end users for entering the plan, budget, and forecast data. The end users write their changes back to the system through these forms. These templates can be stored in any location that is shared with appropriate access permissions to the various users of the system, including the end-users of the planning module and the service account that is used for running the Planning Service. In our example, the templates are located in a subfolder called FormTemplates, under a shared folder called Budget on the PerfPointServer (the server running the Planning Service). After the Budget folder was created, all users (Everyone) were given full control under the Permissions setting.
Report Storage location	This is the location where the reports that make up the layout for the end-user form templates are stored. The same folder access permissions used for the FormTemplates folder apply to the Report Storage folder. In our example, the subfolder called ReportStorage under the shared Budget folder serves as the location for storing the reports.
Assignment Forms location	This is the storage location for assignment forms. The same folder rules as for the previous two entries apply here as well.
Assignment Master Forms location	This is the storage location for Assignment Master Forms. The same folder rules as for the previous three entries apply here as well.

Table 7-1   *Explanation of the Various Fields in the Create Application Dialog Box*

Field	Explanation
Enable native SQL/MDX rules	This check box toggles support of native SQL and MDX business rules in the Models created within an application.
Enable Excel macro support	This check box toggles the support of Excel macros within the end-user data-entry forms.
Root Site name	This is the name of the default model site that is created with the application. Model sites are explained in the next section. The name of the model site in our sample application is Budget. (The root model site name can be a different name than the application name.)
Root Site label	This is the label for the root site, which is also unique internal identifier for the site. This may or may not be the same as the Root Site name.
Analysis Services Computer name	The name of the server that hosts the backend Analysis Service 2005 (SSAS) databases and cubes.
Output Folder location	This is the location where the Application Creation scripts are stored for later manual execution. We are not using this option in our example.

Table 7-1 *Explanation of the Various Fields in the Create Application Dialog Box (continued)*

The completed Create Application dialog box in our example is shown in Figure 7-3. Clicking the OK button after all the information is entered will create both the application and the associated AppDB and StagingDB databases found in the SQL Server and as mentioned in the Create Application dialog box.

Model Sites

As discussed in the previous section, an application forms the highest level of the Planning Server hierarchy. Model sites represent the next level in the hierarchy. Model sites are used to organize the application and data. Each application has one parent model site, also known as the root site, which contains predefined dimensions and global assumption models. All other model sites in the application are referred to as model subsites, which form the third level in the hierarchy.

Model subsites represent the business structure of a company. They can be based on a company's reporting structure, financial processes, operational processes, and so on. For example, a company may create subsites that are based on divisions, on business units, or on security access restrictions that require separation of processes or functions. Model subsites inherit some of the shared metadata that is associated with the parent model site. This includes models, dimensions, and dimension members. Additionally, model subsites might contain models, dimensions, or dimension members that are unique to that model subsite.

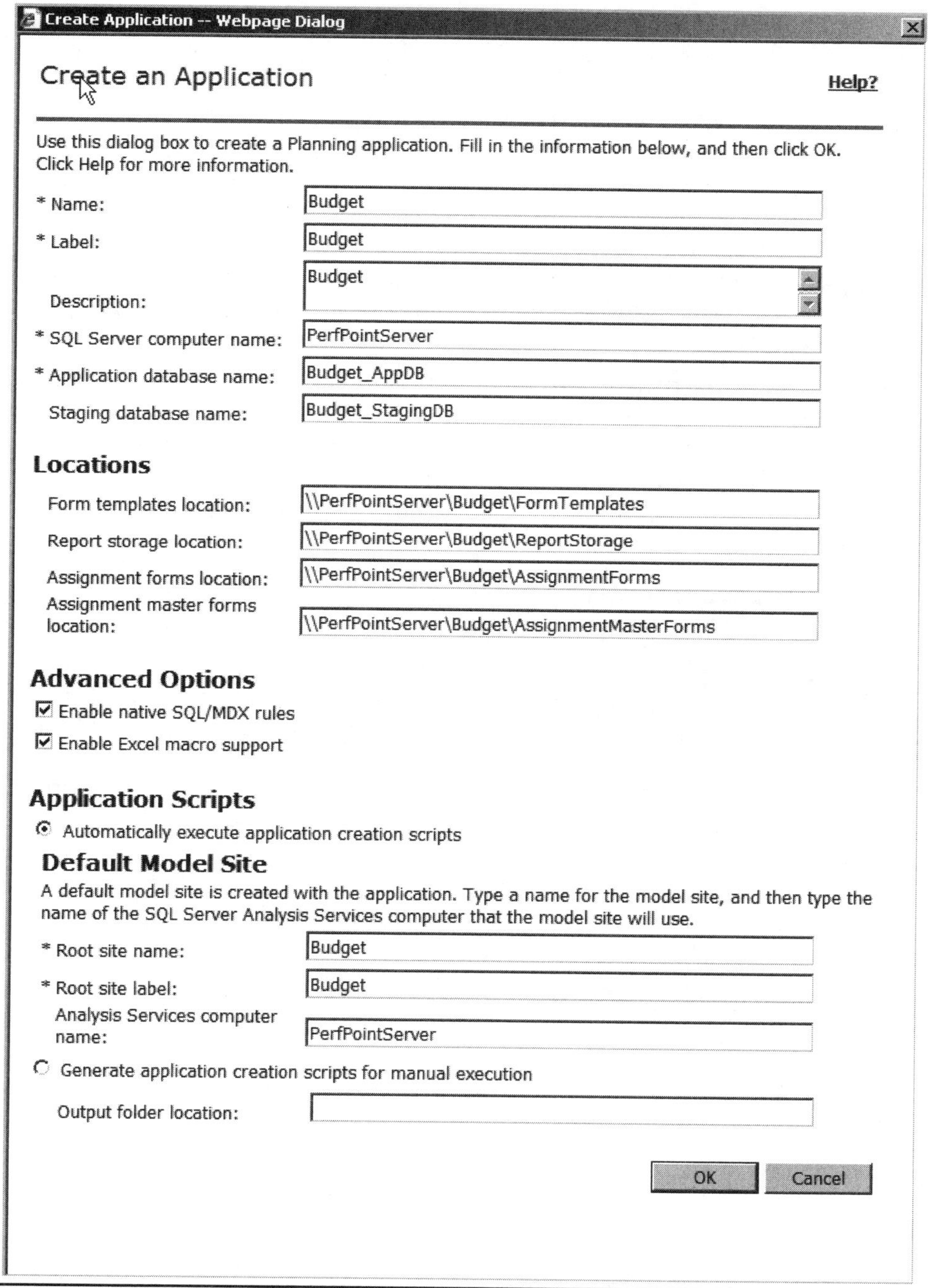

Figure 7-3 *This is the Create Application dialog box shown with the values that are used in our sample application.*

The third link on the left pane of the Planning Administration Console page is called Model Sites. This link opens the Model Sites management page. This page has a drop-down list of all the Applications. Once an application is selected from the drop-down box, all the model sites belonging to the application are listed in the table. The first one in the list is the Root Model site and then the model subsites are listed as belonging to the Root Model site. You might remember that when we created the Budget application in our previous step, we entered the name **Budget** for our Root site as well. Figure 7-4 shows the Budget model site within the Budget Application in the Model Sites Management page. The model site properties can be modified by first clicking inside the radio button for the model site that needs to be modified and then clicking the Edit button.

The model site properties like the name, description, SQL FileGroup and Analysis Services computer name can be edited and modified from the Edit a Model Site dialog box, as shown in Figure 7-5. All the information except the SQL FileGroup was provided in the previous application creation step. In our example, the SQL FileGroup value is set to Primary.

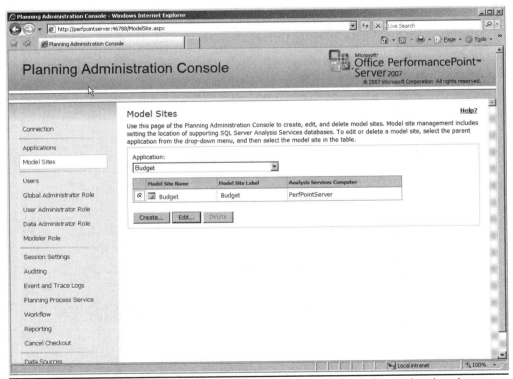

Figure 7-4 *The radio button is clicked on the Budget Model site, located within the Budget Application.*

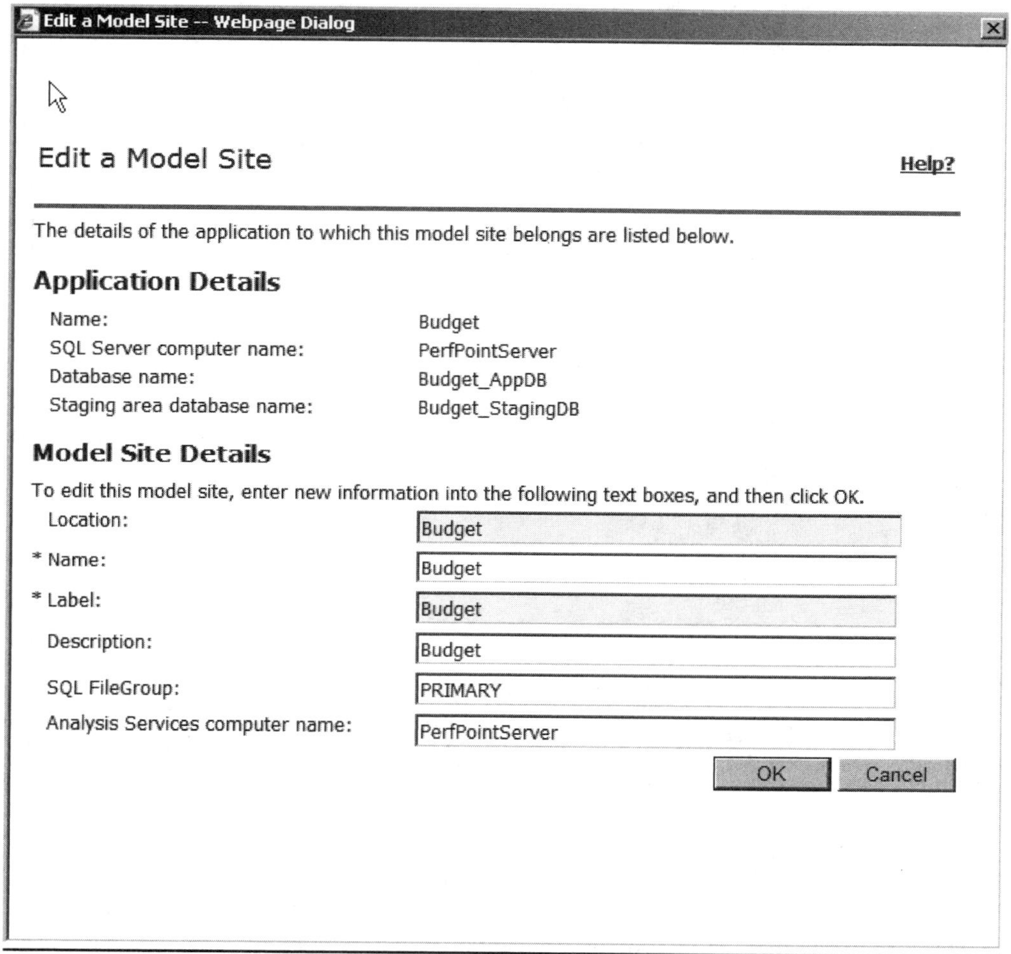

Figure 7-5   *The Edit a Model Site dialog box is shown with the values that are used in the Budget Model site.*

Users

The next step in the configuration of Planning Server is adding the users. Users must be imported or added to Planning Server before they can be assigned to roles or access data through the front-end Excel forms. The fourth link on the left pane of the Planning Administration Console page is called Users. This link opens the Users Management page, as shown in Figure 7-6. There are two options available at the bottom of this page to add users to the Planning Server: Add and Import.

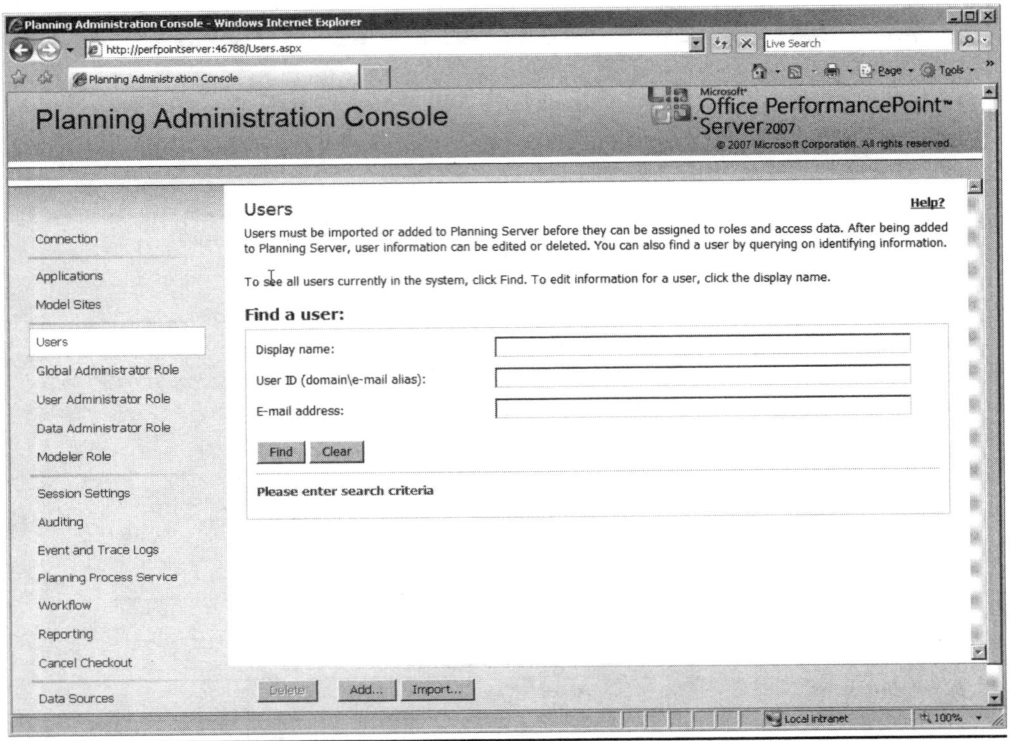

Figure 7-6   *The Users Management page shows the two options available for adding users to the system: Add and Import.*

Clicking the Add button will open up the Add a User dialog box. The fields User ID and Display Name are required fields as denoted by the asterisk next to them. User ID should be provided in the <domain>\<login> format, while the Display Name is typically the users name. The e-mail address is optional, but adding it will allow the PerformancePoint Server Planning system to send e-mail alerts to the users during the various steps in the planning process workflow. Figure 7-7 shows the user Contributor2 being added to the PerformancePoint Server Planning system. The User ID is PerfPointServer\Contributor2. The values Contributor2 and Contributor2@Company. com are entered in the Display Name and E-mail Address fields respectively. After the values are entered, click the Add button to save the values in the system.

If a large number of users need to be added to the system, using the Add button in the Users management page can be a tedious process. The Import button in the Users management page can be used for importing a list of users at once into the system. The list of users should be provided in a Comma Separated Value (.csv) file. The file should contain three columns with the headers Label, Name, and E-mail in the first row.

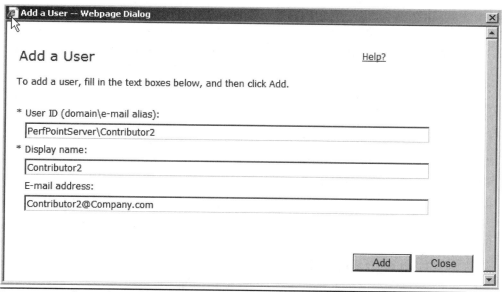

Figure 7-7   *This is the Add a User dialog box shown with the values for the user Contributor2.*

The Label column should contain the User ID values in the <domain>\<login> format, the Name column should contain the Display name values, and the E-mail column should contain the e-mail addresses. Clicking the Import button will open the Import Users dialog box. The developer can then browse to the file that contains the valid list of users to be imported. Clicking OK after selecting the file will import the users listed in the file into the PerformancePoint Server Planning system.

The Users Management page has a Find button to find the users that are already added to the PerformancePoint Server Planning system. Clicking on the Find button while leaving the search criteria empty will list all the users added to the system. Clicking on the hyperlink linked to the Display Name of any user will open the Edit User dialog box for that user. The display name and e-mail address of the user can be modified in this web page dialog box. Users can be deleted from the PerformancePoint Server system by checking the box next to each users Display Name and clicking the Delete button at the bottom of the Users Management page.

The following users have been added to the PerformancePoint Server Planning Server from the Users Management page to be used in the examples given in this chapter. They are the users Contributor1 through Contributor10, Reviewer1, Reviewer2, Approver1, and Approver2. These users are added in addition to the PerfPointServer\Administrator who was added as a user and Global Administrator during the installation of Planning Server.

Global Administrator

The fifth link on the left pane of the Planning Administration Console page is used for managing the Global Administrator Role. Members of the Global Administrator role can configure settings on all computers that are running PerformancePoint Server Planning Server in the system. Members of the Global Administrator role can perform the following tasks in the Planning Administration Console:

► Create or delete applications and model sites

► Modify application and model site properties

► Add users to or remove users from Planning Server

► Manage role membership for the Global Administrator and User Administrator roles

► Edit server system settings (such as session, workflow, and auditing settings)

► Remove the checked-out status for objects on a model site

► Manage data source and data destination connections

On the Global Administrator Role page, users who currently belong to the role are listed in the User ID column. You must belong to the Global Administrator role to add users to or remove users from the Global Administrator role. The first member of the Global Administrator role is designated during the installation of Planning Server. This user will be able to add other members to the Global Administrator role through the Planning Administration Console. Before you can add a user to any Planning Server role, including the Global Administrator role, the user must first be added to the Planning Server from the Users page.

A user can be added to the Global Administrator role by first typing the User ID in the box next to the Add button, and then clicking the Add button. The User ID must be entered in the <domain>\<login> format. A user can be removed from the Global Administrator role by selecting the radio button next to the user and clicking the Remove button.

For the purpose of the examples given in this chapter, the first member of the Global Administrator role designated during the installation of Planning Server is PerfPointServer\Administrator. Note that no additional users were added to the Global Administrator role from the Global Administrator management page.

User Administrator

The sixth link on the left pane of the Planning Administration Console page is used for managing the User Administrator Role. Members of the User Administrator role can add users to or remove users from Planning Server and manage membership for the Modeler, Data Administrator, and User Administrator roles, but not the Global Administrator role. In the Planning Business Modeler client tool, members of the User Administrator role can add or remove Planning Server users from business roles and customize user permissions. The Planning Business Modeler is discussed in detail later in this chapter.

On the User Administrator Role page, users who currently belong to the role are listed in the User ID column next to the appropriate application or model site. Except for the Global Administrator role, which has a system-wide scope, administrative roles have either an application scope or a model-site scope. Application scope permissions apply for all model sites in the application. Model-site scope permissions apply only for the specific model site. You must belong to the Global Administrator or User Administrator role to add users to or remove users from the User Administrator role.

Adding or removing users to the User Administrator role is very intuitive. The first step is to select the appropriate scope for the role—whether it is an application or model site. The scope is then selected by clicking on the radio button next to the appropriate scope. This will enable the Add/Remove Users button. Clicking on this button will open the Add or Remove Users: User Administrator Role dialog box. On this page, a user can be added to the User Administrator role by typing the User ID in the box next to the Add button, and then clicking the Add button. The User ID must be entered in the <domain>\<login> format. A user can be removed from the User Administrator role by selecting the check box next to the user and then clicking the Remove button.

For the purpose of the examples given in this chapter, the user PerfPointServer\ Administrator is added as the only User Administrator at the Budget application scope.

Data Administrator

The seventh link on the left pane of the Planning Administration Console page is used for managing the Data Administrator Role. Members of the Data Administrator role can perform data integration tasks as well as data management, workflow process, and security tasks. Users who are assigned to the Data Administrator role have unrestricted access to all business data within their scope, even if they belong to a business role that has restricted settings. For security reasons, work performed by Data Administrator role members should be carefully reviewed because these individuals can browse databases. It is recommended that Data Administrator role members do not have full database permissions unless it is necessary.

Managing users belonging to the Data Administrator role is similar to managing users belonging to the User Administrator role described previously. On the Data Administrator Role page, users who currently belong to the role are listed in the User ID column next to the appropriate application or model site. Like the User

Administrator role, Data Administrator role has either an application scope or a model site scope. Application scope permissions apply for all model sites in the application. Model site scope permissions apply only for the specific model site. You must belong to the Global Administrator or User Administrator role to add users to or remove users from the Data Administrator role.

Adding or removing users to the Data Administrator role is similar to that described for the User Administrator role. The first step is to select the appropriate scope for the role—whether its an application, or a model site. The scope is selected by clicking on the radio button next to the appropriate scope. This will enable the Add/Remove Users button. Clicking on this button will open the Add or Remove Users: Data Administrator Role dialog box. On this page, a user can be added to the Data Administrator role by typing the User ID in the box next to the Add button, and then clicking the Add button. The User ID must be entered in the <domain>\<login> format. A user can be removed from the Data Administrator role by checking the check box next to the user and then clicking the Remove button.

For the purpose of the examples given in this chapter, the user PerfPointServer\ Administrator is added as the only Data Administrator at the Budget application scope.

Modeler

The eighth link on the left pane of the Planning Administration Console page is used for managing the Modeler Role. Members of the Modeler role can create and configure data, workflow processes, and business roles in Planning Business Modeler. Users who are assigned to the Modeler role have unrestricted access to all business data within their scope, even if they belong to a business role that has restricted settings. However, members of the Modeler role cannot create or delete applications or model sites or manage role membership.

Just like the User Administrator and Data Administrator roles described previously, each Modeler role has either an application scope or a model site scope, and the users who currently belong to the role are listed in the User ID column next to the appropriate application or model site. Managing users who belong to the Modeler role is similar to managing users w to the User Administrator and Data Administrator roles as described in the previous sections.

For the purpose of the examples given in this chapter, the user PerfPointServer\ Administrator is added as the only Modeler at the Budget application scope.

The next four links on the left pane of the Planning Administration Console are used to configure the Session Settings, Auditing, Event and Trace Logs, and Planning Process Service settings. Additional information about these settings can be obtained from the help files for PerformancePoint Server Administrative Console configuration. For the purpose of the examples given in this chapter, all the settings can be left at their default values.

The Workflow link on the left pane of the Planning Administration Console page is used to manage the Planning Server workflow. The OLAP cube refresh interval during the Planning Server workflows and SMTP server/account for e-mail notifications are also configured in the Workflow management page.

Planning Server has two kinds of reports: Operational reports and Business reports. The Reporting link on the left pane of the Planning Administration Console opens the page where the location for the Operational reports and Business reports can be entered. SQL Server Reporting Services can be used to publish both Operational and Business reports. The appropriate path including the URL for the computer running SQL Server Reporting Services and the folder that contains the reports should be entered in the location text box for each type of report.

In the Planning Business Modeler, members of the Data Administrator and Modeler roles can check out models, dimensions, and associations from a model site for maintenance purposes. When objects are checked out, other users cannot write data to them, and pertinent workflow task queues are frozen. The Cancel Checkout page of the Planning Administration Console can be used to remove the checked-out status of all objects in a model site. Clicking Force Cancel Checked Out Objects will check in all objects in the selected model site and then delete any changes that were made to the objects since they were last saved.

Data Connections

The Data Sources link on the left pane of the Planning Administration Console page is used to manage the external data source connections for the PerformancePoint Server Planning Server. A data source connection provides the Planning Server applications access to relevant business data for business intelligence purposes. The source can be external to the Planning Server system, such as an existing data warehouse. A data source connection can point to a database, or Data Source View (DSV), which is an XML file that is created from a Microsoft SQL Server 2005 database. The connections that are created and configured in the Planning Administration Console are logical connections, and these connection names can be used in Planning Business Modeler.

The first step in creating a data source connection is to select the application to which the data source connection should be added from the Application drop-down list. After the application is selected, the model site to which the data source connection should be added is selected by clicking on the radio button next to the appropriate model site. This will enable the Add button. Clicking on this button will open the Create a Data Source Connection dialog box. The fields Connection name and Label are required fields as denoted by the asterisk next to them. The Connection name will be used in Planning Business Modeler, whereas the Label is a unique internal identifier for the connection. One out of the two available types of connection sources can be selected here: database or Data Source View (DSV).

Depending on the type of source selected, the required information such as the
Server Name, Database Name, and File Location (which applies only to a DSV)
should be entered in the text boxes. Figure 7-8 shows the Create a Data Source
Connection dialog box with values entered in it. Clicking on the Show Tables/Views
button will show all the available tables and views from the selected data source. The
tables and views that need to be exposed in Planning Business Modeler should be
moved into the Selected Tables/Views box by selecting items in the Available Tables/
Views box and clicking the > button. Clicking the >> button will move all tables

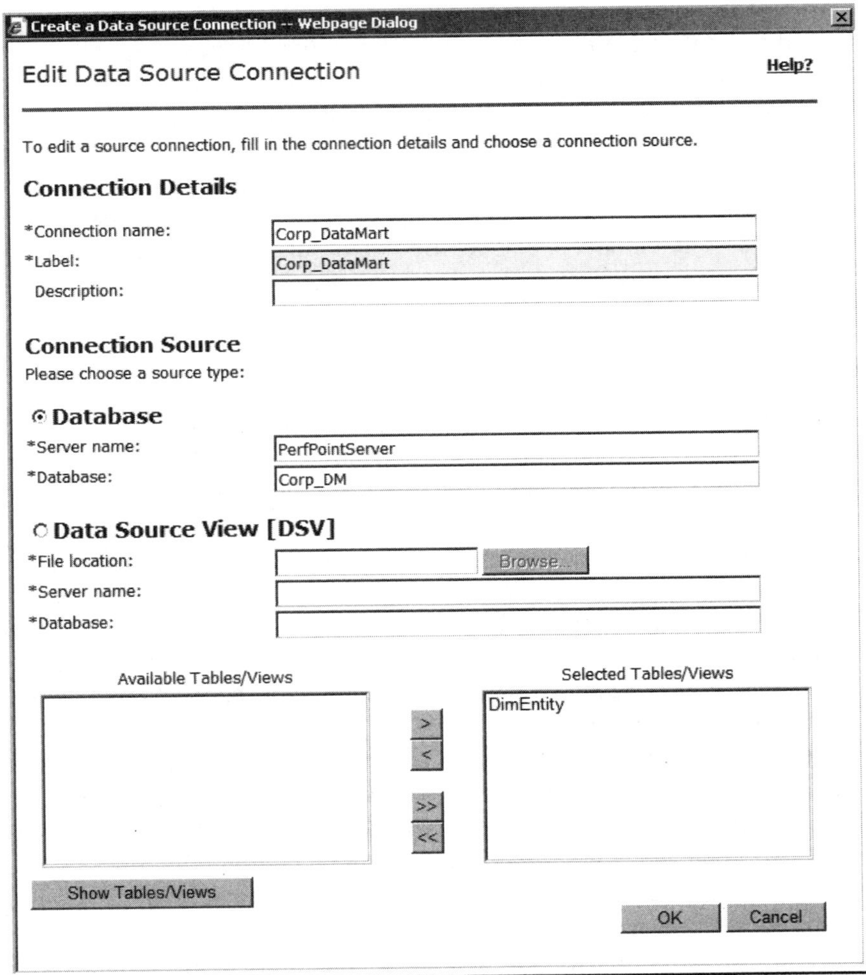

Figure 7-8   *Commonly used external Data Sources include Enterprise Data Warehouses,
which contain dimension and fact data that can be used by PerformancePoint
Server Planning Server.*

and views. If no table or view is specified in the Selected Tables/Views box, the data source will not be available in the Planning Business Modeler. Click OK to close the dialog box, and to save the Data Source connection information in the system.

The Data Destinations link on the left pane of the Planning Administration Console page is used to manage the external data destination connections for the PerformancePoint Server Planning Server. A data destination connection creates or registers a database on the same server that contains the Application database. Data destination connections define locations where data will be exported when outbound rules are run. The outbound rules enable the plan data (forecast, budget, and so on) from the model in PerformancePoint Server Planning system to be exported to an outbound database.

Creating a data destination connection is very similar to creating a data source connection. It is done by selecting the application from the Application drop-down list, selecting the model site by clicking on the radio button next to the appropriate model site, and then clicking on the Add button. This will open the Create a Data Destination Connection dialog box. The only data destination option available is a database connection to the same server that contains the application database. Here you have the choice of creating a new database, or using an existing database. Clicking OK after entering all the required information in the text boxes will save the Data Destination connection information in the system, and close the dialog box. A Data Destination connection is required if you plan to run Outbound Rules, which is one way of exporting the plan data from PPS Planning Server to external data destinations.

Planning Business Modeler

Planning Business Modeler is the main client component of the Planning module within PPS 2007. This is the primary interface for creating and managing business models and their associated metadata. The models that are created using Planning Business Modeler are the basic units of data storage in the Planning Server, and they integrate relevant information about a company. Using the various tools available within the Planning Business Modeler, complex planning, budgeting, forecasting, and consolidation functions can be performed on the models. Planning Business Modeler also facilitates security management for the models and data, creation of business forms and reports, process workflow management, and association between models. Planning Business Modeler runs locally on each users computer, but all the models and schemas are centrally stored in the Planning Server.

When the Planning Business Modeler is opened for the first time, it opens up with a blank environment. The first step is to connect to the computer that is running the Planning Server. To establish a connection to the Planning Server, the developer would first click on Connect... from the File menu. This opens the Connect dialog box. The name of the Planning server is entered in the Select a Server text box using the format - http://<*Server Name*>:46787/. In our example, this would be http://PerfPointServer:46787//, as shown in Figure 7-9. After entering the Planning Server connect string, clicking on the Connect button will connect the Planning Business Modeler client tool to the Planning Server specified by the connect string. This will also retrieve the list of applications and model sites stored in that Planning server. As you may recall from the section on Planning Administration Console earlier in this chapter, you have already created an application called Budget and a root model site called Budget, as shown in Figure 7-3. For the purposes of the example in this chapter, you will select the Budget application from the Select an Application: list box, and then highlight the Budget model site from the Select a Model Site: list box, as shown in Figure 7-9.

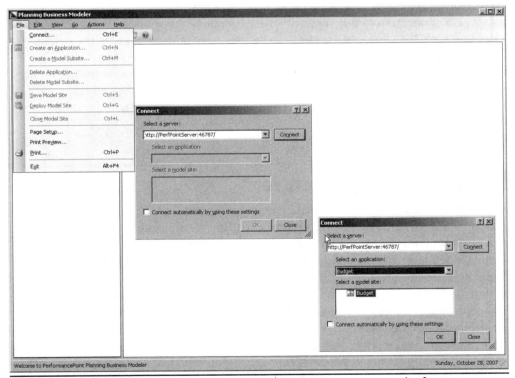

Figure 7-9 *The Connect dialog box (shown as an insert) opens up as the first step in establishing a connection to a PPS Planning Server. The second insert shows the list of applications and model sites stored on the Planning Server.*

After highlighting the Budget model site, clicking on the OK button will open the model site in Planning Business Modeler client tool, as shown in Figure 7-10.

As mentioned earlier in this chapter, a new application can be created from the Planning Business Modeler client tool. The various actions available under the File menu allow the developers to create a new application or model subsite for the current application. The user should have the appropriate role permissions to perform these actions. However, to avoid potential database errors in multiple-server environments, it is recommended that you use the Planning Administration Console to perform all Global Administrator tasks including creating new applications, model sites, or model subsites. This is explained in detail in the section on Planning Administration Console in this chapter.

The models in PPS Planning Server are very similar to Online Analytical Processing (OLAP) Cubes in SQL Server Analysis Services (SSAS). In fact, SSAS OLAP cubes are created for each model in the Planning Server during the model site

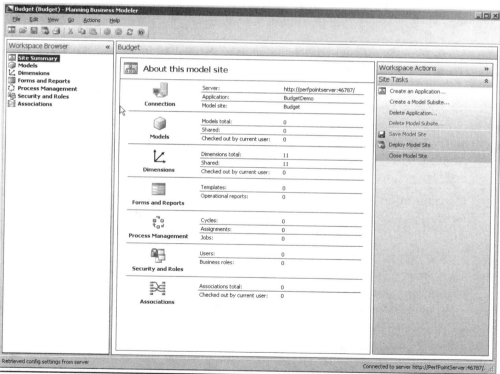

Figure 7-10 *The left pane of the Planning Business Modeler is the Workspace Browser, where the different attributes of a model can be selected by clicking on the appropriate attribute.*

deployment phase. Similar to the design of SSAS Cubes, the Dimensions have to be defined first before a model can be defined in Planning Business Modeler.

Dimensions

A dimension is a structural attribute of a model, and is the primary building block of models. Dimensions offer a concise, intuitive way to organize and select data for retrieval, review, and analysis. The Dimensions workspace within the Planning Business Modeler can be selected by clicking on the Dimensions attribute in the Workspace Browser displayed in Figure 7-10.

Planning Server provides two categories of dimensions: predefined and user-defined. The predefined dimensions are automatically generated by the Planning Server whenever an application is created. Some of these dimensions are populated with members, some with members and member sets (member sets are equivalent to hierarchies within dimensions), some with the specialized NONE member, and yet others with no member at all. The predefined dimensions available within the Planning Server and a short description of each are given next:

▶ **Account**   The Account dimension and its associated rules enable a user to create and maintain a chart of accounts for various financial models.

▶ **Business Process**   The Business Process dimension contains a member set (hierarchy) that enables Planning Business Modeler to store the results from different stages of predefined financial calculations, such as consolidation, allocation, and currency conversion. Since the dimension members store results from each step of these processes, the data that is stored can be useful for auditing and for custom calculations.

▶ **Consolidation Method**   The Consolidation Method dimension is a flat dimension that is intended for financial models that have shares calculations. This dimension defines the basis for the financial consolidation processes, such as specifying equity, full, holding, and proportional consolidations.

▶ **Currency**   The Currency dimension is a flat dimension that stores a list of currencies. This dimension is not automatically populated, but the developer can populate it with the list of currencies that the model requires.

▶ **Entity**   The Entity dimension is used to maintain a list of business entities within the organization.

▶ **Exchange Rate**   The Exchange Rate dimension is a flat dimension that stores values of exchange rates that are used by an Exchange Rate Assumptions model. In addition, this dimension might be used by currency conversion calculations.

▶ **Flow**   The Flow dimension is used with the Account and Time dimensions in a model to track cash flows between periods for financial models.

▶ **Intercompany**   The Intercompany dimension is a system-maintained dimension that contains copies of entities that are involved in intercompany transactions with other entities in the system.

▶ **Scenario**   The Scenario dimension is a flat dimension that holds values that differentiate between different modeling scenarios. For example, this dimension can be used to track values for budget, actual, and forecasted scenarios for any given period of time. (Planning Business Modeler automatically includes the Scenario dimension with every model.) One important consideration when using the Scenario dimension is that only one member of the scenario dimension can be selected to be used for data entry per cycle. If there is a need for selecting two members for data entry in a single cycle, such as budgeting for both best and worst case, a user-defined dimension will have to be built for that.

▶ **Time**   The Time dimension is a system dimension predefined for maintaining a common time scale in an application. The Time dimension is created and maintained by the Application Calendar Wizard. (Planning Business Modeler automatically includes the Time dimension with every model.)

▶ **User**   The User dimension maintains user-related information such as workflow reviewer and approver hierarchies. Members of the User dimension can also be created, updated, or deleted by using the Planning Administration Console.

Planning Server automatically provides the previous set of predefined dimensions to act as starting points in the application development process. The predefined dimensions can be modified or expanded to match the data structure, and naming requirements of the model. By customizing predefined dimensions, and by adding user-defined dimensions, the developer can build the dimension structure of the application. The scope of customization for predefined dimensions is more restricted than that for user-defined dimensions. There is no limit to the number of user-defined dimensions that can be added to an application.

Time Dimension (Application Calendar)

Time is perhaps the most common way to view data in any organization. Therefore, the Planning Business Modeler includes a Time dimension by default. The Time dimension, also called the Application Calendar, is used for maintaining a common time scale within an application. Time is so important that there is a wizard dedicated to maintaining the Time dimension: the Application Calendar wizard.

The Time dimension often includes hundreds or even thousands of members based on the range chosen at creation. A model may include multiple time hierarchies, each of which is created as a member view.

Planning how to create your Time dimension is one of the most important planning considerations you will make for your application, as all aspects of your application refer to the Time dimension in one way or another. Care must be taken to make sure that the Application Calendar is created to accurately match your business processes, as it cannot be modified later without creating a new application, purging the data, and then repopulating the data.

Creating an Application Calendar requires careful consideration before proceeding. The Time dimension is used throughout the application for a variety of purposes and it cannot be modified later without creating a new application, which deletes all the data. However, extending the calendar or creating new calendar views do not require a new application and can therefore be done without affecting existing data.

It is important to understand that an application can have only a single calendar, so if the business must track different business processes with different calendars, those processes will need to be separate applications. For example, sales and marketing might operate on a standard calendar while finance may look at data using a fiscal calendar with different beginning and ending dates.

A custom calendar can be defined for a Planning Business Modeler application by using the Planning Business Modeler application calendar. To be consistent and accurate, the application calendar must be created with great care. The steps described below show how to create a calendar for our sample application. Click on the Dimensions attribute in the Workspace Browser displayed in Figure 7-10 to open the Dimensions workspace within the Budget Model. On the right side of the Dimension Browser is the Workspace Actions, which contains the Dimension Tasks section. The second item under the dimension tasks is the link to Create the Calendar, as shown in Figure 7-11.

Clicking on this link will display the Create Application Calendar Wizard. The first page of the wizard asks for the Label for the calendar and an optional description. The value **Fiscal Calendar** is entered in both of the text boxes for the purpose of the examples in this chapter. Clicking Next will open the Define the Calendar Pattern page.

Though the Gregorian calendar is widely used to schedule events, for many businesses, the Gregorian calendar presents an accounting difficulty, because it contains a varied number of business days from year to year. In Planning Business Modeler, the application calendar is used to set up a concept of time periods that matches the practices that are used in a corporation. From an accounting standpoint, the concept of time and how it is tracked is fundamental to measuring and comparing financial progress over time. An accurate application calendar provides the past,

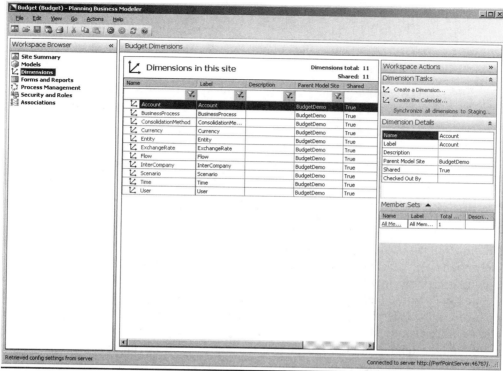

Figure 7-11   *Each application within the PPS Planning system needs an Application Calendar, which is created by clicking the Create the Calendar link in the Dimension workspace.*

present, and forecasted data with the context that is required for successful financial tracking and benchmarking.

Within the Define the Calendar Pattern page the developer can create a calendar that matches the specific patterns of the corporations financial system. For example, a calendar that starts on July 1 and ends on June 30 or a more traditional calendar that starts on January 1 and ends on December 31 can be easily created from this page. The developer can also create complex calendar patterns from this page to model the application calendar to accurately reflect the business calendar. The following are common calendar patterns that are supported in PPS Planning system:

▶ **Gregorian calendar**   In this pattern, all months follow calendar months.

▶ **Gregorian calendar variation**   Months end on same day every month, but the end day differs from the last day of the calendar month.

- ▶ **445 pattern** Months in a year contain weeks as follows: 4 weeks, 4 week, 5 weeks. The pattern is repeated with fixed or variable year ending.

- ▶ **454 pattern** Months in a year contain weeks as follows: 4 weeks, 5 week, 4 weeks. Then the pattern is repeated with fixed or variable year ending.

- ▶ **544 pattern** Months in a year contain weeks as follows: 5 weeks, 4 week, 4 weeks. Then the pattern is repeated with fixed or variable year ending.

- ▶ **13** A year contains 13 equal periods with fixed or variable year ending.

Though a lot of different options are available to define the calendar pattern so that it matches the fiscal/business calendar used in a company, as discussed previously, for this example we will select the simple Gregorian calendar with the Current Year ending on 12/31/2007 (as entered in the Current Year Ends: text box), all other years ending on 12/31 (as selected by the Years Always End on the Selected Month and Day option), and the months within each year corresponding to the Gregorian calendar months (as selected by the Monthly Periods Correspond to the Calendar Months option), as shown in Figure 7-12. The calendar duration is also defined in open the Define the Calendar Pattern page. The number of past years to be included in the calendar (as defined by the Number of Past Years: under the Calendar Duration) cannot be altered once the application calendar is finalized and saved, just like the calendar pattern. This means that careful consideration must be given for selecting the number of past years to be included in the calendar. The number of future years to be included in the calendar is defined by the Number of Future Years: under the Calendar Duration. This can be extended for an application as years roll by. Again for sake of simplicity, we have used the default value of 1 in both the Calendar Duration fields for the examples in this chapter.

The next page in the wizard depends on the calendar pattern selected in the Define the Calendar Pattern page. For complex calendar patterns the next page could be Define Weeks or Add Extra Weeks (Optional). By selecting the appropriate calendar pattern and by correctly utilizing the options that follow, almost all types of fiscal/business calendars can be modeled within the PPS Planning system. In the case of our simple Gregorian calendar example, the next page in the wizard is the Select Optional Frequencies page.

The time frequency is used for grouping data. As can be seen on this page, Year, Month, and Day are required frequencies and cannot be removed. Optional frequencies include half year, trimester, quarter, and week, depending on how you define the monthly periods. For example, if your months correspond with calendar months and the year always ends on the same day, the half year, quarter, and trimester frequencies are available. However, if your year end varies, the half year and trimester frequencies are not available. Optional frequencies can be added to

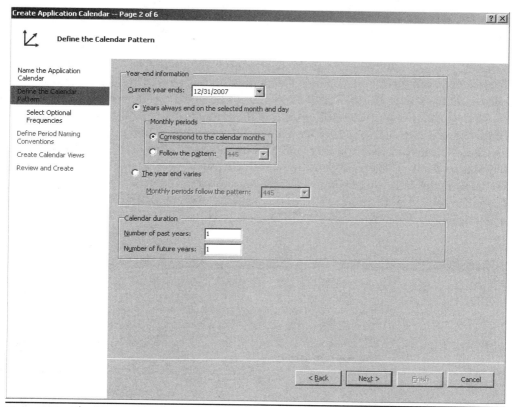

Figure 7-12 *The Year-end information and the Calendar Duration information are defined in the Calendar Pattern definition page. Care must be taken while defining the Calendar Pattern as this cannot be altered for a given application once the calendar is saved.*

the calendar by checking next to the appropriate optional frequencies. The optional frequency Quarter is checked for inclusion in the examples given in this chapter.

The next page in the wizard is the Define Period Naming Conventions page. Here you can modify the naming conventions for each of the calendar frequencies available from the previous page. For the purpose of the examples in this chapter, all the options are left at their default values in this page.

The next page in the Create Application Calendar wizard is the Create Calendar Views page. Additional custom views of the calendar data can be created when the Application Calendar is created for the first time, or when the calendar is extended. Calendar views are used to display members of the Time dimension in a convenient way. For example, if the calendar includes the frequencies year, quarter, month, and day as it does in our sample calendar, views of the data can be created to show only year, quarter, and month data. These views can be used in models and fulfill the role of Hierarchies or Member Sets within the Time dimension. For the purpose of the examples given in this chapter, a new year-quarter-month (YQM) Calendar view is created by clicking on the Create a View link on this page. The value **YQM** is entered in the text boxes for Label and Description in the top right of this page.

This new name—YQM—will appear in the Calendar Views box on the left side of this page. First select the new view by clicking on it once and then click on the check boxes next to Year, Quarter, and Month in the Included Frequencies box on the bottom right of this page. Now the new YQM view with year, quarter and month levels from the Time dimension is defined, as shown in Figure 7-13. Unwanted Calendar views can be removed from this page by clicking on the Delete Selected View link on this page.

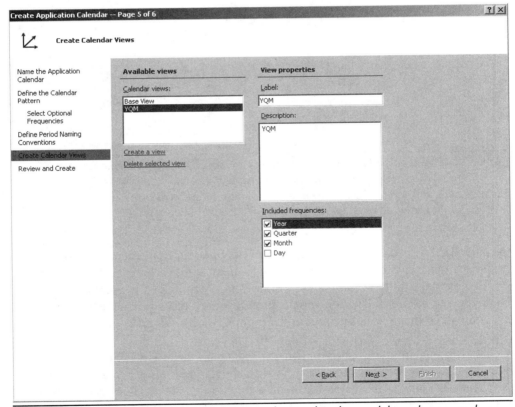

Figure 7-13 *The Time dimension hierarchies to be used in the model can be created as Calendar Views while creating or extending the application calendar.*

Click Next to open the Review and Create page. Review the information that is displayed. If the new calendar contains any errors, the Back button can be used to return to the appropriate page to correct it. If the new calendar is accurate, clicking the Finish button will create the new calendar and will take you back to the Dimensions workspace where the newly added members of the Time dimension can be seen.

Though the Application Calendar is now created, it is not saved into the PPS Planning system until the Time dimension is explicitly saved by clicking on the Save this Dimension link under the Dimension Tasks on the right side of the Dimensions workspace, as shown in Figure 7-14. The Check In link will automatically save the changes and check them in as well. It is recommended that you check in the changes on a regular basis and after any major changes or modifications to any dimension or model.

The menu bar within the Member Maintenance tab in the Dimensions workspace shows a drop-down list on the left side. Clicking on the arrow next to the drop-down list will show the list of all available member sets within the Time dimension. This is the same for every other dimension as well. In the case of Time dimension

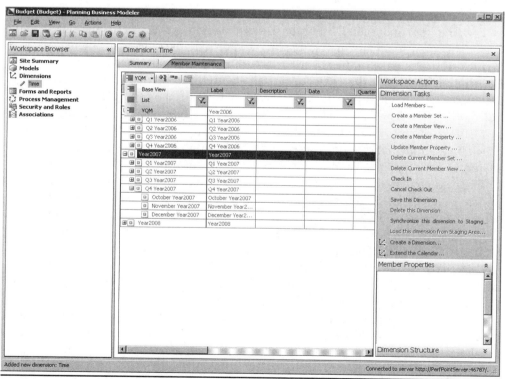

Figure 7-14   *The YQM Calendar View within the Time dimension is displayed after expanding some members.*

this drop-down list shows the calendar views that were created including the YQM calendar view (hierarchy). Clicking on the YQM will change the display of the Time dimension members to show the YQM member set. To the right of the drop-down list in the same menu bar is a plus (+) sign button that will expand the member set to display all the members within the member set, and a minus (-) sign button that will collapse the member set to the top level members. Figure 7-14 shows the drop-down list along with the YQM member set being displayed.

Creating User-Defined Dimensions

More often than not, the predefined dimensions that come with the PPS Planning Server may not be sufficient to accurately model the planning needs of a business. User-defined dimensions can be created in the Planning Business Modeler, which in turn will extend the functionality and flexibility of the business models created in the Planning application. There is no limit to the number of user-defined dimensions that can be added to an application. The user-defined dimensions can then be customized to suit the business models requirements. This section will discuss how to add a user-defined dimension to a Planning application.

The first item under the Dimension Tasks shown in Figure 7-11 is the link to Create a Dimension. Clicking on this link will display the Create a Dimension Wizard. The first page of the wizard asks for the Name, Label, and an optional Description of the new dimension. The value **Employee** is entered in all the three text boxes (as shown in Figure 7-15), for the purpose of the examples in this chapter. Select the Allow This Dimension to Be Shared check box to make this dimension available to other model subsites. When a dimension is shared by selecting this check box, all members and member sets that are contained in the dimension are shared with all model subsites below the model site in which they are created.

The next page in the Create a Dimension wizard is the Select Dimension Structure Source page. There are three options on this page that you can use to select the source for the new dimension structure. These options include creating a new dimension structure, defining the dimension structure from a Comma Separated Values (CSV) file, and defining the dimension structure from a data source that has already been added to the Data Sources link on the left pane of the Planning Administration Console page. The first option for Create a New Dimension Structure was selected for the purpose of the examples in this chapter.

The next page in the Create a Dimension wizard is the Define Member Creation page. Out of the two options on this page, the first option of Define Members Later is selected for this example. Selecting this option will create only the default NONE member within the dimension.

The last page in the Create a Dimension wizard is the Review and Create page. Here the developer can review the information that is displayed. If any of the

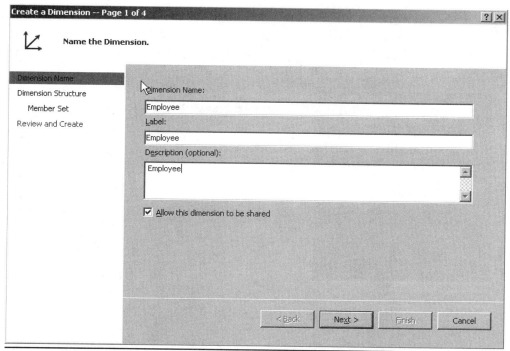

Figure 7-15   *The Name, Label, and Description information is entered in the first page of the Create a Dimension wizard.*

previous choices need to be modified, the Back button or the left navigation bar can be used to return to the appropriate page to change it. Clicking the Finish button will create the new dimension, and will take you to the newly created dimension. The Member Maintenance tab of the new dimension is open by default, as shown in Figure 7-16.

Dimension Member Property

Dimension member properties define the behavior and characteristics of each dimension member. Dimension member properties are similar to dimension attributes in SSAS OLAP cubes and, in fact, will be defined as such when SSAS OLAP cube is created for the model during the model site deployment phase. There are two types of dimension member properties: system-defined and user-defined.

System-defined dimension member properties are part of the predefined dimensions that are provided with Planning Business Modeler. Like the predefined dimensions themselves, the system-defined dimension member properties cannot be deleted, because these properties are used for the internal logic of Planning Business Modeler.

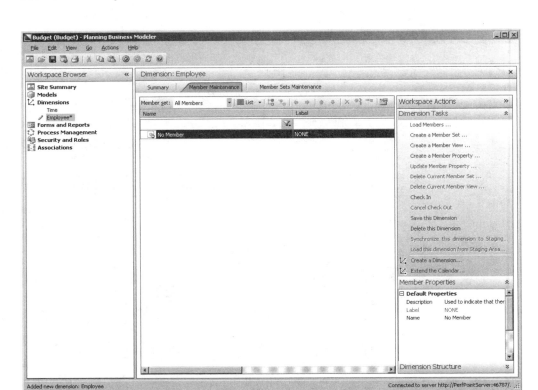

Figure 7-16   *The Member Maintenance tab of the new Employee dimension shows the default NONE member. The right pane shows the Dimension Tasks available for this dimension.*

For example, in the Account dimension, the Account Type dimension member property is system-defined. It is required for all models that use the Account dimension.

All dimensions—whether predefined or user defined—also have three required member properties. The required properties are Name, Label, and Description. The purpose of the Name property is to provide a user-friendly descriptor for the dimension member, and each dimension member is assigned a name when it is created. The Label is the primary identifier of objects throughout the system, and each dimension member is assigned a label when it is created. The Description property provides a description of the dimension member. Though this is a required member property and must exist for each dimension, populating this property with values is optional. Planning Business Modeler uses the previously mentioned required dimension member properties to manage dimension members.

User-defined dimension member properties are a very powerful feature in PPS Planning System, which can be used to track any behavior or characteristic of dimension members of both predefined and user-defined dimensions. The rest of this section will describe how a user-defined dimension member property can be created.

The first step in creating a user-defined dimension member property in any dimension is to check out that dimension. You can be check out a dimension by clicking on it in the Dimension Workspace, and then clicking the Check Out link in the Dimension Tasks pane on the right side. Once a dimension is checked out, it will appear similar to the newly created Employee dimension shown in Figure 7-16. Please note that in this example we have not yet saved or checked in our newly created Employee dimension from our previous example. We will be using this example to create the new user-defined dimension member property. If the dimension has been checked in, it has to be checked out as was just described.

From the Dimension Tasks pane on the right side, click the link Create a Member Property. This will open the Create Member Property dialog box, as shown in Figure 7-17. The various aspects of the dimension member property are defined in this dialog box. The value **Entity** is entered in the text boxes titled Label and Description for the purpose of the examples in this chapter. The next step is to select the type of data that the dimension member property will contain. The various available data types are listed in the drop-down list titled Data Types. Most of the data types listed here are self explanatory, with the exception of Member of Dimension data type. This data type allows you to create referential relationships among dimensions, by allowing you to select a member belonging to another referenced dimension as the member property for the referencing dimension. For the purpose of the examples in this chapter, the Member of Dimension data type is

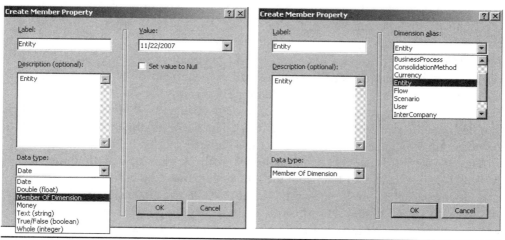

Figure 7-17 *The Member of Dimension data type allows you to create referential relationships among dimensions.*

selected from the drop-down list (as shown in the left half of Figure 7-17). Once the Member of Dimension data type is selected, the text box on the right side of the dialog box will change from Value to Dimension Alias:, and a dimension list will appear to select the referenced dimension. The Entity dimension is selected as the referenced dimension, as shown in the right half of Figure 7-17 for the example in this chapter. The default value for the referenced dimension can be selected by clicking on the Ellipsis (…) button that is available to the right of the text box titled Member: in the Create Member Property dialog box. Clicking the Ellipsis (…) button will open the Member Selector, which then displays the available members in the referenced dimension, from which the default member of the referenced dimension can be selected. After you've defined the various aspects of the new dimension member property, clicking OK will close the Create Member Property dialog box. It will also display the Dimension Workspace for the Employee dimension where the newly created Entity member property can be seen as the right-most column. Click the Check In link in the Dimension Tasks pane on the right side to save and check in the Employee dimension.

The user-defined dimension member property will be available to all members of the dimension. It is important to note that the user-defined dimension member properties cannot be deleted after they are created and saved.

Loading Dimension Data

There are four commonly used ways for loading members into dimensions within a PPS Planning Application. The choice of the data loading method depends on the volume, the original source, the complexity, and the volatility of the dimension data. The following sections will explain each of the commonly used data loading mechanisms with examples.

Direct Data Entry   The dimension member data can be directly entered to the dimension from the Member Maintenance tab in the dimension workspace. The direct data entry method is recommended for dimensions that have few members that are fairly static, and where the dimension data cannot be derived from any other sources including an existing data warehouse. The Scenario dimension is selected to demonstrate direct data entry method in this chapter.

The first step is direct data entry method is to check out the Scenario dimension by clicking the Check Out link from the Dimension Tasks pane. After checking out the dimension, select the Member Maintenance tab in the dimension workspace. In the next step, go to the Actions menu and select action New Sibling. This will add a new member to the Scenario dimension with the Name and Label values of NewMember1, as shown in the top half of Figure 7-18. You can then double click on the text NewMember1 under the Name column and change the name to **Actual**.

The label value can be similarly changed to **ACT** after double clicking on the text NewMember1 under the Label column. An optional description of **Actual** can be added by double clicking in the Description column. In the direct data entry method, new dimension members can be added by selecting New Sibling from the Actions menu. Every time the New Sibling is selected from the Actions menu, a new member with Name and Label values of NewMember*x* is added to the dimension. The names and labels can then be modified by double clicking on the text, and entering the desired values. For the purpose of the example in this chapter, another member with Name, Label, and Description values of **Budget**, **BGT**, and **Budget** respectively is added to the Scenario dimension. The final Scenario dimension member list is shown in the bottom half of Figure 7-18. After all the dimension members are entered by the direct data entry method, the dimension can be saved or checked in. Checking in will automatically save the dimension data to the PPS Planning system.

Load Members from Data Source   The dimension member data can be loaded from a data source that has already been added to the Data Sources link on the left pane

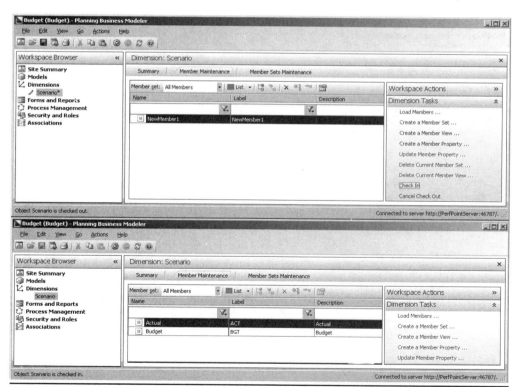

Figure 7-18   *The direct entry of dimension data is feasible for small dimensions with fairly static data.*

of the Planning Administration Console page. Loading dimension members from a data source is recommended for dimensions that have a large number of members that are fairly static, and where the dimension data is readily available from other sources including an existing data warehouse. The Entity dimension is selected to demonstrate loading of dimension data from a data source in this chapter.

The first step in loading dimension data is to Check Out the Entity dimension. After checking out the dimension, select the Member Maintenance tab in the dimension workspace. From the Dimension Tasks pane on the right side, click the first link—Load Members... to display the Select Member Source page in the Load Members Wizard, as shown in Figure 7-19. Select the Load members from source option in this page. Associated with this option is a drop-down list titled Source, which will show a list of all the data sources that are associated with the model site in the PPS Planning Server. Select the Source named Corp_DataMart (defined earlier in this chapter) as the data source, as shown in Figure 7-19.

The next page in the Load Members Wizard is the Specify Dimension Properties page, as shown in Figure 7-20. The Source Dimension: drop-down box will list all

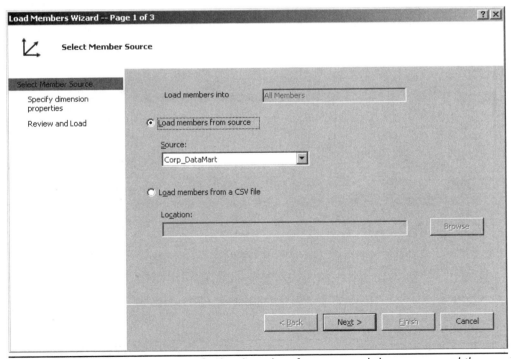

Figure 7-19 *There are two options for loading data from external data sources while using the Load Members Wizard.*

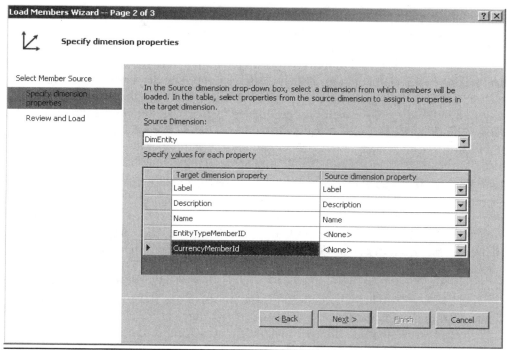

Figure 7-20 *The PPS Application dimension properties should be correctly mapped to the data source fields while using a previously defined Data Source Table or View.*

the Tables and Views that were selected while defining the Data Source Connection in Planning Administration Console, as shown in Figure 7-8. From this drop-down list select the table or view that contains the dimension data. The DimEntity table is selected here for the purpose of the examples in this chapter.

The next step is to map the PPS Planning Application dimension properties to the fields in the source table or view. The Application dimension properties are listed under the column titled Target dimension property to the left of the Specify dimension properties page. Clicking on the down arrow button to the right of each row in the Source dimension property column (to the right side of the page) will display the list of fields available in the selected source table or view. Using these buttons on each row, map the Application dimension properties to the appropriate fields in the source table or view. The Label and Name are required fields and should be mapped to data source fields. The optional fields can be mapped if data is available, or they can be left unmapped by selecting <None> in the Source dimension property column. The completed mapping for the Entity dimension is shown in Figure 7-20.

The last page in the Load Members Wizard is the Review and Load page. Here the developer can review the dimension and property mapping information. The Back button or the left navigation bar can be used to return to the appropriate page to change any of the selected options. Clicking the Finish button will close the wizard and load the dimension data from the selected source. The display is automatically changed to dimension workspace where the newly loaded members can be reviewed.

After all the dimension members are loaded from a data source, the dimension can be saved or checked in. Checking in will automatically save the dimension data to the PPS Planning system.

Load Members from CSV Files   The third option for loading dimension data is to load members from a Comma Separated Value (CSV) file. Loading dimension members from a CSV file is used in situations where the modeler working with the Planning Business Modeler client tool has to load a dimension that has a large number of members that are fairly static, the dimension data is obtained from an external source like an ERP system in a flat file, and the modeler does not have the know-how or permission to load the data into one of the data source databases defined in the PPS Planning Server. The user defined Employee dimension is selected to demonstrate loading of dimension data from a CSV file in this chapter.

The first step in loading dimension data from CSV file is to click the link Load Members from the Dimension Tasks pane after the Checking Out the Employee dimension. This will open the Select Member Source page in the Load Members Wizard, as shown in Figure 7-19. Select the Load members from a CSV file on this page and provide the location of the file containing the dimension member data in the Location text box.

The dimension member data should be provided in a Comma Separated Value file format. The CSV file should contain columns headers in the first row and the first column header should be titled Label. This column should contain the dimension member labels, which is the primary identifier of objects throughout the system. The Name column is also required, and the column header must be titled Name exactly. If the optional description column is included in the CSV file, the column headers must be titled Description. Figure 7-21 shows a sample CSV file that is loaded to the Employee dimension for the purpose of the examples in this chapter.

The last page in the Load Members Wizard is the Review and Load page. Here the modeler can review CSV file path. The Back button or the left navigation bar can be used to return to the first page to change the file path if needed. Clicking the Finish button will close the wizard, and load the dimension data from the CSV file. The display is automatically changed to dimension workspace where the newly loaded members can be reviewed. After all the dimension members are loaded from the CSV file and verified, the dimension can be saved or checked in. Checking in will automatically save the dimension data to the PPS Planning system.

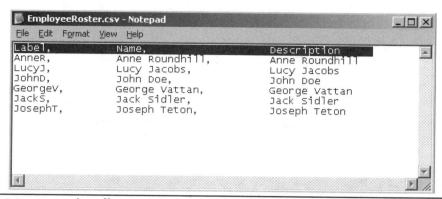

Figure 7-21   *CSV Files offer a quick and easy way to load dimension data to the PPS Planning system during development and testing.*

You may remember from the earlier section on Dimension Member Property that we have created a referential relationship between the Employee dimension and Entity dimension, with Employee being the referencing dimension and Entity being the referenced dimension. There we had selected the NONE member of Entity dimension as the default value for the Entity member property of Employee dimension. Once the Employee and Entity dimensions are loaded with members, the appropriate relationship between the dimensions can be defined for each member of the referencing Employee dimension.

For each member (row) in the referencing dimension, the corresponding value for the referenced dimension can be selected by clicking on ellipsis (…) button that is available to the right of the current value of the dimension property that serves as the link between the referencing and referenced dimensions, and then selecting the appropriate referenced dimension member from the Select Members dialog box. In the example given in this chapter, clicking the ellipsis (…) button next to the NONE value in the Entity column for any member in the Employee dimension (as shown in the top half of Figure 7-22) will open the Member Selector. This in turn displays the available members in the referenced Entity dimension. Select the check box next to the Name of the appropriate Entity dimension member and then click OK to establish the referential relationship. The bottom half of Figure 7-22 shows the Entity dimension property values for all Employee dimension members. The referential relationship can be defined for dimension members during the data loading process as well. But a detailed explanation of those techniques is beyond the scope of this chapter.

Loading Dimension from Staging Database   Data Integration within Planning Business Modeler refers to the processes involved in moving the business data from multiple sources to the Staging database, validating the data, and moving it from the Staging

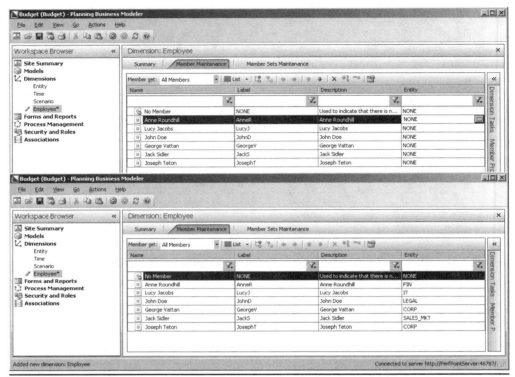

Figure 7-22 *The before and after of populating the Member of Dimension data type in a dimension.*

database to the Application database. Data Integration uses a set of stored procedures provided with the PPS Planning Server to accomplish the data validation and the loading of the Application database. The Staging database that was defined in an earlier section of this chapter (see Figure 7-3) plays an indispensable role in Data Integration within Planning Business Modeler. The various aspects of Data Integration are explained in the relevant sections in this chapter.

Synchronizing the staging database is an important step in preparing the staging database for populating data from various sources, and later loading the data to application database. Synchronizing a dimension to the staging area is accomplished by clicking the Synchronize this dimension to Staging Area link in the Dimension Tasks pane after Checking Out the dimension. In this section we will use the Account dimension to demonstrate loading of dimension data from the staging database. When a dimension is synchronized with the staging area for the first time, it creates a table named D_<DimensionName> in the Staging Database and populates the table with all the members that are currently defined for that dimension in the PPS Planning Application. In our example, synchronizing the Account dimension will create dbo.D_Account table in the Budget_ StagingDB database. The default NONE member from the Account dimension is also loaded into that table.

The Account dimension members from any external source can be loaded into D_Account table using ETL process and/or tools such as SQL Server Integration Services (SSIS). As always, the fields Label and Name are required fields. Another required field that should be populated by the ETL process in the case of any dimension is the BizSystemFlag. Any other required field, such as the AccountTypeMemberId in the case of Account dimension, should also be populated in the Staging Database before data can be loaded from the Staging Database to the Application Database.

When you are loading dimension data from the staging database to the application database in Planning Business Modeler, all changes to dimension data in the staging database will be integrated into the application database. This includes new dimension member rows, updated dimension member rows, and deleted dimension member rows. Dimension members that are not changed in the staging database remain unchanged in the application database. This makes the process of loading data from the staging database to the application database, the recommended process for loading dimension data in all cases as long as the data is available from external sources including an existing data warehouse. However, the proper integration of staging database changes to the application database is controlled by the value of the BizSystemFlag field mentioned in the previous paragraph. The possible values of BizSystemFlag, and the operation performed by the data integration process for each of these values, is given in Table 7-2.

By looking at Table 7-2, you can see that any ETL process that populates the dbo. D_Account table in the staging database for the first time should set the value of BizSystemFlag to 200, at least for the purpose of the examples in this chapter. After populating the staging database table, the next step in loading dimension data from staging database is to click the Load This Dimension from Staging Area link in the

BizSystemFlag Value	Data Integration Action Taken
100	Indicates that the record is loaded from the Application database to the Staging database via synchronization. No action is taken during loading from Staging database.
200	Insert records during loading from Staging database.
300	Update records during loading from Staging database.
400	Delete records during loading from Staging database.
900+	Indicates that errors were detected during validation of load operations. The actual value corresponds to the error code generated.

Table 7-2 *Explanation of the Various BizSystemFlag Values Used in the Data Integration Process within PPS Planning System*

Dimension Tasks pane. Click OK when you see the warning message that appears to remind the developer to synchronize and populate the staging area. After the data load is completed, a completion message will appear on the Status Bar at the bottom of the Planning Business Modeler client tool. A successful load can be verified by the BizSystemFlag value of 100 for all the records in the dbo.D_Account table in the Budget_ StagingDB database.

The newly loaded members in the Account dimension can be viewed by first selecting the Refresh option from the View menu, and then opening the Member Maintenance tab in the Dimensions workspace for Account dimension. After loading dimension data from staging database, the dimension can be saved or checked in. Checking in will automatically save the dimension data to the PPS Planning system.

Dimension Member Sets

Planning Business Modeler helps to manage dimensions by organizing dimension members into member sets. Member sets are used to create models, with dimension members belonging to an unlimited number of member sets. A member set can be flat, with all dimension members organized as siblings, or members can be organized into a hierarchy, with some dimension members designated as parents and other members designated as child elements, nested below the parents in the hierarchy. When organized into a hierarchy, parent members in member sets represent dimensions subtotals of child members. Thus member sets can be easily used to create subtotals in a form or report generated by the PPS Planning Application. The dimension member sets are similar to dimension hierarchies in SSAS OLAP cubes and, in fact, the member sets are defined as parent-child hierarchies when a SSAS OLAP cube is created for the model during the model site deployment phase.

A member set should include all the members that are required from a dimension for the calculations that will be performed by a model or group of models. One approach to designing member sets is to determine which calculations will be used in a given model. Then you should work backward from those calculations to determine the members that will be required from each dimension, and include those members in member sets from each dimension. The rest of this section will describe how member sets can be defined for dimensions. The Entity dimension is selected to demonstrate creation of member sets in this chapter.

The first step in creating a member set is to click the link Create a Member Set from the Dimension Tasks pane after Checking Out the Entity dimension. This will open the Specify Member Set Name, Label and Description page in the Create a Member Set Wizard. The value Corporate is entered in the text boxes titled Label and Description for the purpose of the examples in this chapter.

The next page in the wizard is the Select Member Set Creation Option page. Select the first option that says Create an Empty Member Set on this Page. The next page in the wizard is the Review and Create page. Clicking the Finish button will close the wizard, and creates the new member for the Entity dimension. The display is automatically changed to dimension workspace where the newly member set titled Corporate is displayed in the Member Maintenance tab. Since we chose to create an empty member set, there are no members displayed in this member set at this stage.

The next step in the process is to add members to the newly created Corporate member set. Click on the Member Sets Maintenance tab to go to the member sets workspace. Make sure that the newly created Corporate member set is selected from the Member Set drop-down box on the left half of the workspace titled Destination Member Set. The right half of the workspace titled Source Member Set should have All Members selected from the Member Set drop-down box.

Right-click on the Demo Corporation member on the right half of the pane and then select the Add as Sibling option, as shown in the top half of Figure 7-23. The same option is available from the Actions menu, after highlighting the Demo Corporation member on the right half of the pane. On doing so, the Demo Corporation member is moved from the Source Member Set on the right half of the pane to the Destination

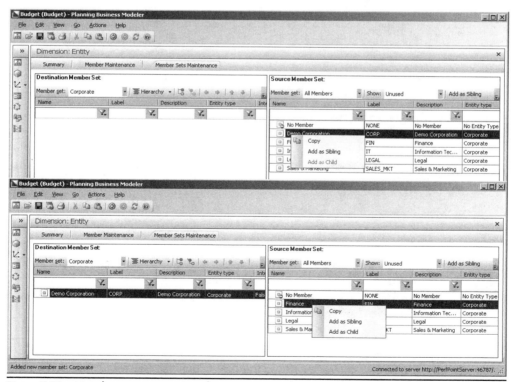

Figure 7-23 *Member sets organize dimension members to create powerful analytical hierarchies*

Member Set on the left half of the pane, as shown in the bottom half of Figure 7-23. Right-clicking on other members in the Source Member Set on the right half of the pane will show the options Add as Sibling and Add as Child. Select the appropriate option to add the next member as a sibling or a child of the first member to the Destination Member Set on the left half of the pane. Follow the previous steps for all the members in the Source Member Set.

After all the required members are added to the new member set, click on the Member Maintenance tab to go back to the dimension workspace. From the drop-down box titled Member Set, select the newly populated Corporate member set. The members that belong to the Corporate member set are displayed in the dimension workspace. After creating and populating a new member set, the Entity dimension can be saved or checked in. Checking in will automatically save the dimension data to the PPS Planning system. Figure 7-24 shows the member sets that are created for the Entity and Account dimensions for the purpose of the examples in this chapter.

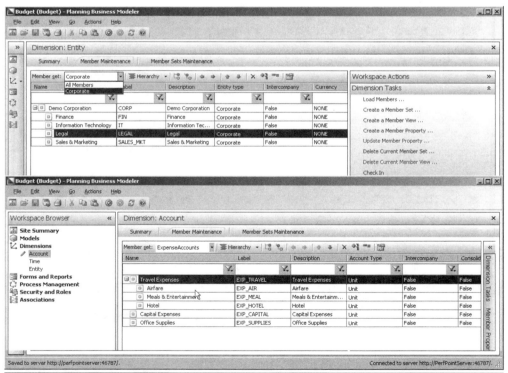

Figure 7-24 *The top half of this figure shows the Corporate member set of the Entity dimension, while the bottom half shows the ExpenseAccounts member set of the Account dimension.*

Models

In the PerformancePoint Server Planning module, a model is the basic unit of data storage. Models contain dimension member sets that define the structure of the model and for what levels and members the data is stored. Different business scenarios may require a different number of models. For example, you may have seen a catalog that comes with a separate printed price list, so that the life of the catalog is longer since it doesn't have prices printed in it. This way, a business might schedule monthly or quarterly price updates, so a pricing model would have a monthly or quarterly grain, while the sales model would have a daily grain.

As mentioned previously in this chapter, model sites organize the application and data. Every application has a single parent model site that contains predefined dimensions and global assumption models. All subsequent model sites in the application are referred to as model subsites.

The Models workspace within the Planning Business Modeler can be selected by clicking on the Models link in the Workspace Browser displayed earlier in Figure 7-10. A new model can be created by clicking the Create a Model link in the Model Tasks pane to the right side of the Models workspace or by selecting the Create a Mode under the Actions menu. This will open the Create a Model Wizard. The first page of the wizard asks for the Name, Label, and an optional Description of the new model. The value **CorpBudget** is entered in all the three text boxes, as shown in Figure 7-25 for the purpose of the examples in this chapter. Select the Allow This Model to be Shared check box to make this model to allow this model to share its data with model subsites. When sharing with model subsites, they can see but not modify the root model. Subsites can, however, add their own data or dimensions which will not be visible to the root model.

On the next page of the wizard select the first option to Create a New Model. Here the modeler has a choice of several different model types to choose from.

▶ **Generic model**   Two predefined dimensions, Scenario and Time, are added to the model automatically, but predefined accounting rules are not added.

▶ **Global Assumption model**   This model contains assumptions available to all model sites. The predefined dimensions Scenario and Time are automatically added to this model type. To fully use assumption model functionality, assumption models should be linked to other models in Planning Business Modeler.

▶ **Exchange Rate model**   This model is a special-purpose assumption model that tracks foreign exchange rates for a specified time across all currencies in the system. In addition to Scenario and Time, the following dimensions are automatically added: Currency (Destinations), Exchange Rate, Currency (Source), and Entity.

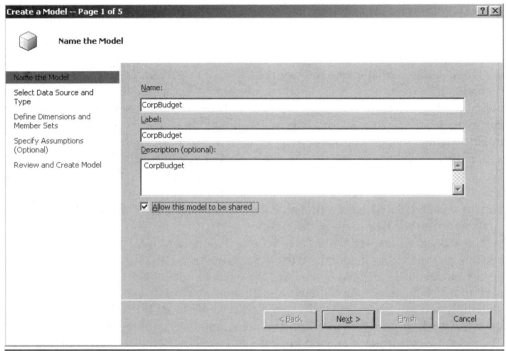

Figure 7-25 *A model is the basic unit of data storage within the PerformancePoint Server Planning module.*

▶ **Financial model with shares calculations** This model contains built-in logic for performing consolidation with shares calculations. It automatically contains the following dimensions: Scenario, Time, Account, Entity, Business Process, Time Data View, Consolidation Method, and Flow.

▶ **Financial model without shares calculations** This model contains built-in logic for performing consolidation without shares calculations. The dimensions include Scenario, Time, Account, Entity, Business Process, and Time Data View, and are automatically added to this model.

The Generic Model option is selected for the purpose of the examples in this chapter.

The next page in the Create a Model wizard is the Define Dimensions and Member Sets page. This is where the dimensions and the member sets that make up the model are selected. As you can see on this page, and as we mentioned earlier in this chapter, the Scenario and Time dimensions are automatically included in the model. Additional dimensions can be added to the model by selecting the required dimension from the Dimension drop-down box, and the appropriate member set for that dimension from the next drop-down box titled Member set:. A user friendly name for the dimension to be displayed in forms and reports can be entered in the Alias: text box. Clicking the > button to the right of the Member set: box will add the selected member set of the selected dimension to the model and will be displayed in the dimension list on the right side of the page. The member sets can be changed for the automatically added Time and Scenario dimensions, and for any other dimension that is already added to the model by clicking in the Member Set column in the right window for the dimension whose member set needs to be changed. This will bring a drop-down box that lists all of the member sets belonging to that model. The appropriate member set can be selected from here. For the purpose of the examples in this chapter, the All Members member set of the Scenario dimension, the Corporate member set of the Entity dimension, the ExpenseAccount member set of Account dimension, and the YQM member set of Time dimension are selected in the model, as shown in Figure 7-26.

The last page in the Create a Model wizard is the Review and Create Model page. Here the developer can review the information that is displayed. If any of the

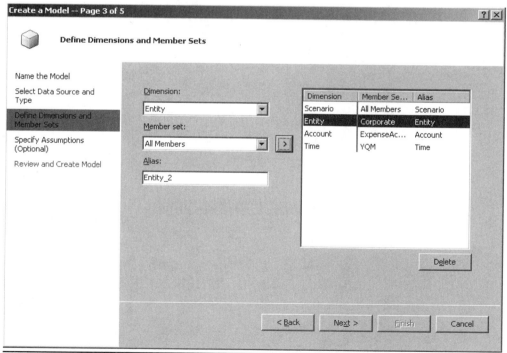

Figure 7-26 *Designing models is critical to the success of PerformancePoint Server Planning applications.*

previous choices need to be modified, the Back button or the left navigation bar can be used to return to the appropriate page to change it. Clicking the Finish button will create the new model, and will take you to the newly created model. The Summary tab of the new model is opened by default, as shown in Figure 7-27.

The second tab in the Model workspace shown in Figure 7-27 is titled Model Properties. Model properties are actually similar to variables; they can be set and then referenced elsewhere in the model. An example is the setting of a fixed conversion factor and then using that factor in calculations in the model; this way, a single change to the factor can impact all the data in the model. The model designer is free to add new model properties, but there are a number that come with the model. For example the property Enable Offline Cube determines whether or not a user can download assignments and work with them in Excel while disconnected from the server. The Model Data Has Changed property determines whether or not changes are tracked.

The third tab in the Model workspace seen in Figure 7-27 is titled Business Rules. Business rules are executable programs that work with the multidimensional data in

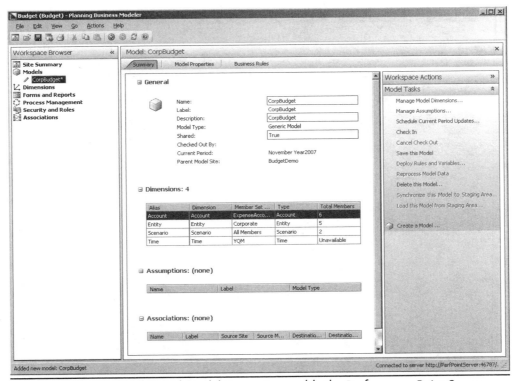

Figure 7-27   *Business Rules and Model Properties enable the PerformancePoint Server Planning module to model complex business processes.*

a model. These programs might generate forecasts or find outliers in the data. Given what business rules can do, they can vary from simple to extremely complex, and the syntax for working with multidimensional data is sometimes confusing even for those experienced with relational data. A detailed discussion on Business Rules within PPS Planning application models is beyond the scope of this chapter.

The Schedule Current Updates link allows the model designer to set one or more scheduled updates to the Current Period model property, and this property can then be used in calculations of rolling cycles. For example, if a budgeting process is done each quarter for the following quarter, a cycle could be set up that sets the budgeting period to the start and end dates of the next quarter. This process could run on the thirtieth day of each quarter in order to set up the time periods for the next quarter, and dole out assignments for people to enter their budgets for the upcoming quarter.

After the model has been designed, the business rules have been written, and the current period has been set, the model can be saved or checked in. Checking in will automatically save the model to the PPS Planning system. The model is ready to be deployed at this stage. Deployment is separate from saving. Saving a model site saves the data on the server running the Planning Server, while deploying a model site updates the data in the OLAP Cube which is the data source used by the PerformancePoint Add-in for Excel. Deployment does save the model changes first, and all the models in the model site are checked to ensure that it they are valid. Assuming the models are valid, the data is updated in the source systems so that end users can perform their assignments.

The model can be deployed by clicking on Deploy Model Site under the File menu of the Planning Business Modeler. Successful deployment of the model (which can be verified from the Messages dialog box) will result in a SSAS OLAP Cube being built in the Analysis Services computer specified in the Planning Administration Console. The OLAP cube will have the same name as the PPS Planning Application model. It will also have the same dimensions that were selected during the model design. Each of the dimensions will have a parent-child hierarchy in the OLAP cube for the member set that was selected during cube design.

Forms and Reports

Clicking on the Forms and Reports link in the Workspace Browser (displayed in Figure 7-10) will open the Forms workspace within the Planning Business Modeler. The Form Templates used by PPS Planning Application are created and published using the PPS 2007 PerformancePoint Add-in for Excel client tool. A detailed discussion of the creation and publishing of Business Reports and Form Templates is given in the section on the PerformancePoint Add-in for Excel client tool later in this chapter. From the drop-down box in the Forms workspace, the view can be toggled between Form Templates and Operational Reports.

Process Management

Once the form templates are created and published, the next step in the Planning process is the creation of planning cycles, commonly referred to as budget cycles. The planning cycles can be created to coincide with the budget or forecast cycles within your corporation. These planning cycles are created within the Process Management workspace. Clicking on the Process Management link in the Workspace Browser will open the Process Management workspace within the Planning Business Modeler, as displayed in Figure 7-28.

A new cycle can be created by clicking on the Create a Cycle under the Actions menu or clicking on the Create a Cycle link on the Process Scheduling Tasks pane that appears to the right of the Process Management workspace. This opens the Create a Cycle wizard. The Name, Label, and an optional Description of the cycle is provided on this page. The owner of the cycle can be selected by clicking on the Ellipsis (...) button to the right of the Owner: text box at the bottom of this page. Clicking this button will open another pop-up window that displays all the users that

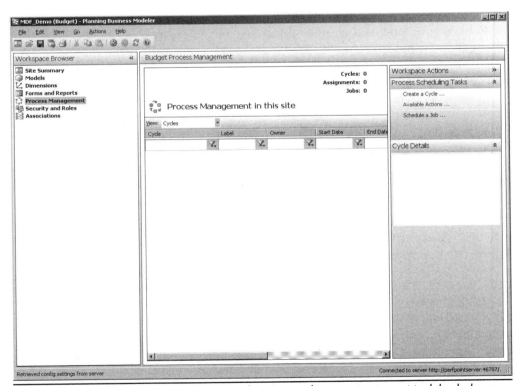

Figure 7-28   *The Process Management workspace in Planning Business Modeler helps to create and manage planning cycles throughout the organization.*

are added to the PPS Planning Server. In this Select Owner dialog box, highlight the name of the user that should own the cycle. Then click on the Add Selected button at the top to add the selected user as the owner of the cycle. One cycle can have only one owner and any user that is assigned to a business role within the PPS Planning system can be selected as the owner of the cycle. The owner is granted permission to change the status of the cycle at any time, regardless of its current state. The value Corporate Budget 2008 is entered in the Name and Label text boxes and PERFPOINTSERVER\Administrator is selected as the owner of the cycle for the purpose of the examples in this chapter, as shown in Figure 7-29.

On the next page, you will select the model that your data will be submitted to through this cycle. You can select it from the drop-down list of all the models available within the application; a process cycle can reference only a single model. In this example the CorpBudget model that we created in the previous section is selected from the drop-down list.

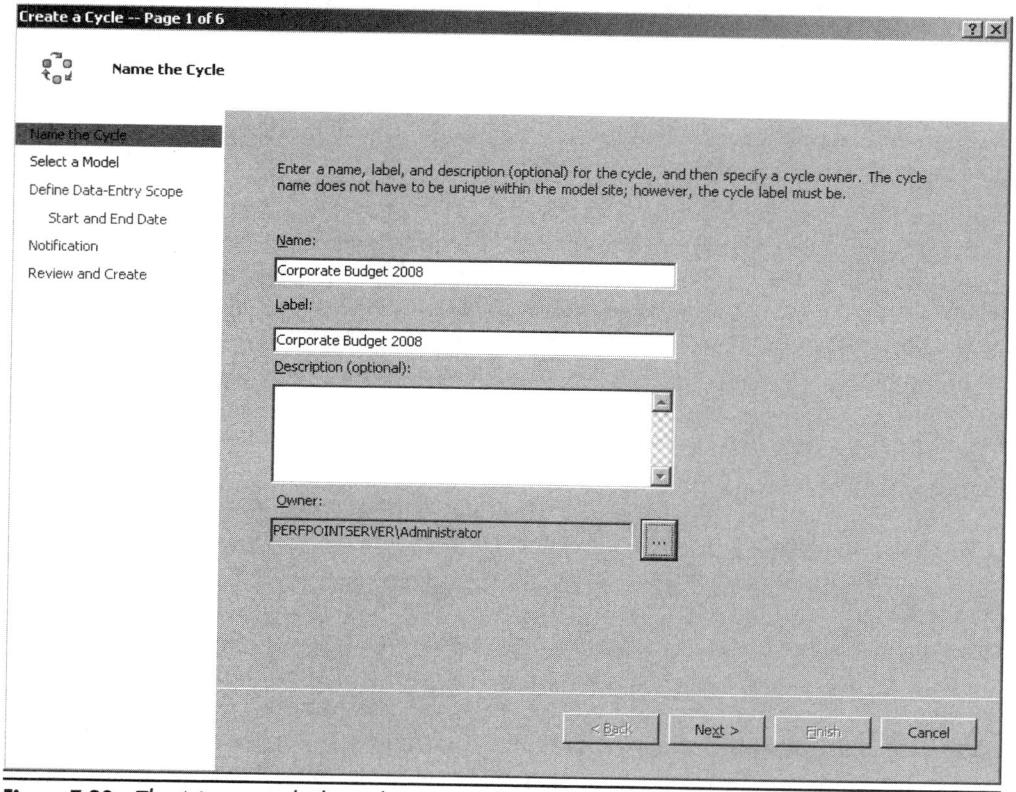

Figure 7-29   *The Name, Label, and Owner of a cycle are defined in this page.*

The next page in the Create a Cycle wizard is the Define Data Entry Scope page. On this page you'll select the Time dimension members and Scenario dimension members to unlock for data entry in the newly created cycle. The values you enter on this page determine which cells in the Planning Forms are open for data entry by end users when they open their Assignments. Clicking the Edit... button to the right of the Data Period: Start: text box in this page will open the Select Member dialog box which shows all the members within the YQM member set from the Time dimension that was selected for the CorpBudget model. Only the leaf-level members of the Time dimension member set can be picked for the data entry period start and end dates. This is another consideration in the selection of the appropriate time member set in the model. In our example YQM member set, Months are the leaf-level members. If the Planning applications within your corporation need a different granularity of time for planning, budgeting, or forecasting purposes, the Time dimension member set should be defined and selected accordingly within the model. For the purpose of the examples in this chapter, the Time dimension member **January Year2008** is selected as the starting month which will be unlocked for data entry for all the form assignments within this cycle. The dimension member can be selected by checking the check box next to the appropriate Time dimension member in the Select Member dialog box. Similarly, the Time dimension member **December Year2008** is selected as the ending month which will be unlocked for data entry. The selection of January Year2008 and December Year2008 as the start and end time members for the data entry scope means that all the cells that belong to Time dimension members January 2008 through December 2008 are unlocked for data entry within the form assignments for this cycle. This will be demonstrated later in this chapter when we discuss the actual data entry and submission. The Scenario dimension member that defines the unlocked cells for data entry is selected in a similar manner. The scenario dimension member Budget was selected to define the data entry scope for the purpose of the examples in this chapter. Figure 7-30 shows the data entry scope that is selected for the Corporate Budget 2008 cycle described in this chapter.

The next page in the Create a Cycle wizard is the Start and End Date page. This is where the cycle start date and end date are defined. This is not to be confused with the data entry scope dates defined in the previous page. The cycle start and end date determines how long a cycle is available to the users for entering and submitting data. In a typical corporate scenario, the budgeting analyst will have a two- to three-month window during to enter the budget for the next year. This two- to three-month window is captured in the cycle Start and End Date page, whereas the next year for which the budgeting is done is captured in the previous data entry scope definition page. The start date of December 1, 2007 and an end date of January 31, 2008 is selected as the cycle start and end dates for the purpose of the examples in this chapter.

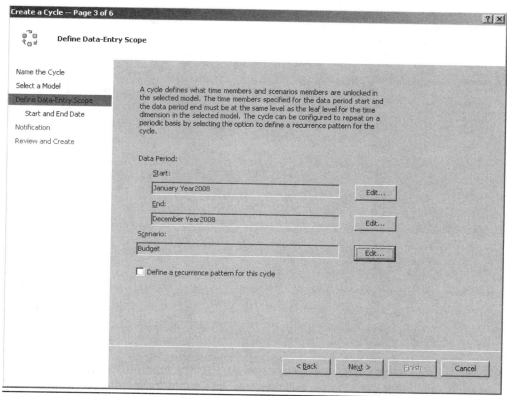

Figure 7-30 *The data-entry scope of a cycle determines the cells that are unlocked for data entry while using the PerformancePoint Add-in for Excel.*

Enabling notifications in the next page of the Create a Cycle wizard will send e-mail notifications to the end users of PPS Planning Application whenever they have assignments available for data entry, review, or approval. The last page in the Create a Cycle wizard is the Review and Create page. Here the developer can review the information that is displayed. If any of the previous choices need to be modified, the Back button or the left navigation bar can be used to return to the appropriate page to change it. Clicking the Finish button will create the new cycle, and will take you to the newly created cycle. The Summary tab of the new cycle is opened by default, as shown in Figure 7-31.

After a cycle is defined and created, forms templates should be assigned to the cycle. The cycle workspace can be enabled by single clicking on the appropriate cycle in the process management workspace. Once you are in the cycle workspace, click the Assign Forms... under the Actions menu to open the Create an Assignment Definition wizard. The value Budget 2008 is entered in the Name, Label, and

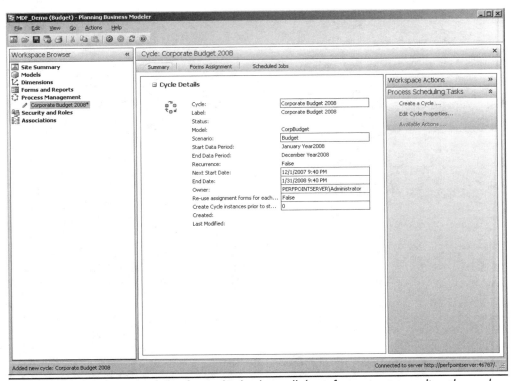

Figure 7-31   *The Summary tab of a cycle displays all the information regarding the cycle.*

Description text boxes in the first page of the wizard for the examples in this chapter. The next page of the wizard is the Data Submission page, which defines the users that can contribute data in a given assignment. Select the check box next to Contributors and click on the Edit… button to open the Select Contributor dialog box, as shown in the bottom right of Figure 7-32. In this dialog box, any combination of Business Users and Business Roles can be selected as the contributor for the assignment. The Business User or Business Roles can be selected in this dialog box by highlighting the appropriate user or role and clicking the Add Selected button at the top of the dialog box. The user Contributor1 is selected as the contributor for the purpose of the examples in this chapter, as shown in Figure 7-32.

The Form Template to be used for data submission in an assignment is also defined in the same Data Submission page of the Create an Assignment Definition wizard. Clicking the Edit… button next to the Form box will open the Select Forms dialog box. All the Form Templates that are available in the PPS Planning Server are listed on the left side of this dialog box. A form template can be selected by highlighting the required form template and clicking on the > button in the middle of the dialog box.

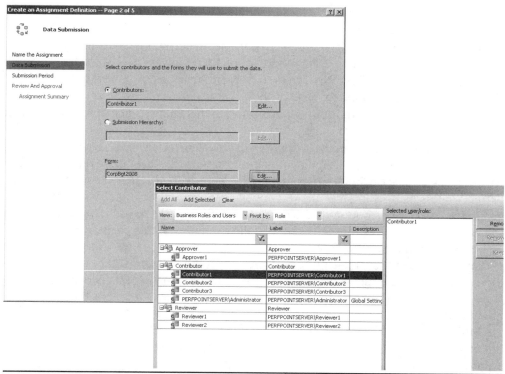

Figure 7-32 *The Data Submission page defines the Contributors and Form Template used in an Assignment.*

The selected form template is listed on the left side of this dialog box. The form template CorpBgt2008 is selected for the purpose of the examples in this chapter. Creation of this form template is discussed in a later section of this chapter.

In the next Submission Period page of the Create an Assignment Definition wizard, the developer can select the priority, start, and end dates for submission, as well as the no-submission options. The default options on this page are selected for the purpose of the examples in this chapter. In the Review and Approval page of the wizard, the required workflow for the data submission can be selected. Depending on the option selected in this page, a submission may go through a review and approval process, or may go through no additional review or approval process. The Review and Approval option is selected for the examples in this chapter.

The next page in the wizard depends on the options selected in the previous Review and Approval page. If the Review Only or the Review and Approval options are selected, the next page will be the Review page. Adding any combination of Business Users and Business Roles as Reviewers is similar to adding Contributors, as you saw in an earlier step. The PPS Planning System allows the Reviewers and Approvers to edit and modify the data that is submitted by contributors. This is a powerful feature of the tool that is used by many corporations using the PPS Planning Server applications. Data modification by reviewers is enabled by selecting the check box next to Allow Reviewers to Edit Submissions. A review deadline can also be specified in the Review page of the wizard. The user Reviewer1 is selected as the reviewer for the purpose of the examples in this chapter. The other two options on this page are not selected.

Since the Review and Approval option was selected earlier in the wizard, the next page in the Create an Assignment Definition wizard is the Approval page. The Business Users and Business Roles that are the approvers for the data submission are defined in this page. Similar to the Review page, data modification by approver(s) and approval deadline options can be enabled in this page. The user Approver1 is selected as the approver for the purpose of the examples in this chapter. The other two options on this page are not selected.

The last page in the Create an Assignment Definition wizard is the Assignment Summary page. Here the developer can review the information that is displayed. If any of the previous choices need to be modified, the Back button or the left navigation bar can be used to return to the appropriate page to change it. Clicking the Finish button will create the new assignment for the cycle. Multiple assignments featuring multiple Form Templates and Users (Contributors, Reviewers, and Approvers) can be defined for each cycle. All the assignments defined for a cycle will follow the rest of the cycle properties, including the data-entry scope and cycle start and end dates.

The next step in making the assignments available to contributor users for data submission is to create assignment instances. From the process management workspace, select Assignments from the drop-down box titled View at the top of the workspace. This will display the assignment Budget 2008 created in the previous section. Highlight this assignment and click on the Available Actions... link under the Process Scheduling Tasks pane to the right side of the workspace, as shown in Figure 7-33. This will open the Available Actions dialog box, as shown in the inset of Figure 7-33. From the drop-down list Select action:, choose Instantiate to create a new instance of the assignment. Under the Parameters: section in this dialog box, set the value of Start to True, as shown in Figure 7-33. Clicking OK will exit the dialog box, and create assignment instances for all Business Users and Business Roles that can be selected as contributors for this assignment. One assignment instance is created per business user. The business user can either be added individually as a contributor or belong to a business role that was added as a contributor when the assignment was defined using the Create an Assignment Definition wizard described earlier. The newly created assignment instances are visible in the cycle workspace after refreshing the Planning Business Modeler client tool.

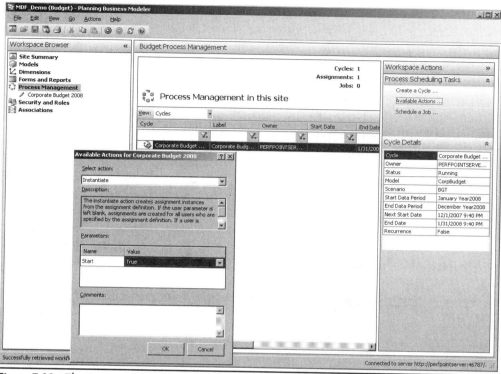

Figure 7-33 *The Instantiate action creates assignment instances from assignment definitions.*

Security and Roles

As with most Microsoft products, security is role-based. This means that users are assigned to one or more roles, and that their inclusion in those roles determines the permissions they have in the system. There are actually two different kinds of roles in the Planning Server: Administrative and Business. Administrative roles are for those creating and maintaining the infrastructure of the Planning Server, while Business roles deal with the access to the data in the Planning Server.

Business roles are a predefined collection of Business Users in the PPS Planning Server and can be defined in the Security and Roles workspace in the Planning Business Modeler client tool. Business roles are designed to include users who require similar access to business data. Adding users to Business roles allows the developer to manage a group of users at once. The security permissions for all the users belonging to that role can be set at the at the role level. While defining Assignments as described in the previous section of this chapter, multiple users can be added to the Contributors, Reviewers, or Approvers list by selecting the appropriately defined Business Roles that contain the users—rather than selecting multiple users individually. Even within a given role, a user can have customized permissions that are different from the overall permissions for the role. A user can also belong to multiple roles. In the case of users belonging to multiple roles with different permission scope, the least restrictive permission scope will prevail.

To successfully submit data to the assignment instances created in the previous section, access to the Model—CorpBudget—should be turned on for the all the Business Users or Business Roles defined as contributor, reviewer, or approver in the assignment. To do this, go to the Security and Roles workspace by clicking on the Security and Roles link in the Workspace Browser, as shown in Figure 7-10. All the Business Users and Business Roles are listed in this workspace. Next, click on the user Contributer1, which will open the Role or User workspace (depending on whether the user belongs to a role or not). In the bottom half of the Summary tab, set the access to On for the model CorpBudget, as shown in Figure 7-34. Repeat the same steps for users Reviewer1 and Approver1 (for the purpose of the examples in this chapter). After all the changes are made, save them to the PPS Planning Server.

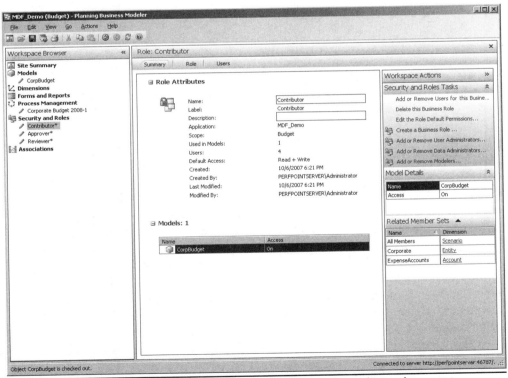

Figure 7-34 *Model access should be turned on for every role and user that requires access to the business forms and reports.*

Associations

Associations are the final link in the Workspace browser. While no associations are used in this chapter, it is important to understand what they are and what they can do. Associations provide a way to tie together two models, with one model acting as the source and the other model acting as the destination. Data from the fact table of the source model can be moved into the destination model, with the option of aggregating data as it is moved. Imagine a scenario where each division has its own model and does its own forecasting and budgeting. These divisions might have different rules for when things should be done, but when each is completed they could have an association with a master model that is company-wide, with the data from each division moved into the master model via associations.

PerformancePoint Add-in for Excel

The PerformancePoint Add-in for Excel is a tool that plays two primary purposes. First, it allows for the creation of business reports and form templates. Form templates can be created that define that data that will be entered, the way it will look, and the rules that apply to it. Second, the add-in allows users to enter plan data and push it to the Planning server. The benefits of having an Excel add-in are obvious: most people using the Planning server will be intimately familiar with Excel, and because they are working in a comfortable environment they will face a very small learning curve. In addition, Excel provides powerful formatting, macros, cell formatting, and other great features that can be incorporated in the form templates.

Creating Reports and Forms

The form templates that are available under the Forms workspace within the Planning Business Modeler are created using the PerformancePoint Add-in for Excel. This section explains in detail how the business reports are created in Excel and published as Form Templates to the PPS Planning Server.

The PerformancePoint menu is available in Excel on a computer where the PerformancePoint Add-in for Excel is installed. Clicking on the PerformancePoint menu will open the PerformancePoint ribbon within Excel 2007. The first step in using the PerformancePoint Add-in for Excel is to establish a connection with the PPS Planning Server where the model information is stored. Clicking on the Connect icon in the PerformancePoint ribbon will open the Configure PerformancePoint Add-in for Excel dialog box. In the text box below the title PerformancePoint Server system, enter **http://<Server Name>:46787/**, which in our case will be **http:// PerfPointServer:46787/**, as shown in Figure 7-35. The Add to Favorites button can

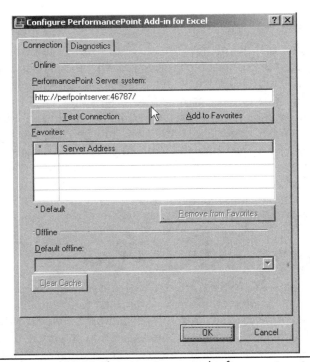

Figure 7-35 *Connecting to the PPS Planning Server is the first step in using PerformancePoint Add-in for Excel.*

be used to add the address to the Favorites: section, which will make it available to the developer for later use.

The Form Templates that are available within the Planning Business Modeler client tool are first created as Business Reports and later published as Form Templates within the PPS Planning System. After connecting to the PPS Planning Server from Excel, click on the New… link under the Reports ribbon icon to create a new business report. This will open the Choose Application dialog box. From the drop-down list titled Application, choose the application where the business report and form template are created. Choose the Budget application from this drop-down list for the purpose of the examples in this chapter. Click OK to establish a connection to the Budget application. If the reader is using the PerformancePoint Add-in for Excel for the first time, the PerformancePoint action pane will open at this stage. It is easier to work with Excel if this pane is docked to a side of the Excel worksheet. Double-clicking on the caption bar of the action pane will dock it to the left of Excel worksheet.

To create a new business report, the developer must select the Authoring pane by clicking on the Authoring link at the bottom of the Action pane. The Authoring pane as it appears for the first time is shown in left half of Figure 7-36. The next step is to add report matrixes in the worksheet. A business report and the corresponding form template can have multiple Excel worksheets, and each worksheet can have multiple report matrixes. There are two ways to create a new report matrix: by clicking on either the Add a New Matrix icon or the Add a New Matrix with Wizard icon. We will use the Add a new matrix icon for the examples in this chapter.

Clicking on the Add a New Matrix icon will open the New Matrix dialog box. In the General tab of the dialog box, we will keep the default values for the Name:

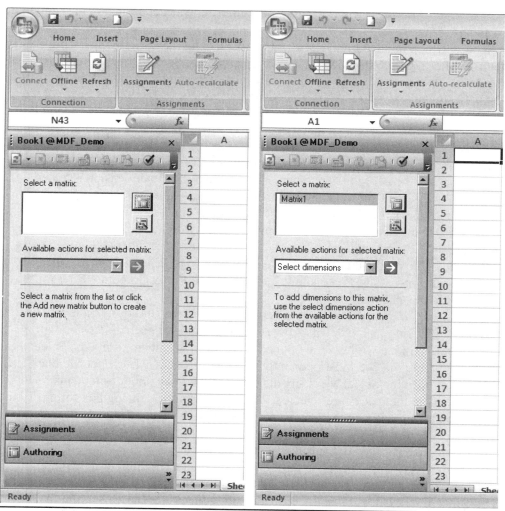

Figure 7-36 The left and right sides of this figure show the before and after of the creation of the report matrix—Matrix1.

and Start in Cell: text boxes. The value entered in the Start in Cell: box determines the location of the report matrix within an Excel worksheet. Space can be provided in the Excel worksheet for customized report titles by appropriately selecting the matrix start cell. The Model: box lists all the models available in our Budget application. Highlight the CorpBudget from Budget to select the CorpBudget model for the purpose of the examples in this chapter. The Options tab in the New Matrix dialog box allows the developer to select the various report matrix options, including allowing data entry, removing blank rows and columns, and so on. The selections on this tab are left at their default values. Clicking OK will close the dialog box, and the new matrix—Matrix1—will appear in the Authoring pane, as shown in the right half of Figure 7-36.

The next step in creating a report matrix is selecting the dimensions for the matrix. After highlighting Matrix1 in the top box, pick Select Dimensions from the Available Actions drop-down box. Clicking on the green arrow button next to the drop-down box will open the Select Dimensions for Matrix dialog box. All the dimension member sets used in the model CorpBudget are available on the left side of this dialog box. Selecting a member set from any dimension will enable the three buttons in the middle bar of the dialog box. These buttons can be used to add the selected member set to Columns, Rows, or Filters. For the purpose of the examples in this chapter, the All Members member set of the Scenario dimension is added to the Columns, the Corporate member set of the Entity dimension is added to the Filters, the ExpenseAccount member set of Account dimension is added to the Rows, and the YQM member set of Time dimension is added to the Columns, as shown in Figure 7-37. If any dimension member set is added to the Filters, then the Select Filters dialog box will appear to help the developer to pick the default members for the filter dimensions. Select the value FIN for the Entity.Corporate filter for the examples in this chapter.

The selected dimension member sets will appear in the Authoring pane at this point. Clicking on the down arrow next to the name of each dimension will open a pop-up menu with several options. The Select Members... and the Select Properties... are the two most frequently used options here. The Select Members... option will open the Select Members dialog box where the dimension members to be displayed in the matrix are selected. The Select Members dialog box for the Time dimension, along with the member selection used in the examples in this chapter, is shown in Figure 7-38. The Select Properties... option can be used to pick the dimension properties to be displayed in the report matrix.

A single Excel work sheet in a multi-sheet report can contain multiple report matrixes. There are several properties that can be defined for the matrixes within a business report. Clicking on the Properties link under the Reports icon in the

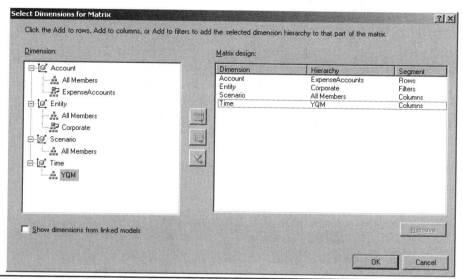

Figure 7-37 *The arrangement of dimension member sets within a report matrix determines the final layout of the form used by end users for data entry.*

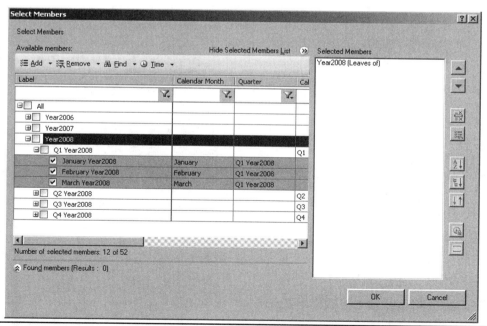

Figure 7-38 *The dimension members to be displayed in the final form are selected while defining the report matrix.*

PerformancePoint ribbon will open the report properties dialog box, as shown in Figure 7-39. The value **True** is selected for the Auto-indent row members property for the purpose of the examples in this chapter.

The reports and form templates created using PerformancePoint Add-in for Excel supports Global Filters. Global Filters are filters that are applied to all the matrixes within an Excel workbook, irrespective of whether the matrixes are on the same worksheet or not. Once the report or form is rendered, changing the member selection in a global filter will change the member selection for all the matrixes that use the global filter. This feature is useful in cases where multiple matrixes on one or more worksheet are required to generate a single report that pertains to any member belonging to a filter dimension. In the example report used in this chapter, using

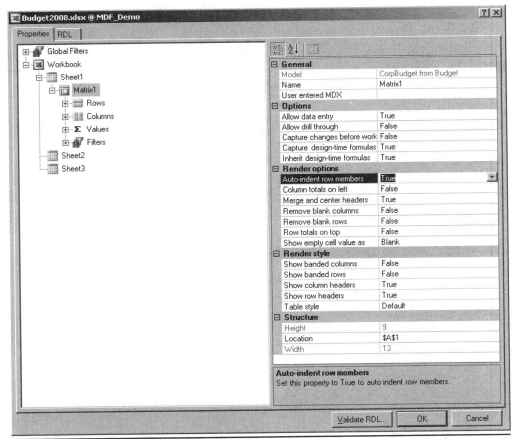

Figure 7-39   *Report properties can be used to fine tune the functional and display characteristics of PPS Planning forms and reports.*

a global filter will change the Entity dimension member selection for all the matrixes if the dimension member selection is changed in any one matrix in the report.

Once the business report is finalized with all the required work sheets and matrixes, it must be saved using the Save link under the Reports icon in the PerformancePoint ribbon. The report will be saved to the default Report storage location for the application defined in the Planning Administration Console. It is important to use the Save link under the Reports icon, since the regular save action in Excel will not save the report to the PPS Planning Server. Once the business report is saved, it can be published as a form template by selecting the Publish -> As Form Template... option under the Reports icon in the PerformancePoint ribbon. Selecting this option will open the Publish as Form Template dialog box. The value CorpBgt2008 is used as the Name and Label for the purpose of the examples in this chapter. The Budget model site is selected from the drop-down list for Model Site:. Clicking OK will close the dialog box and save the report as a form template in the PPS Planning Server. These form templates are visible in the Forms workspace within the Planning Business Modeler as described in the section on Forms and Reports earlier in this chapter.

Submitting Plan Data

Submitting the plan data is the ultimate goal of PPS Planning system. This means budget, forecast, or any other planning data is submitted to a centralized data store, where users with appropriate permissions have real-time access to the plan data, and can report on that single version of truth throughout the enterprise, along with actual operational data from other systems. Submitting the plan data is done using the PerformancePoint Add-in for Excel installed on the end users computers.

In the earlier section on Process Management under Planning Business Modeler we discussed how assignment instances are created for the end business users. We used the specific example of creating the assignment Budget 2008 for user Contributor1. The PerformancePoint action pane is available when Contributor1 logs into the PPS Planning Server using the PerformancePoint Add-in for Excel. To open an assignment, the user must select the Assignments pane by clicking on the Assignment link towards the bottom of the action pane. The assignment pane will then display a link for each active assignment assigned to the user. In the case of the example used in this chapter, the link named Budget2008-1 is available for Contributor1 as can be seen in the top left quadrant of Figure 7-40. The suffix -1 at the end of the assignment name denotes that this is the first instance of the cycle. This number then increments for subsequent cycles of the assignment.

When the user clicks on a link for any active assignment, the assignment Form opens up in the Excel work space, similar to the one seen in the top right quadrant of Figure 7-40. The data entry region where the user can enter the plan data is highlighted in yellow color in the Excel worksheet. Here the user can enter the plan data. By default, the users can enter data only in the cells that represent the leaf level of all the dimensions. However, Spreading of Data Entry can be turned on in the Options, which will allow the users to enter data at non-leaf levels as well. Spreading can be done evenly across all the children of the data-entry level, or based on the ratio of pre-populated data in the cells. In the example shown in Figure 7-40, the Account dimension members Airfare, Meals and Entertainment, and Hotel represent some of the leaf levels of the Account dimension, whereas member Travel Expenses is not a leaf level member. So, by default, the user will not be able to enter data directly to the Travel Expenses row. The data that is entered at the leaf level members of Airfare, Meals and Entertainment, and Hotel will automatically be summed up and presented at the Travel Expenses level. If Spreading is turned on, data can be directly entered at the Travel Expenses level and it will be allocated to the leaf levels of Airfare, Meals and Entertainment, and Hotel depending on the spreading type selected.

The user can also use the same form for entering plan data for multiple members of the Entity dimensions. The different Entity dimension members are selected using the Select Filters dialog box that opens up when the user clicks on the down arrow next to the Entity member currently selected. This kind of Form design eliminates the need for multiple forms for similar planning needs across the various work centers within a corporation. The users' access to the data can be controlled by setting the right permissions in the Planning Business Modeler client tool.

There are three options available for a user to save the plan data, as can be seen under the Actions: drop-down box in the bottom-left quadrant of Figure 7-40. The Save Privately option saves the changed data privately to the users local hard drive, and the changes are not propagated to the PPS Planning server. The Submit Draft option saves the data changes to the server. This allows the contributor to share the changed data with other users who have the appropriate permissions. The user can still modify or update the data. The Submit Final option saves the assignment status and populates the changes to the PPS Planning server. This will promote the assignment to the next step in the workflow process such as review or approval. The data cannot be modified by the contributor after the Submit Final action.

The Submit Final action should be selected once the user has entered all the plan data, and ready to submit the data to the PPS Planning Server. Clicking the green arrow button next to the drop-down box will initiate the selected action. The user can enter an optional comment in the next step and then click OK to finalize the action.

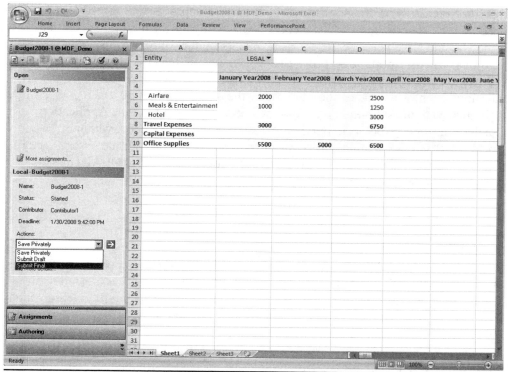

Figure 7-40 *The PPS Planning data entry form appears to the business end users in the familiar Excel interface.*

Once the Submit Final action is executed, the contributor user will not be able to make any more changes to the plan data stored on the PPS Planning Server.

If a reviewer is defined for the assignment, the reviewer will receive e-mail notifications when a contributor submits the data. The reviewer can open the assignment just like the contributor opens the assignment by clicking on the link for the assignment in the Assignment pane. Towards the lower half of the Assignment pane is a link that says Review or Approve Submissions of this Form. Clicking this link will open the Review and Approve Assignments dialog box. This box will display all the assignments that are assigned to that user for reviewing. The reviewer can select multiple submissions by checking the check box next to each submission in the dialog box. There are various options available to the Reviewer under the Actions drop-down box. If data modification is enabled for the reviewer, the reviewer will be able to modify the data submitted by the contributor and re-submit it. He can also review the submissions with or without any modifications.

If an Approver is defined for the assignment, the approver will receive e-mail notifications after the review is done; the approver opens the assignments in the same way the reviewer accesses the assignments. In the Actions drop-down box, Approver has the option to Approve the submission or Reject it. Rejecting a submission will automatically send it back to the contributor that is responsible for the submission, where he or she can modify the data and submit it again.

If approved, the submitted plan data will be available in both the Application Database, Budget_AppDB in our example, and in the OLAP cube, which is CorpBudget in our example. This data can be exported to an external system using data export rules, queried directly from the relational database or OLAP cube, or accessed using any of the several reporting tools.

Summary

The Planning Server is a large product by itself, yet is represents just one of the three main pillars of PerformancePoint Server 2007. Planning Server was created to allow organizations to more easily manage the budgeting and forecasting processes, which are often tedious, complex procedures. PerformancePoint Server seeks to ameliorate the process by providing a strong security model that focuses users on just what they can do. This is achieved first by defining an approval process that flows though the system, so that changes are submitted to the approver automatically and once approved, changes flow into the system. Finally, it's achieved by taking the new data and integrating with the other pieces of PerformancePoint Server. This means that the budget and forecast data can be used as the targets in the monitoring module, so that KPIs can be comparing actual data against the budget submitted through the planning module. When users perform analysis, they can examine the variances between the actual performance and the expectations set forth during the business planning process.

As can be seen by the length of this chapter, there is significant work involved in setting up the Planning Server and creating models. Once this work is done, however, the process is designed to be as simple as possible for end users. The use of Excel as the front end for entering data for the Planning server allows users to work in a familiar environment, and the form templates can leverage the full power of Excel to apply business rules as necessary. Having a centralized Planning server enforces standards on the planning process across the entire business as well.

PART

III

Additional Tools and Security

PerformancePoint Deployment and Security

erformancePoint Server is a somewhat unusual product in that it contains three distinct areas of focus: Monitoring, Analysis, and Planning. Many companies may find themselves using the Monitoring and Analysis components only, while other businesses are excited about the Planning module, but do not have plans to deploy the Monitoring and Analysis pieces. Of course, some businesses will seek to implement all three. In addition, with the first release, there is little doubt that some people will also install various components of ProClarity. As was seen in Chapters 5 and 6, dashboards will be deployed to SharePoint, so either Windows SharePoint Services or Microsoft Office SharePoint Server is added to the software mix. Combine all this software with SQL Server, Analysis Services, and Reporting Services, and it is clear that there is a wide variety of applications that can combine to deliver the BI experience. The good news is that in most cases, all the software does not have to be, and in most cases *should* not be, installed and run on a single server.

Given this wide array of components, it is important to understand the installation process and how PerformancePoint Server can be configured and secured. This chapter will in no way provide a complete resource on the subject, because changes are coming soon in the forms of Windows Server 2008 and SQL Server 2008. Future service packs to SQL Server, PerformancePoint, or the operating system may change recommendations significantly.

Deploying PerformancePoint Server

PerformancePoint Server may encompass three specific areas, but the installation is broken into two separate setup routines. The Monitoring Server includes both the monitoring and analysis pieces and covers the items discussed in Chapter 5 and the first half of Chapter 6. This is where the Dashboard Designer resides, and allows for the creation of KPIs, indicators, scorecards, reports, dashboards, and so forth. The Planning Server is a separate installation and includes all the components for creating and working with the planning items as discussed in Chapter 7. Because there are two separate installation components, this chapter will first discuss deployment of the Monitoring Server, and then describe deployment for the Planning Server.

It's important to understand that while there are two separate installations, there are several files that make up the suite of tools for the Planning Server. In addition, there is a single setup page, similar to the one for SQL Server 2005, which allows administrators to install the Planning Server and its components, as well as the Monitoring Server. Despite this single setup page, the installations will frequently be done separately.

Installing the Monitoring Server

The Monitoring Server consists of the server itself, which is made up of ASP.NET pages, web services, and related components. These will be installed on a web server running Internet Information Services, or IIS. The Monitoring Server will also need access to a SQL Server 2005 server, on which the monitoring database will be installed. The database is required because it stores the metadata for KPIs, scorecards, dashboards, and so forth. SharePoint will have to be installed, and this can be either Windows SharePoint Services 3.0 (WSS) or Microsoft Office SharePoint Server 2007 (MOSS). There are other requirements as well, such as the .NET Framework 2.0, ASP.NET 2.0 AJAX Extensions 1.0, and ADOMD.NET 9.0 SP2 (if the dashboards will be accessing data from Analysis Services), but these requirements are subject to change so make sure you check the latest installation guide.

There are six separate components plus the Monitoring Server database that can be installed with the Monitoring Server. These components, as well as the database, are listed in Table 8-1.

The hardware requirements for the Monitoring Server are quite minimal by today's standards. The recommendation is for two dual-core 64-bit processors with 2GB RAM, but the server runs on a single processor with one core and 1GB RAM. Again, check the current recommendations because changes are likely as patches and service packs are issued.

Component	Description
PerformancePoint Monitoring Server Web Service	This component allows the Dashboard Designer to communicate with the Monitoring database.
PerformancePoint Monitoring database	This is the database holding metadata for KPIs, scorecards, and other elements in the Monitoring Server.
PerformancePoint Dashboard Designer installation site	This site allows users to download and use the Dashboard Designer.
PerformancePoint Dashboard Viewer for SharePoint Services	This component is a web part that allows SharePoint to display dashboards from the Monitoring Server.
PerformancePoint Dashboard Web Preview	This component allows dashboards to be deployed and viewed as ASP.NET pages.
PerformancePoint Scorecard Viewer for Reporting Services	This component allows for the viewing of scorecards in Report Definition Language (RDL) format.
PerformancePoint Monitoring Plug-in for Report Designer	This plug-in allows Visual Studio 2005 to edit scorecards that are saved in RDL format.

Table 8-1   *Components Making Up the PerformancePoint Monitoring Server*

The initial installation of the Monitoring Server is extremely straightforward. Other than choosing the installation location, there are no options for the administrator to choose, and installation will proceed. However, once the basic installation is done, the administrator must run the Monitoring Server Configuration Manager before the Monitoring Server is ready for use. The Configuration Manager starts out by checking for all necessary prerequisites, and then moves to the screen shown in Figure 8-1.

Figure 8-1 shows only five options, while Table 8-1 listed seven; this is because the Monitoring Web Service, Dashboard Web Preview, and Dashboard Designer Installation Site components are all included under the Monitoring Server check box. All other components match those as found in Table 8-1.

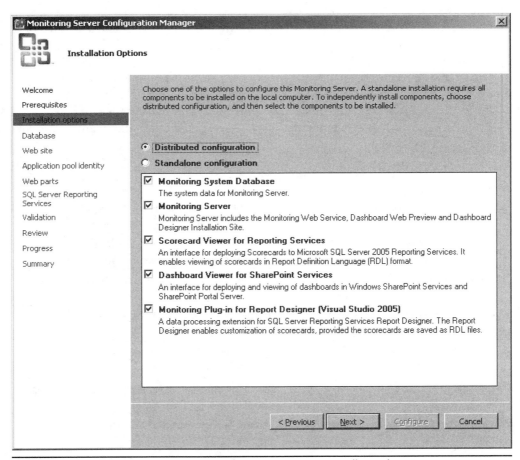

Figure 8-1   *The Monitoring Server Configuration Manager allows the Monitoring Server components to be deployed on a single server or across multiple servers.*

The primary purpose of this screen is to allow administrators to choose whether or not the Monitoring Server will be installed on a single machine or distributed across multiple machines. In scenarios that include web farms for scale-out processing, or with clustered SQL Server machines for high availability, it often makes sense to separate components. The Monitoring Server Database will be installed only on the server running SQL Server, and these machines might not even have IIS installed. The web servers, meanwhile, would have the Monitoring Server installed, but might not have the Monitoring Plug-in for Report Designer. The server or servers running SharePoint will host the web parts that display PerformancePoint Server dashboards, but PerformancePoint Server itself might be running on separate servers. Separating the components across servers can lead to increased scalability and improved uptime. Choosing a standalone configuration installation grays out all the check boxes and installs everything on the local machine.

Choosing to install the Monitoring System Database presents the administrator with a screen to specify the server name and database name to use for the monitoring database. This allows the administrator to change both the server and database name to conform to any existing standards and allows for the installation of a database to occur on another server instead of requiring the setup routine to be run on both servers. Installing the database on a different server requires that the user account running the installation has administrative privileges on the SQL Server machine or that the user person performing the installation use the Provision an Existing Database option. The Provision an Existing Database option allows the database administrator on the target SQL Server machine to create a blank PPS Monitoring database. This means that installers of PerformancePoint Server can provision it and can have their tables created on that centralized SQL Server machine.

The next step in the installation process is to specify the account under which the Monitoring Server service will run. This is called the Service Identity, or SI, account, and all Monitoring Server work is done under this SI account. The SI account is used by the IIS application pool, which is where all the Monitoring Server processes run. The default is to use the Network Service account, but a good practice is to create a domain account specifically for PerformancePoint Server. The reason for this is that the SI account will have to have permissions to Analysis Services cubes, and having the SI run under Network Service account means granting cube permissions to the Network Service account, an account under which many other applications may be running. In fact, Microsoft is recommending that the Monitoring Server SI account be the same as the SharePoint SI account and that the SI account should only be assigned to the IIS_WPG group on the machine on which Monitoring Server is installed. Figure 8-2 shows this page of the Configuration Manager and has been set to a domain user.

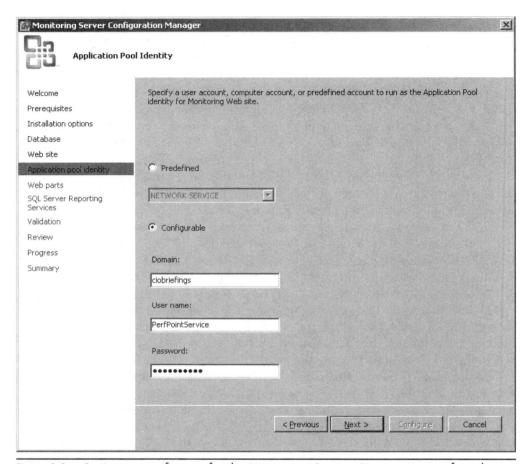

Figure 8-2   *Setting a specific user for the Monitoring Service SI account is preferred to leaving the default of Network Service.*

   The reason that Microsoft is recommending that the SharePoint SI account be the same as the Monitoring Server SI account is because the PerformancePoint Server web parts will access data as the SharePoint application pool SI account. All SharePoint data connections happen under the control of the SharePoint SI account. The PerformancePoint SI account is only used to connect to data sources from the Dashboard Designer. Note that any chosen user will have to be granted permissions to any Analysis Services cubes that data is being retrieved from.
   The next two screens ask for the SharePoint site and the SQL Server instance on which to install the web parts and the Report Server viewer, respectively. After entering these, the Configuration Manager validates all the entered data and allows the administrator to complete the configuration. This process configures

the IIS application pool, grants permissions to the database and IIS as needed, adds components to SharePoint and Reporting Services, and creates the relational database to hold the Monitoring Server metadata, among other steps.

It is not necessary to run the user interface for the Configuration Manager. The command line tool is called PMServerConfigManger.exe and is located in %program files%\Microsoft Office PerformancePoint Server\3.0\Tools\MonitoringConfiguration by default. There are a number of command line switches that can be used; not specifying any switches loads the GUI, as shown previously in Figures 8-1 and 8-2.

After installing and configuring the Monitoring Server, the Monitoring Central site can be shown by navigating a browser to http://<servername>:<port number>/central, where the server name is the name of the server running the Monitoring Server Web Service, and the port number is the port specified during installation (the default is 40000). Monitoring Central contains only two buttons: the first downloads and runs Dashboard Designer, while the second takes the user to the Dashboard Designer Preview Site.

Once Monitoring Server is up and running, it creates two log files in the %temp% directory. These files are named MonitoringStatus and MonitoringVerbose, and each has the date appended, as well as an extension of .log. Therefore, the status file for January 5, 2008, would be MonitoringStatus1-5-2008.log if the system's date format is configured for US English.

Perhaps one of the biggest areas of confusion in PerformancePoint Server is how connections are made. Most people think that the SharePoint web parts connect to the Monitoring Server machine, which then connects to the data source. This is not the case; the Monitoring Server supports the Dashboard Designer and the preview sites, but does not come into play when dashboards are viewed through SharePoint. Instead, SharePoint connects directly to the data sources, so all caching and security for the user's session occurs on the SharePoint server. This is true even if you export the dashboard directly to SharePoint and don't use the web parts directly.

On a related note, administrators might want to consider setting up ConnectionPerUser in the web.config file. ConnectionPerUser sets up dedicated connections per user rather than pulling existing connections from a connection pool. This is useful when applying security on individual users because connections in a connection pool can only be reused if all the connection information is the same, and this includes the username and password.

Installing the Planning Server

The Planning Server consists of two different web services: a remote administration service and a database. These are installed on a web server running Internet Information Services. The Planning Server will also need access to a SQL Server 2005 server, on which the planning database will be installed. The planning database will run on SQL Server 2005 Standard Edition, but access to Analysis Services requires the Enterprise Edition. There are also other requirements, such as the .NET Framework 2.0, ASP.NET 2.0, and a post-SP2 cumulative update. Make sure to check the current requirements, because they may change as updates are made to the Planning Server.

There are three separate components plus the Planning Server database that can be installed with the Planning Server. These components and the database are listed in Table 8-2.

The hardware requirements for the Planning Server are nearly the same as the ones for the Monitoring Server. The recommendation is for two dual-core 64-bit processors with 2GB RAM, but the servers will run on a single processor with one core and 1GB RAM. Again, check the current recommendations as changes are likely as new patches and service packs are issued.

While the Monitoring Server had just a single installation file, the Planning Server contains multiple files, and thus includes a setup.hta file to guide the installation process. In fact, one of the links on the page is for the Monitoring Server, so the setup. hta file works as a single point of installation for all the PerformancePoint Server components. There are three options in the Planning section of the installation page:

▶ Install Planning Server

▶ Install Planning Business Modeler

▶ Install PerformancePoint Add-in for Excel

Choosing to install the Planning Server results in a process that is similar to the one resulting from the installation of the Monitoring Server. After entering only the installation path, the server installs and then seeks to run the Planning Server Configuration Manager. After verifying that the requisite software is already installed, the Configuration Manager presents the user with the option of performing a distributed or standalone installation. Like the Monitoring Server, the Planning

Component	Description
PerformancePoint Planning Web Service	This component is used by the Planning Business Modeler and the PerformancePoint Add-in for Excel.
PerformancePoint Planning Process Service	This service is used for jobs and workflow tasks in PerformancePoint.
PerformancePoint Planning database	This is the database holding all the data of the Planning Server.
PerformancePoint Planning Remote Administration Service	This service is used by the Planning Administration Console and can be used to modify server settings, manage roles, and so forth.

Table 8-2 *Components Making Up the PerformancePoint Planning Server*

Server can be installed on multiple separate machines in order to work in a web farm environment. Figure 8-3 shows that there are four options for what may be installed at this point: the SQL Server databases, the Planning Process Service, the Planning Web Service, and the Planning Administration Console.

After selecting the components to install, the Configuration Manager allows the administrator to enter the name of the SQL Server machine that the database will be installed on. At this point, a screen asks for the name of a user with administrative privileges for the server that the Planning Server is being deployed to. This user will be the first user added to the Global Administrator role and will be used to add other administrators through the Planning Administration Console. Note that this screen asks for the name of the user, but not the password.

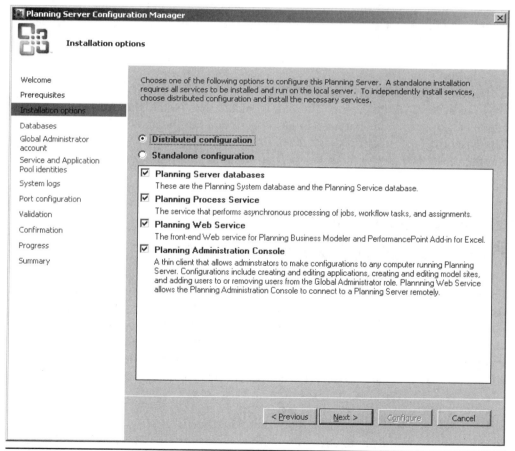

Figure 8-3 *The Planning Server Configuration Manager allows the Planning Server components to be deployed on a single server or across multiple servers.*

The next screen asks for the server running Analysis Services. You should simply enter the name of the server and click Next.

The next screen asks for the name of a domain user to act as the Planning Server Service Identity (SI) account. This account is separate from the SI account for the Monitoring Server. In addition, this screen does not include a drop-down box as seen with the Monitoring Server in Figure 8-2. Instead, the only option is to add a domain user, and in this case the password will be necessary. Microsoft explicitly recommends against this account having administrative privileges to any server running Planning Server.

The next screen asks for the location of both the audit logs and the trace logs. It also allows the administrator to enable or disable audit and trace logging; both are on by default.

A page now appears that asks for the ports that you would like to run the servers on. The default port for the Planning Web Server is 46787 and the default port for the Planning Administration Console is 46788.

The remaining screens simply verify the previous information and complete the installation.

The Planning Business Modeler follows the same installation process as the previous servers, simply asking for a location and then installing. The Business Modeler, however, does not need to be configured after the installation is complete. Likewise, the PerformancePoint Add-in for Excel simply asks for an installation path and then installs itself, without any post-installation configuration required.

Security Considerations for PerformancePoint Server

There are a number of places that security can be applied to when dealing with PerformancePoint Server. These include standard network security, using NTLM or Active Directory, IIS security, SharePoint security, and security in SQL Server and Analysis Services. This next section will assume that standard network security has been set up and that you can log on and is a member of some groups on the system. Upon launching Internet Explorer, the user attempts to access a SharePoint site hosting a PerformancePoint Dashboard—this is where security issues enter the picture.

Internet Information Services Security

IIS contains several different security options for each virtual directory. First is anonymous access, which allows anyone to access that particular site. Anonymous access works by logging all users in as the same user, which is IUSR_<servername>

by default. Windows manages this user and password so administrators don't have to worry about maintaining this account. The good news is that this option is incredibly easy, as nothing has to be done and things just work. This is not recommended when dealing with PerformancePoint, however, as all users look like the same user to PerformancePoint and there is no way to restrict access at that point. All users will be able to see exactly the same things.

Basic authentication is another option. This setting in IIS opens a dialog box in Internet Explorer that requires the user to log in. This option works but there are a couple of disadvantages. First, the user must log in with each visit to the site and if they are internal users, they're already authenticated on the network. Second, the username and password are sent as clear text if encryption is not being used.

The only recommended setting for PerformancePoint is integrated authentication, officially known in IIS as Integrated Windows authentication. Integrated authentication passes the credentials of the current user to the web server automatically, and does so in an encrypted fashion, even if the web server connection is not encrypted with Secure Sockets Layer (SSL). Using this method, the server sees the user as their true network identity.

Secure Sockets Layer

Secure Sockets Layer is a standard technology for encrypting the data stream between a browser and a web server. SSL works by generating a key that lasts just for the current session and sharing that key with the browser; the browser and server then use keys to encrypt and decrypt data in a bidirectional manner throughout the length of the session. The good news is that SSL works at a lower level than the application, so no application changes are necessary; in fact, the web application will be unaware if SSL is being employed or not.

Microsoft recommends that SSL be used for PerformancePoint Server work. In fact, PerformancePoint Server is set to require SSL by default during installation. This is a good best practice, but it requires the installation of an SSL certificate on the server, which may not be available in all cases.

Kerberos and Delegation

One of the most confusing aspects of security is determining the users who may be logging into SQL Server and Analysis Services. By default, the users seen by both SQL Server and Analysis Services are users set up through the SI account. No matter what method is used in IIS, the servers run under an SI account and it is those SI accounts that appear as the calling user to the databases.

If security in SQL Server or Analysis Services is set up to only show certain data to certain users, it is important to know the originating user of a request; the identity of the SI account isn't good enough. In this case, the SI account must take on the credentials of the original calling user.

In order for the SI account to mimic the original caller, either basic or integrated authentication must be used. Next, Kerberos must be installed; this is because it is only through Kerberos delegation that the current user can be impersonated through IIS back to the data source. Kerberos allows IIS to take the user token and present that to the data source as the user making the request, and in this fashion SQL Server or Analysis Services can send back just the correct data to the user.

In many cases, IIS can impersonate the user without Kerberos if both IIS and Analysis Services are on the same server, but if IIS and Analysis Services are on separate machines, this leads to the "double hop" scenario. In this case, the user requests a page from their browser, so data flows from the client machine to the web server (the first hop). The web server now needs data from Analysis Services and makes a call to the server running Analysis Services (the second hop). Even if integrated authentication is used, the user's credentials cannot be passed from IIS to Analysis Services on another server, unless Kerberos is installed and configured.

When working with PerformancePoint, there is a setting in the web.config file that must be changed in order to enable impersonation when using Kerberos. This property is called Bpm.ServerConnectionPerUser and it must be enabled to allow the impersonation token to be passed. This only applies to the Monitoring Server, as the Planning Server is set up to always pass user credentials.

Summary

Installation of the various PerformancePoint modules is relatively straightforward. There are actually few options to choose during installation and configuration. Most commonly, people will set the Service Identity the Monitoring Server to a domain user account created for that purpose, while the Service Identity for the Planning Server must be a domain account. Once the servers are installed and configured, they will run under the context of the Service Identity assigned to them.

PerformancePoint exists in an environment in which many components have security settings, such as IIS, SharePoint, SQL Server, Analysis Services, and so forth. Using Kerberos is the easiest way to get all the components working and have the user's identity flow from the front-end client through IIS and SharePoint back to the data source. Since not every company uses Kerberos, there are considerations for handling data communications in a double hop scenario, in which either custom security solutions must be created or the data sources must accept a single user account for all requests.

Analysis with Excel 2007

Prior to Microsoft's acquisition of ProClarity Corporation, their primary client tool for working with Analysis Services was Excel. Excel was an adequate client tool that worked for users who didn't need the power and flexibility of ProClarity and who were already familiar with Excel. It made sense to use Excel as a client, since many organizations run much of their business on Excel (often to the chagrin of the IT department).

With the advent of Office 2007, Microsoft significantly enhanced the analytic capabilities of Excel 2007, moving it closer to a true analytics tool. It's still not as powerful as the ProClarity Professional client—which is obviously dedicated to doing nothing but analysis against an Analysis Services cube—but Excel 2007 contains significant improvements for performing analytics, and has moved into the realm where it is a real option for all but pure data analysts. Once again, the key point is to know the users and what they need when looking at data. It's entirely possible that Excel 2007 will satisfy the needs of many knowledge workers in the organization when they need to perform analysis beyond that provided by the Analytic Chart or Analytic Grid of PerformancePoint Server.

Performing Analysis with Excel 2007

In late 2006, Microsoft released Office 2007 and SQL Server Service Pack 2. The reason these two releases roughly coincided was that SQL Server Service Pack 2 included a number of Analysis Services enhancements designed to better integrate with Office 2007. The Office and Analysis Services teams worked closely to ensure that Excel 2007 would support nearly all the features of Analysis Services 2005 and would be a powerful client tool for analyzing the data in cubes.

Excel 2007 achieves this through many enhancements to the PivotTable and PivotChart reports in Excel. The PivotTable and PivotChart tools are nothing new in Excel, but they now provide significantly stronger tools and capabilities for performing analytics. Excel 2007 now understands measure groups, KPIs, actions, and many other features of Analysis Services 2005. This chapter will describe how Excel 2007 can be used as an analytics tool for working with Analysis Services 2005 cubes.

Using the PivotTable

The first step in working with Analysis Services 2005 from Excel 2007 is to connect to the Analysis Services database or a specific cube. On the Data ribbon in Excel 2007, users can click on the From Other Sources button and then choose From Analysis

Services from the menu. This opens the Data Connection Wizard, which has a first screen that asks for a server name and login credentials. After clicking next, the user is presented with a page that has a drop-down list box of all the databases, and for each database, a list of cubes. As shown in Figure 9-1, there is a check box that asks whether the user wants to connect to a specific cube or table; unchecking this box merely prompts the user later in the process, which means that leaving it checked and selecting a cube now is often easier.

As Figure 9-1 shows, a database may contain both cubes and perspectives. A perspective is similar to a view in a relational database, in that it restricts what is seen to just what the cube developer has specified. For example, a cube may contain a number of dimensions, measure groups, measures, KPIs, and so forth, covering a broad range of the business. A cube developer may choose to create one perspective that includes just the items related to finance and another related to just human resources, for example. From an end-user standpoint, perspectives and cubes work exactly the same way, so in this case the user should select just what they want to see. This chapter will assume the user has the entire Adventure Works cube selected.

The next screen of the wizard has several options on it. The first is the name of the data connection file as it will be stored on the hard drive. There is also a check box to allow for the saving of a password if the user chose to enter a username

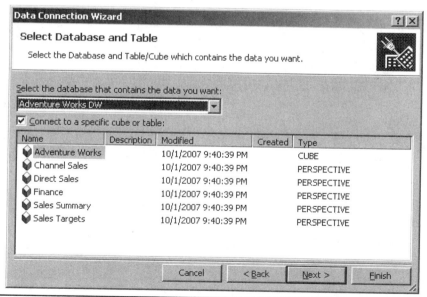

Figure 9-1 *The Data Connection Wizard allows users to connect Excel 2007 PivotTables and PivotCharts to many different data sources, including Analysis Services cubes.*

and password on the first screen of the wizard. There is an optional description field available, and then a field for a friendly name. This is the name of the data connection as it will appear in the future if the user clicks on the Existing Connections button on the Data ribbon. By default this is server name, database name, and cube name, but shortening it often makes sense. Figure 9-2 shows it renamed to a much simpler name. The Wizard screen also enables the user to type in search keywords and then click on a check box that attempts to use the file to refresh data. Checking that particular box means that if any changes have been made to the connection file, those changes will be picked up by the PivotTable when the data is refreshed. Finally, there is a button to set the authentication method if Excel Services is being used.

After clicking the Finish button, the Import Data dialog box appears as shown in Figure 9-3. This dialog box offers several options, including the ability to view the data in a PivotTable, both a PivotChart and PivotTable, or just create the connection

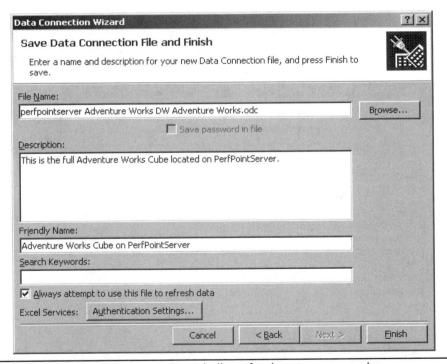

Figure 9-2 *The Data Connection Wizard allows for the connection to have a name, description, and keywords, along with a saved password and a flag to always view the connection information in the file before refreshing the data.*

Figure 9-3   *The Import Data dialog box allows users to add a PivotTable, both a PivotTable and PivotChart, or just create the connection, and choose where to display the data.*

file without importing any data. The dialog box also asks where the PivotTable should be placed.

Also on the Import Data dialog box is a Properties button that opens a Connection Properties dialog box. This box, shown in Figure 9-4, contains several options that may be important when dealing with data from a cube. The Refresh Control section has a check box for enabling background refreshes, which is checked and disabled so the user cannot change it; this option means that the user can continue to use Excel while the data is refreshed in the background. Understand, however, that in this case the refresh is kicked off manually by the user. A second check box allows for an automatic refresh in minutes, ranging from one to 32,767, or once every minute to once every approximately 23 days. Finally, a check box can force the data to be refreshed each time the spreadsheet is open, and then a check box under that can have the data removed before the spreadsheet is saved. Removing the data before saving the spreadsheet prevents users from ever seeing old data in a situation in which the data cannot be refreshed.

The OLAP Server Formatting section determines whether or not formatting options from the cube are honored when the data is rendered in Excel. Cube developers have the option of setting a number of properties on cube data, including the four shown here: Number Format, Font Style, Fill Color, and Text Color. If these check boxes are selected, the data displayed in the PivotTable will use any formatting for these properties that might have been specified in the cube.

The OLAP Drill Through section determines the maximum number of records that will be returned by a drill through operation on a cube. Drill through is taking

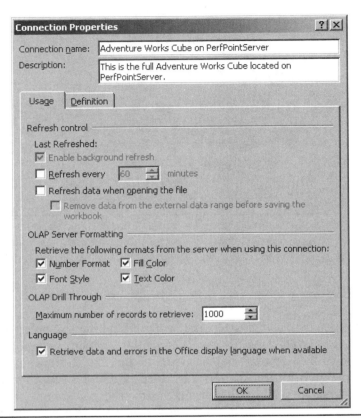

Figure 9-4   *The Connection Properties dialog box can control data refreshes, cube formatting options, and the number of records to retrieve when drilling through, among other options.*

a measure in a grid and asking for all the records in the cube that contribute to that particular value. The challenge with drilling through is that users may not understand what they are doing, and drilling through from a high level could return millions or even billions of records. To prevent users from having to wait long periods of time for the data, or possibly consume the available memory on their local machine, the number of records returned for a drill through operation can be capped. The default is 1000 records, although this can certainly be changed.

After changing any properties as desired and choosing the location of the PivotTable report from the Import Data dialog box, the PivotTable is added to the spreadsheet and the Field List window is placed on the right-hand side of the spreadsheet. Figure 9-5 shows the default layout for the Field List as well as the empty PivotTable on the spreadsheet.

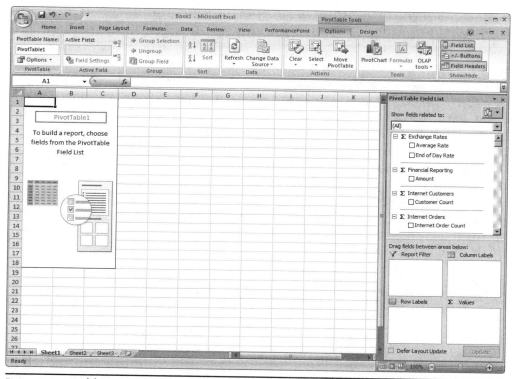

Figure 9-5   *Adding a PivotTable to a spreadsheet shows an empty PivotTable and opens the Field List along the right side of the page.*

The Field List is broken into two sections: a Fields section and an Areas section. By default the Fields section is on top and the Areas section is below the Fields section and contains four boxes for the filter, columns, rows, and values (the measures). The Fields section contains the measures first, broken down in measure groups. Next come the KPIs, followed by the dimensions and their attributes and hierarchies.

The layout of the Field List can be changed. At the top of the Field List is a button that can alter the layout to show the Areas section beside the Fields section, the Fields section only, or the Areas selection only in a couple of different layouts. On the Options tab of the ribbon bar, which appears under a larger PivotTable Tools tab, there is a button labeled Field List that can toggle the entire panel on and off.

With the Field List visible, it's now possible to create a report by simply dragging and dropping or by clicking the check boxes beside the items in the Field List. Assume that the user scrolls down to the Sales Summary measure group and selects the Sales Amount measure. Clicking the check box next to this measure will add it to the Values box in the Areas section. The value will now appear in the grid as the total sales amount for all time, all products, all customers, and so forth; it will be the total sales amount in the cube, which is just under $110 million.

Scrolling down to the Date dimension, expanding Calendar, and selecting Date.Calendar adds that to the Column Labels box, while moving to the Product dimension and selecting Product Model Categories adds the Product Model Categories to the Row Labels box. In addition, the PivotTable updates to show the members on the rows and columns, as expected. Totals are also turned on for both rows and columns automatically. Figure 9-6 shows what this simple report looks like, along with the layout shown in the Field List.

There are a number of things to notice about the PivotTable in Figure 9-6. First, the upper left-hand corner is labeled Sales Amount. This is because there is only one measure on the report at this time, and so the name appears there. Adding additional

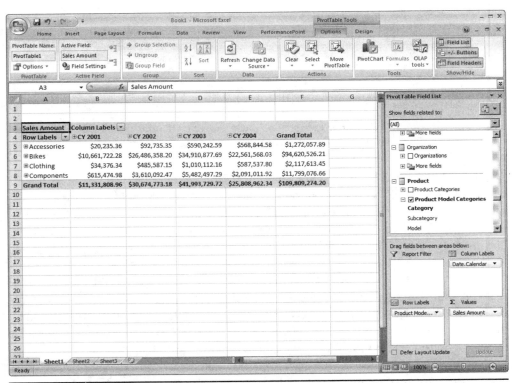

Figure 9-6 A simple report created in a PivotTable. The data ties back to an Analysis Services cube.

measures will place the measure names over additional columns under the time values, which will be seen later.

The members in both the rows and columns have plus signs next to them to indicate that they can be expanded. Not surprisingly, clicking on one of the plus sign buttons expands that member and shows its children, while the parent remains on the screen. Clicking on the plus sign to show the children for that member changes the plus sign to a minus sign, of course. There is a way to hide the plus and minus signs; the Options ribbon contains a button labeled +/- Buttons that will toggle the plus and minus signs on and off. Even if the plus and minus signs are removed, double-clicking on the member will either expand or collapse it, depending on its current state. Figure 9-7 shows that the year 2003 has been expanded one time to show the semesters of 2003. In addition, a subtotal for the year 2003 now appears in the grid. This will be discussed in a moment.

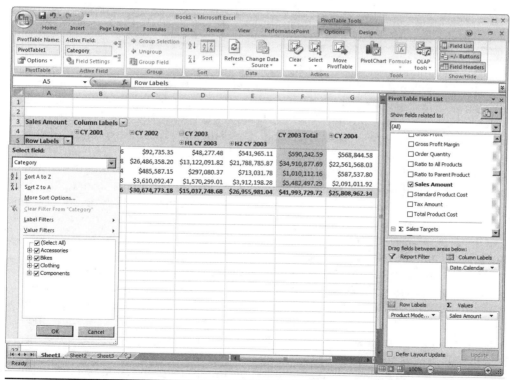

Figure 9-7   *The report showing an expanded 2003 and the drop-down list for the Row Labels*

Sorting and Filtering

There are also two drop-down list boxes: Column Labels and Row Labels. Dropping down either list reveals a series of options, as shown in Figure 9-7. There are two sort options at the top, and they allow you to sort either in ascending or descending order. A third option, labeled More Sort Options, opens a dialog box that allows users to sort in other ways, including manually, by simply dragging and dropping the members in the preferred order.

The drop-down list also allows users to apply label filters and value filters to the data. Label filters restrict the data based on the label that is being shown. For example, Figure 9-7 shows Accessories, Bikes, Clothing, and Components for the row labels. Clicking on Label Filters and choosing Begins With opens a simple dialog box that asks for a value on which to filter the data. Putting in just the letter **c** and then clicking OK immediately reduces the values in the list to just Clothing and Components. Begins With is just one of the many options for filtering data, with others including Equals, Does Not Equal, Contains, Greater Than, Between, and so on. The Column Labels drop-down list provides the same options as for Row Labels, although in this case the column contains dates. This means that the Label Filters are changed to Date Filters, and that filter methods include Last Month, Next Month, This Month, and similar values for days, weeks, and quarters.

Value Filters limit the items in the rows or columns based on the values of the particular measure. For example, dropping down the list for Row Labels, selecting Value Filters, choosing Greater Than, and entering a value of 90,000,000 will restrict the members on the rows to just Bikes, since it is the only one with a Sales Amount of greater than $90,000,000.

The Row Labels and Column Labels drop-down list boxes can be toggled on and off using the Field Headers button on the Options ribbon. This helps clean up the report a bit, but also hides the easiest way to perform sorting and filtering options. An alternative way to reach the sorting and filtering options is to click the down arrow that appears to the right of hierarchies in the Field List. Figure 9-8 shows this option highlighted and the resulting menu for the Product Model Categories dimension.

There is another way to add filtering to a report, but this filtering works like the parameters on Reporting Services and ProClarity, creating a drop-down box that allows users to make selections to perform analysis. For example, users might want to easily filter by Sales Territory. Scrolling to the Sales Territory dimension in the Field List and then choosing the Sales Territory hierarchy by clicking the check box next to it will add it to the Row Labels box by default. The user can drag the hierarchy from the Fields section to the Report Filter box in the Areas section, or if it's already in another box in the Areas section, it can be dragged from that box into the Report Filter box. Adding the Sales Territory hierarchy to the Report Filter

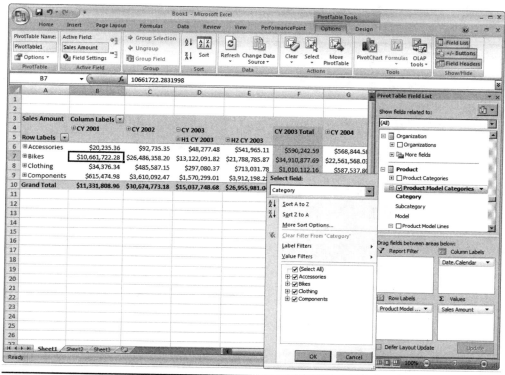

Figure 9-8   Selecting the drop-down arrow next to a hierarchy or member will bring up a menu that allows for sorting and filtering.

box adds a drop-down list at the top of the report that includes the members of the various levels of the hierarchy in a tree view format. Figure 9-9 shows what the filter looks like by default.

By default, the filter only allows a single selection. There is a check box on the filter itself labeled Select Multiple Items. Checking this box allows the user to select multiple items at once, even if they are from different levels of the hierarchy. Making multiple selections changes the display of the filter to (Multiple Items), but there is no indication of the items that have been selected. The only way to discover this is to open up the filter and look to see what is checked.

Multiple Dimensions, Subtotals, and Grand Totals

Adding multiple dimensions to either the rows or columns is simple. Checking the box next to a dimension in the Field List adds it to the Row Labels box and immediately adds it to the grid. If the user wants it on the columns instead of the rows, it can be

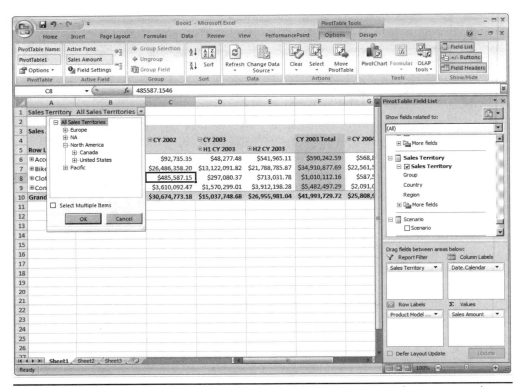

Figure 9-9   *Items added to the Report Filter box of the Areas section show up as a drop-down list that allows users to make selections without using the Field List.*

dragged from the Row Labels or, if the user hasn't checked the box, it can be dragged directly from the Fields section and dropped in the Column Labels box.

Figure 9-10 shows the results of adding the Sales Territory Group attribute hierarchy to the Row Labels. The product category is shown first, and then each territory group is shown for that category. Not surprisingly, the order of the dimensions in the row and columns boxes matters; if the user reverses the order of the Sales Territory Group and the Product Model Categories, the grid will change to show the territory group first, and under each territory group will be the product categories.

Figure 9-10 shows that the subtotals for each product category are on the same line as the category itself; in other words, the subtotals are at the top, above the breakdown by territory. This is common in many financial situations, but some users might want the subtotals turned off or to appear after the territories.

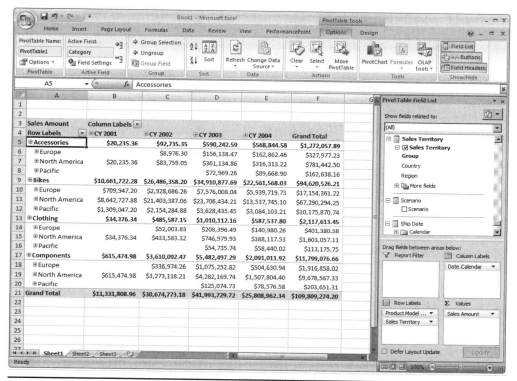

Figure 9-10 *Multiple dimensions can be added to the rows and columns. The order in which they appear in the row and column boxes determines how they will be displayed in the PivotTable.*

Measures cannot be moved to the Row Labels and Column Labels boxes directly. Choosing more than one measure lists the measures in the Values box, but it also adds a Values item to either the Column Labels or Row Labels box. This Values item can be moved from Column Labels to Row Labels or vice versa, and this will determine where the measures are displayed.

In order to control the subtotals, users can right-click on one of the labels and choose Field Settings. For example, right-clicking on Accessories and choosing Field Settings opens the Field Settings dialog box as shown in Figure 9-11. This dialog box is not specific to Accessories, but covers all the product categories that are displayed. The first tab covers options for subtotals and filters, and the first section can turn off subtotals or apply custom subtotals. Simply changing this option to None turns off the subtotals. Figure 9-11 shows the results of this in the background;

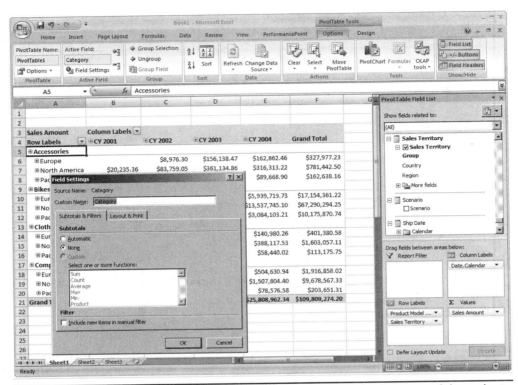

Figure 9-11 *Multiple dimensions can be added to the rows and columns, and the order in which they appear in the row and column boxes determines how they will be displayed in the PivotTable.*

as you can see, the subtotals are no longer shown for the Accessories product category, or for any other category.

A simpler method exists for turning subtotals on and off; users can simply right-click on one of the product category members and choose Subtotal "Category" (where "category" is the name of whatever member is being chosen). Clicking on the Subtotal "Category" will turn subtotals off; selecting it again will turn them back on. If the only desire is to toggle the display of the subtotals, this is an easy way to do it.

If the user wants the subtotals to appear but move to the bottom of the group, this can be done by again opening the Field Settings dialog box and moving to the Layout & Print tab. There is a check box on this tab labeled Display Subtotals at the Top of Each Group, and it is checked by default. Unchecking it moves the subtotals to the bottom of each group, provided that subtotals are being displayed. This adds a new row to the PivotTable for each group that contains the subtotals for that group.

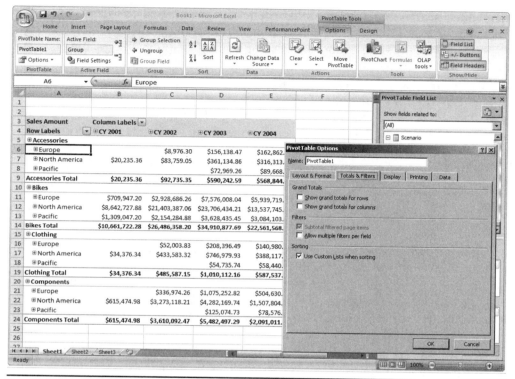

Figure 9-12   *Subtotals can be turned off or moved to the bottom of the group. Grand totals can be turned off for either rows or columns or both.*

Not only are subtotals shown by default, but the PivotTable also shows grand totals by default. These appear at the bottom and right of the PivotTable but can be turned off as part of setting properties for the entire PivotTable. Right-clicking anywhere in the PivotTable and then choosing PivotTable Options opens the PivotTable Options dialog box. There are many properties that can be altered via this dialog box, but grand totals are found on the Totals & Filters tab. Here, two check boxes control the row and column grand totals so they can be turned on and off independently. Figure 9-12 shows this dialog box with both the row and column grand totals turned off. The PivotTable reflects these changes, and also moves the subtotals to the bottom of the group as described in the previous paragraph.

Conditional Formatting and KPIs

Excel 2007 includes additional formatting capabilities that allow end users to apply conditional formatting to their Excel spreadsheets. One such feature is conditional formatting, which is not limited to PivotTables but can be used anywhere in Excel. There are several different kinds of conditional formatting available, and the choices can be found on the Home ribbon by clicking on the Conditional Formatting button. Figure 9-13 shows the various types of conditional formatting that can be applied, and these types are also described in Table 9-1.

Figure 9-13 shows the results of choosing to apply green Data Bars to the value area of the PivotTable. This was done by selecting all the value cells (not including the grand totals) and then selecting the green data bars from the Conditional Format, Data Bars menu. The cells clearly show the bars, with long bars representing higher values.

Multiple rules can be applied to cells, although changing the background or foreground colors in multiple rules can lead to confusion. Clearing the rules is as simple as clicking on the Conditional Formatting button and choosing Clear Rules. This gives the options of clearing all the rules in the spreadsheet or just the rules for the selected cells.

While conditional formatting includes icons similar to the indicators in PerformancePoint Server, it is possible to use KPIs that are embedded in Analysis Services cubes. These KPIs may or may not be the same as used in PerformancePoint Server scorecards, as PerformancePoint Server may contain its own KPIs that are not reflected in the cube. Regardless, in order to use KPIs found in cubes, the user need only select KPIs from the Field List. The KPIs appear just after the measures, and each KPI consists of four separate items: Value, Goal, Status, and Trend. Each of these acts like a separate measure, so they can be placed on the PivotTable independently of each

Conditional Format	Description
Highlight Cells Rules	These rules are very similar to the exception highlighting found in the ProClarity Desktop Professional client and they allow for highlighting to be applied if numbers are greater than, less than, equal to, between, or one of several other options.
Top/Bottom Rules	These rules allow for formatting to be applied to the top or bottom X%, to values above or below average, or to the top or bottom X items.
Data Bars	Data bars shade the background of the cell. The longer the bar, the larger the value in relation to all other cells in the selected range.
Color Scales	Color scales can apply formatting based on the values in the cell, often employing a red-yellow-green format, although this can be modified. The default is to take the highest and lowest values in the range as the endpoints of the color scheme, but this too can be modified.
Icon Sets	Icon sets are very similar to the indicators found in the Dashboard Designer for PerformancePoint Server. These include stoplights, flags, arrow, and so forth.

Table 9-1   *The Various Types of Conditional Formatting that Can Be Applied*

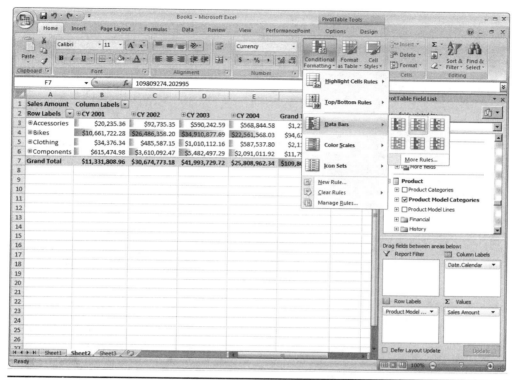

Figure 9-13 *Conditional formatting can be applied to a range of cells. In this instance, Data Bars have been added to the values in the PivotTable.*

other if desired. Figure 9-14 shows just such an example. The date is across the top, where it has been restricted to just the year 2003 for the sake of simplicity. On the rows are the sales territories, because the KPI in question, Channel Revenue, was defined by territory. The first column represents the actual value for 2003, while the second column represents the goal. The column for the status shows the indicator representing the health of the KPI. The final column shows the trend for that particular sales territory. The ability to include KPIs and their associated indicators and trend icons makes the KPIs built into the cube even more useful.

Using the PivotChart

Earlier in the chapter, Figure 9-3 showed that when the user creates a new report, she can choose to create a PivotTable or a PivotTable and PivotChart. This is one way to create a PivotChart. Another way is to be on a PivotTable and click on the Options

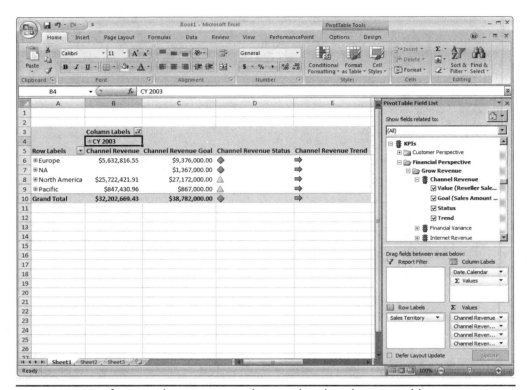

Figure 9-14   *KPIs from Analysis Services cubes can be placed in PivotTable reports, including the actual value, the goal, the status, and the trend.*

tab under the PivotTable Tools tab. This opens the Options ribbon, which contains a button labeled PivotChart. This button opens the Insert Chart dialog box, shown in Figure 9-15. The PivotChart contains a wide variety of chart templates including bar, column, line, pie, and many others. Each template may include a number of different styles, which are selected in the right pane of the Insert Chart dialog box. Figure 9-15 shows the selection of the 3-D Clustered Column chart.

After clicking the OK button, the PivotChart is added to the page. (It is not terribly considerate about where it appears, often overlapping with the PivotTable.) Fortunately, it can simply be dragged and moved anywhere on the spreadsheet. Because this PivotChart was created from the PivotTable, it is tied to the same Field List, and updates to the PivotTable, such as expanding or filtering, will affect the PivotChart.

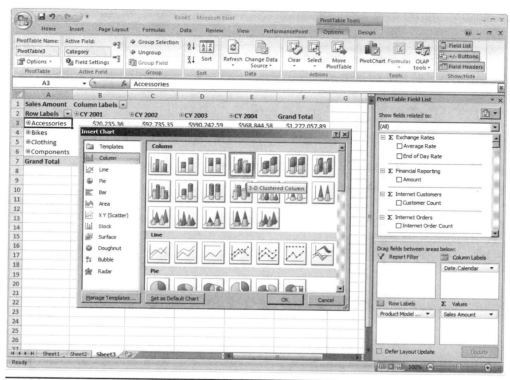

Figure 9-15 *The Insert Chart dialog box shows the variety of chart types that can be used by the PivotChart.*

While the PivotChart has the focus, a new window appears, called the PivotChart Filter Pane. There are two drop-down fields labeled Axis Fields and Legend Fields. Dropping down either list reveals the same menu as seen on the drop-down lists in the PivotTable, as shown earlier in Figure 9-7, when the Row Labels drop-down list was opened. In addition, the labels of the boxes in the Areas section of the Field List have changed to Axis Fields and Legend Fields as well. These labels will change depending on whether the focus is on the PivotTable or PivotChart. Figure 9-16 shows what the PivotChart looks like on the same page as the PivotTable, along with the PivotChart Filter Pane.

Changing the chart type after the PivotChart has been created is as simple as right-clicking on the chart and choosing Change Chart Type. This opens a dialog box entitled Change Chart Type, but it is identical to the Insert Chart dialog box shown in Figure 9-15. The chart can also be customized by right-clicking in a blank area

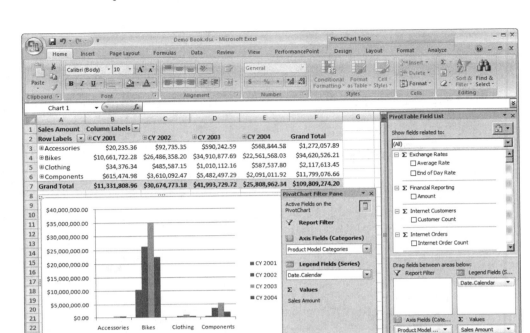

Figure 9-16   A PivotChart is added to the same worksheet as a PivotTable. The two use the same Field List because the PivotChart was created from the PivotTable.

and choosing Format Chart Area. This allows for the customization of colors, border styles, drop shadows, and more. Right-clicking on the bottom axis and choosing Format Axis allows for many customizations to the axis. Likewise, right-clicking on the legend and choosing Format Legend allows for customizations to the chart legend.

The PivotChart is live, meaning that users can expand values to see lower levels of detail. This can be done within the chart by double-clicking on a bar or pie slice or data point, depending on the chart type. For example, if the user double-clicks on a bar on the PivotChart shown in Figure 9-16, the chart expands to show the data for the two semesters of each year. In other words, double-clicking on a bar drills the user down on the dimension shown in the Legend Fields. The PivotTable updates to show the semesters as well, but the chart also continues to show the year values. Fortunately, the PivotChart is smart enough to show only the lowest level of detail currently available, rather than showing both the years and semesters at the same time.

Instead of double-clicking on a bar, the user can also double-click on a member in the legend, which has the same effect as double-clicking on a bar. Likewise, the user can double-click on a value along the X axis to drill down on the dimension on the Axis Fields. Double-clicking on any of the members shown on the X axis will expand to the subcategory level.

Sometimes having the PivotTable and PivotChart on the same page is too restrictive due to a lack of screen real estate. Fortunately, it's possible to move the PivotChart to another spreadsheet while leaving it linked to the same PivotTable. Simply right-clicking on a blank area of the chart shows an option on the menu labeled Move Chart. Selecting this item opens a Move Chart dialog box and allows the user to move the PivotChart elsewhere on the same worksheet or to a new worksheet. Moving to a new spreadsheet works well and the PivotChart and PivotTable remain linked; a change in one will be reflected in the other.

Summary

In the past, companies wanting to provide analytics tools to users had two options: buy a full-featured, third-party analytics program, or give users a weak analytics tool in the form of Microsoft Excel. Fortunately, this is no longer a problem because Excel 2007 provides vastly more powerful analytics than previous versions. While it is not as powerful as ProClarity or some third-party applications, it is now powerful enough for the majority of users in a business. In addition, it is a familiar application to almost everyone in business and is therefore a comfortable environment for people to use while analyzing data.

Like ProClarity, Excel 2007 includes a variety of chart types to help with data analysis. The combination of the charts and the formatting options available to both the PivotChart and PivotTable make Excel 2007 a powerful, highly-customizable analytics tool. And now, with Excel Services, PivotTable reports can be published to the server for easier consumption by others.

SQL Server Reporting Services

S QL Server Reporting Services is a server-based reporting tool that is included with SQL Server. It can connect to many different data sources, including both relational and OLAP stores. Reporting Services runs on a web server, which means that no distribution is necessary for end users. One of the most important features for our purposes is that Reporting Services includes functionality that allows for analytics, albeit in a limited fashion. Reports can allow for items to be expanded so that they show lower levels of detail, with one report linking to another to mimic drill-down or cross-drill behavior. Not only can a report link to other reports, but it can link to anything that can be viewed in the browser, which means that it can call PerformancePoint dashboards, ProClarity Analytics Server views, and more.

Given that the focus of this book is on PerformancePoint Server and not Reporting Services, this chapter will cover the analytic capabilities of Reporting Services. It will specifically cover the ways Reporting Services can access data from cubes and the ways that interactive reports can be created to allow end users to perform analysis. For books dedicated to Reporting Services, check out *Microsoft SQL Server 2005 Reporting Services 2005* and *Delivering Business Intelligence with Microsoft SQL Server 2005*, both by Brian Larson. A discussion of how Reporting Services and PerformancePoint Server interact will close out the chapter.

Creating Reports with Reporting Services

Reporting Services reports are created through the Business Intelligence Development Studio, or BIDS, which is simply a version of Visual Studio that has templates for business intelligence projects. If it seems strange that the reports are created in a tool specifically geared to developers, you should understand that there is an end-user tool, called the Report Builder, for performing ad-hoc queries.

Reporting Services ships with SQL Server 2005 and today requires Internet Information Services (IIS) to be running on the server. Microsoft has announced that SQL Server 2008 will drop Reporting Services' requirement for IIS, meaning that Reporting Services will be handling its own requests and supplying the results to the calling applications. Today, however, the installation of Reporting Services checks for IIS and configures a couple of virtual directories: one for the reports themselves, and one for the management site, called the Report Manager.

While Reporting Services is often used when reporting against relational databases, this discussion will focus primarily on using Reporting Services to access a cube. This is in no way intended to diminish Reporting Services' strength as a relational reporting tool, but since most PerformancePoint scorecards and charts are built off of cubes, and PerformancePoint's planning module can generate forecast cubes, it's reasonable that one of the primary uses for Reporting Services will be to access cubes in the organization.

Accessing Cubes with Reporting Services

Reporting Services projects are created through BIDS with several types of projects that can be created. Figure 10-1 shows the New Project dialog box containing three templates specific to Reporting Services: Report Server Project Wizard, Report Server Project, and Report Model Project. The Report Server Project Wizard template will create a new Reporting Services project and then guide the user through setting up the project and creating the first report. Subsequent reports can also be created by walking through the wizard. While there is certainly nothing wrong with using the wizard, after gaining some experience with Reporting Services many developers walk through the creation process manually, as will be shown later on in this chapter.

The Report Model Project template guides the developer through the process of creating a reporting model, which is an abstraction layer designed to make it easier for

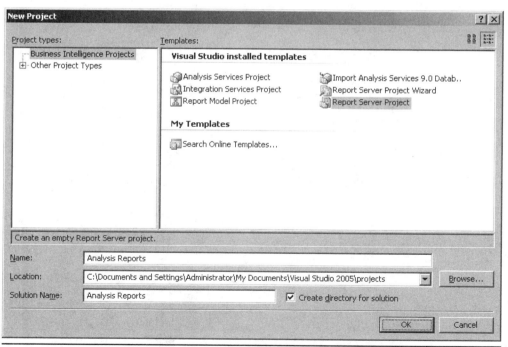

Figure 10-1 *The New Project dialog box shows that there are three different templates that can be used to create Reporting Services projects.*

end users to build their own reports. Many end users lack the knowledge of relational databases necessary to understand the joins that are needed to produce the report they are after. A report model can simplify the view of the underlying database in ways that make it much easier for end users to work with as they create their reports.

The Report Server Project template creates the new project and then stops without running any wizards. This is the starting point employed in this chapter. Notice in Figure 10-1 the Report Server Project template has been chosen. The name of this project will be Analysis Reports; a space in the name of the project isn't always smart, but it's easy enough to work with as will be shown throughout this chapter. Note also that there is a location on the local drive; just like PerformancePoint Server, Reporting Services creates a local copy of all the files for the development process. These files are then deployed to the server where they are made available to others and eventually executed. At this point, the project is not asking for the name of the server to which the reports will be deployed, and this setting will be examined later.

Once the new project is created, the view of the project in the Solution Explorer window is relatively simple, as there are only two folders: Shared Data Sources and Reports. Right-clicking on the Shared Data Sources folder and selecting Add New Data Source opens the Shared Data Source dialog box as shown in Figure 10-2. The name of the data source should reflect the data that is being accessed and in Figure 10-2,

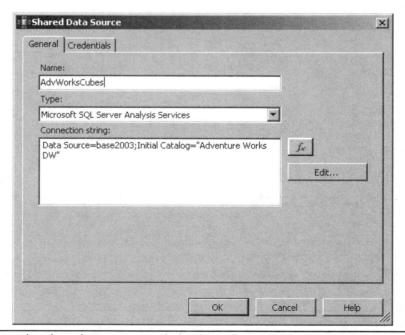

Figure 10-2   *The Shared Data Source dialog box allows developers to create a data source that will feed data to the report.*

the name includes the words "cubes" tacked on the end. This is certainly not necessary, but in projects that have connections to both Analysis Services and a relational database, it's easier to keep them separate using some sort of naming convention to easily identify what they are accessing. Unfortunately, the symbol shown in the Solution Explorer window is the same for all data sources. The Type drop-down list includes items such as SQL Server, Analysis Services, and Oracle among others, while also including far more generic items such as OLE DB, ODBC, and XML. The connection string can simply be typed in manually but in many cases, it's better to click on the Edit button, which opens the Connection Properties dialog box shown in Figure 10-3. When using Analysis Services as a source, the developer uses this dialog box to enter the server name and then choose the name of the Analysis Services database. By using this dialog, the developer is assured that the connection string is formatted properly. Figure 10-2 includes the connection string that matches the settings for the Connection Properties dialog as shown in Figure 10-3.

Once a data source is in place, it's time to create the first report. Simply right-clicking on the Reports folder and choosing Add New Report launches the Report Wizard. Again, there is nothing wrong with using the wizard, because it guides the developer

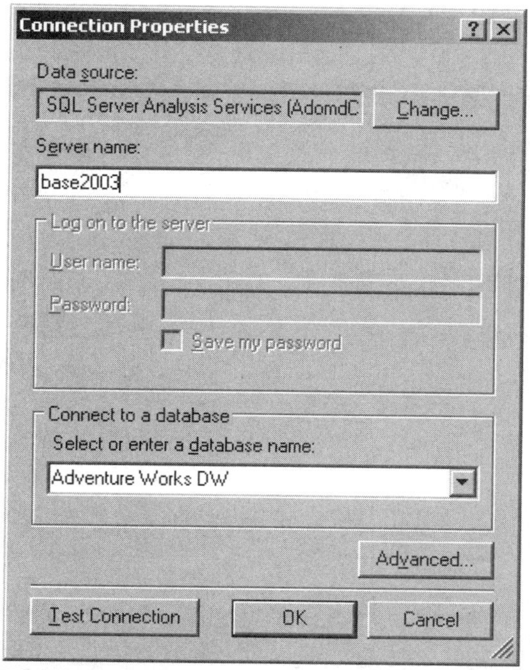

Figure 10-3 *The Connection Properties dialog box lets developers build the connection through a wizard, ensuring the connection string is properly formatted.*

through the process of picking a data source, constructing a query, and then building the report. It even applies some nice color and font formatting to the final report. In this case, however, the walkthrough will show everything being done manually—since all reports will eventually have to be edited manually anyway—and this will give you a feel for how the process works. Instead of clicking on Add New Report, the developer can click on Add, then New Item, and from the dialog box that appears, choose Report (not Report Wizard, which is the default). The report should be given a meaningful name and once it's created, it will appear in the Visual Studio work area.

There are three tabs in the main work area of a report: Data, Layout, and Preview. A new report will default to the Data tab, since no data has yet been accessed for this report. The Dataset drop-down box is blank and dropping the list down shows only New Dataset. It is important to note for any .NET developers that the dataset mentioned here is *not* the same as an ADO.NET Dataset, and while similar in concept, they really have nothing in common.

Choosing New Dataset opens the Dataset dialog box, shown in Figure 10-4. A name will be assigned to this dataset though, unlike many names in Reporting Services, this one cannot contain blanks. The dataset will then be tied to a data source. A report may contain data from many different data sources, and these sources may be relational, OLAP, XML, or a variety of other sources, but each

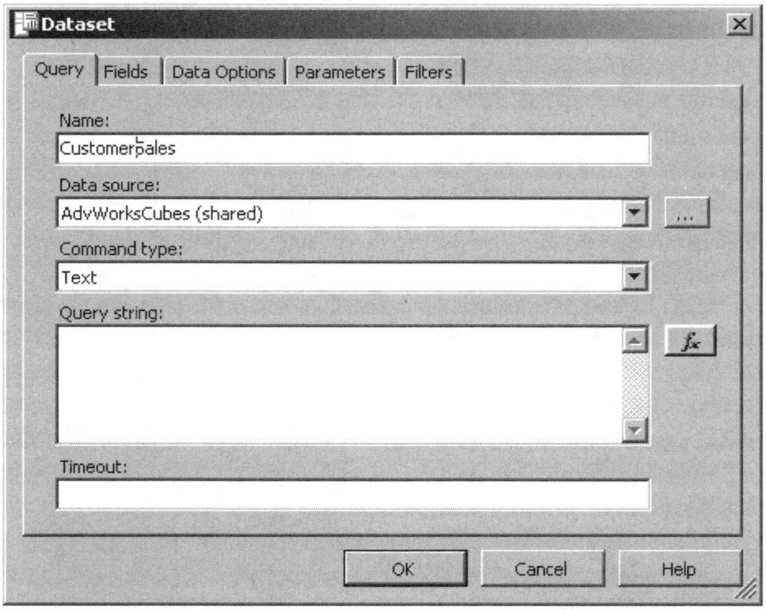

Figure 10-4 *The Dataset dialog box is where developers choose the data source to use, set parameters, and more.*

dataset can relate to only a single data source. The command type for a dataset tied to an Analysis Services data source can only be of type Text, although relational sources can present other options. Finally, there is a box for the query string. At this point, the developer is certainly free to start typing in the appropriate MDX statement, but often this box is left blank and the query is designed using the graphical query builder tool that will be examined next. Note too that there are a number of tabs along the top of the Dataset dialog, some of which will be examined during the chapter.

Assuming that the developer has set only the options shown in Figure 10-4, clicking the OK button returns her to the report's Data tab with a designer loaded. Actually, there are two views for the query designer: one is the design view, as shown in Figure 10-5, and the other is simply a view of the text of the query with a results pane below it. Flipping back and forth between the two views is accomplished by clicking the Design View button, which is the right-most button to the right of the Dataset drop-down list box.

When working with cubes, it's easy at this point to construct a query simply by dragging and dropping items from the Metadata tab to the main work area of the Query Designer. In this case, this particular report will look at the orders by customer location. Also, in the Adventure Works sample, the end customer is known only for Internet orders. Therefore, the Internet Sales Amount measure is brought over from the appropriate measure group and dropped on the design surface. A value now appears immediately; this is the sum of all Internet Sales for all time, all products, all customers, and so forth.

Since this will be a report about customers and their sales, it might be tempting to simply drag the entire Customer Geography hierarchy onto the design surface. Certainly this will work, but you should understand the impact: the query will now go down to the lowest level of the hierarchy, which in this case is the individual customer. That means that the query in the background will be retrieving a dataset that is potentially very large, and both time and memory constraints may enter into the picture. Figure 10-5 actually shows the entire Customer Geography hierarchy in the design surface. For small cubes this may not be an issue, but in the real world you may find that going down to the leaf level can lead to issues, especially when there are multiple dimensions on the report, as there will be in a moment.

By simply having the Customer Geography hierarchy you know that there is only one dimension in the report at the moment. This might work in some cases, but many reports also include time, so for this report the Date.Calendar hierarchy will be dragged from the Metadata window and dropped on the design surface. Once again, dragging the entire hierarchy over means that the dataset now includes individual customer sales at the day level; this is potentially a huge dataset and on cubes of any decent size, this could be a very slow query.

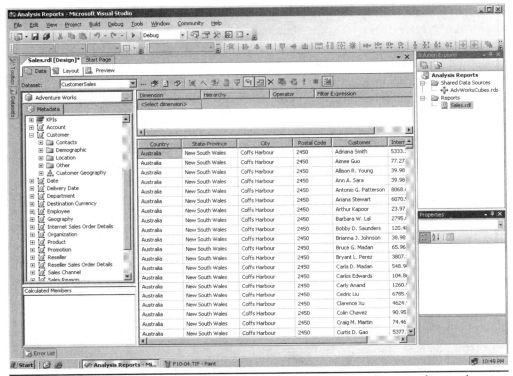

Figure 10-5 *All levels of the Customer Geography hierarchy are shown in the result set due to Reporting Service's flattening of the data.*

The alternative to dragging an entire hierarchy to the design surface is to drag over only the levels of the hierarchy that are needed for the report. For example, if only the Year and Quarter are needed, those two levels could be dragged and dropped on the Query Designer, resulting in a much smaller dataset, and therefore a report that executes much faster. In addition, the default setting is for the query designer to immediately execute the query as soon as anything changes. In order to stop this, the developer can click the Auto Execute button on the designer's toolbar to toggle the automatic execution off and on.

Another point of interest when building OLAP queries using the graphical query designer is that there is no concept of rows and columns. Instead, the result set that is returned from the cube—that lovely, multidimensional cellset—is flattened into simple tables and rows, a two-dimensional format. Therefore, the query designer shows the results in a flattened format as the query is being built.

Once the query is built, the developer can click on the Layout tab to begin the layout of the report itself, which includes mapping data elements to the page.

By default the design surface of the report is blank and elements from the Toolbox can be placed on it. Oftentimes with OLAP data, the matrix control is used. This certainly isn't the only control that can be used and many reports of OLAP data are done using the table control, but the matrix is the most popular for dealing with multidimensional data.

The matrix starts out with a single column, a single row, and a single cell for the data. Normally, the measure will go in the Data box, and additional boxes can be added if there are multiple measures. The developer can simply drag the measure from the Datasets window and drop it on the Data box in order to tie these two elements together. Similarly, dragging the Country field from the Datasets window, dropping it on the Rows, and then dragging Calendar_Year and dropping it on the Columns will set up the matrix to do some simple reporting.

Figure 10-6 shows what the matrix looks like after the fields from the dataset have been tied to it, and the columns have been expanded to show all the text. Notice that the values all start with an equal sign; this is because nearly every property

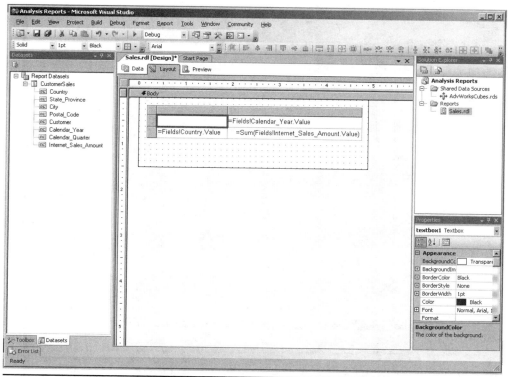

Figure 10-6 *This is the matrix control, which contains a single measure and a single level from two different dimension hierarchies.*

in Reporting Services is an expression, which means that it can contain logic and change its behavior on the fly if necessary. Note also that the measure is wrapped with a Sum function automatically. This is part of the matrix control's default behavior and while Sum is usually correct, developers are free to replace Sum with other functions for averages, minimums, maximums, and so on.

In this example, before clicking on the Preview tab, some simple formatting is applied. The lines of the grid are shown by setting the BorderStyle property of each cell to Single. The columns are resized and both cells in the second column, containing years and the measure, have their TextAlign properties set to Right. Finally, the Format property of the data cell is set to the letter "c" which means a currency format. At this point, clicking on the Preview renders the report, which means the query is executed and the data placed in the cells. The end result is shown in Figure 10-7. This image clearly shows how the rows and columns both expand automatically to show the years across the columns and the countries along the bottom.

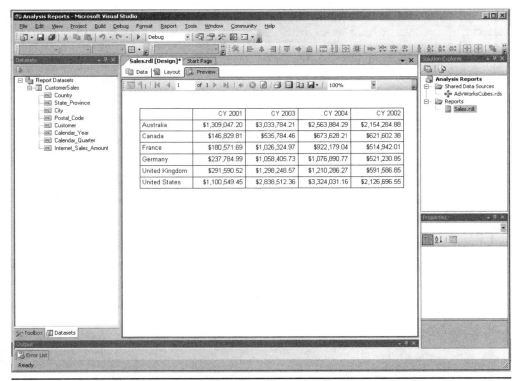

Figure 10-7 *This is the matrix displaying data from a cube, although at this point the report contains no interactive features.*

Recall from the earlier discussion that the query is returning all the data contained in the query that was built, regardless of what is displayed. This report shows only twenty four cells of data, not counting the member values in the column and row headers. This is an extremely limited amount of data but if the query went all the way to the day and individual customer levels, all that data would be returned for this report even though it isn't needed. That particular query would be overkill for this simple report and again, on large cubes, it could take minutes to execute. Therefore, it's important to return only what is necessary for a particular report.

Adding Subtotals to a Matrix

One of the items that users may want to see on such reports is subtotals. On this simple report there are two places to which subtotals can be added: the columns and rows. Later reports will show that it isn't always this simple, because there might be multiple levels of data from the same dimension on either rows or columns, which can lead to multiple levels of subtotals. For now, however, it's enough to see how to turn on the subtotals and apply some formatting to the subtotal cells.

In order to add subtotals, the report developer simply needs to right-click on the cells for the row or column headers; in the case of this sample report, the cell for Calendar_Year or the cell for Country. Right-clicking on one of these cells opens the pop-up menu and the third item on this menu is Subtotal. Selecting Subtotal adds a new cell below the row or to the right of the column that simply says "Total" and has a green triangle in the upper right-hand corner. The word "Total" is simply a label in a textbox and therefore can be changed.

The subtotal textbox itself can be formatted by changing the background color, the font style and weight, and so forth, just like any other textbox. However, making these changes does not in any way affect the display of the subtotal values when they appear. Instead, to change the format for the subtotal cells, the developer must click on the green triangle. Clicking this triangle opens the subtotal properties in the properties window, and here the background color, font, numeric format, and other properties can be changed. This is useful when the subtotals for reports should have a shaded background or the fonts should appear bold or italicized.

Figure 10-8 shows the same report as Figure 10-7, but with subtotals added. Subtotals were turned on for both rows and columns. The new textboxes had their labels changed to Years Total and Country Total. The next textboxes had their background colors set to a light grey color, and the subtotal backgrounds were also set to the same light grey color by first clicking on their small green triangles to access the subtotal properties. In addition, the column and row headers were given a pale blue background to help distinguish them from the measure. It might appear that the Format property of the subtotals was set to "c" (for currency.) In fact, that is not the case. Because the cell containing the measure was set to a Format property of "c," the subtotals pick this formatting up automatically. It's still possible to override

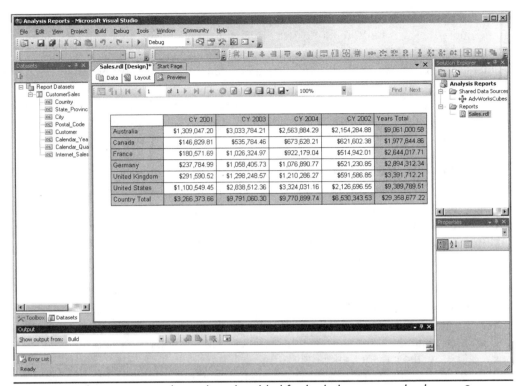

Figure 10-8 *The matrix now has subtotals added for both the rows and columns. Some simple formatting has been applied to change the background color for the row and header columns as well as the subtotals.*

that format by changing the Format property of the subtotal, but in most cases businesses will want the same format as the data it is totaling.

The reports shown in Figure 10-7 and Figure 10-8 are static, meaning that they do not contain interactivity. For example, users cannot see the data at the quarter level for each year, nor can they expand countries into the states or provinces that make up those countries. Adding such interactivity to the report is examined next.

Adding Parameters

Adding parameters to a report is perhaps the easiest way to add interactivity that allows users to perform some of the own simple analysis. The good news is that adding parameters is relatively simple, but there are several ways to modify parameters so that they are more effective and allow users to perform the analysis they need.

The first step in adding a parameter is to return to the Data tab. When the graphic query designer is shown, there is an area above the data grid that allows for filters to be added. The developer can click on the Dimension drop-down box or drag the dimension attribute or hierarchy from the Metadata tab and drop it on the Filters area. When this happens, the name of the dimension and hierarchy are displayed. An operator column can be changed from Equal to a number of other items, such as Not Equal, Contains, and Beings With. Next, the developer can choose members from the hierarchy in the Filter Expression drop-down list. This is useful when the report has a hard-coded filter on the data that the user can neither see nor modify.

The final column in the filter area is a check box named Parameters. Simply checking this box makes the current hierarchy a parameter, and this causes at least three things to happen. First, while nothing changes on the report at design time, the report at runtime will have a drop-down box for the parameter. Second, the original query is modified to now include the value of the parameter in the report. Finally, a new dataset is created that retrieves the data to fill the parameter drop-down list for the report at runtime. Figure 10-9 shows what the query looks like in design mode with a parameter added.

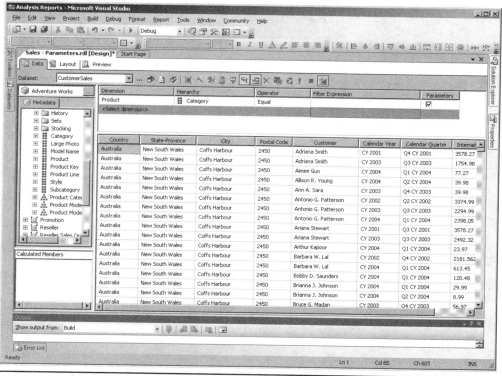

Figure 10-9 *The query for the sales report now has a filter added to it, and the filter is marked to be used as a parameter.*

In Figure 10-9, a parameter has been added for product categories. This means that end users will be able to select one or more product categories and see the sales data for just the selected categories. Inside the original query, changes were made that will now only retrieve from the cube the data that matches the selected parameters; in other words, the query does not retrieve all the data and then filter it locally; instead, Reporting Services is smart enough to write the query to only ask for the data necessary for the report.

Figure 10-10 shows what this parameter looks like when previewing the report, which is also the way it will look to users at runtime in the web interface. You should notice two things about the parameter: the list allows for multiple selections and that there is a (Select All) selection as well as an All Products selection. Developers have the ability to control whether or not a parameter allows for multiple selections, and they can modify the query to control whether or not two All choices show up in a multiple selection list.

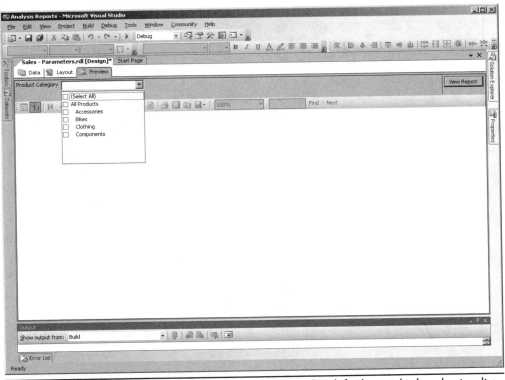

Figure 10-10 *The parameter, as viewed on the report, is by default a multiple selection list.*

In some cases, it may not make sense for a parameter to allow multiple selections. Developers are able to control the type of list that is used for a report by clicking on the Data or Layout tab and then selecting Report Parameters from the Report menu. The Report Parameters dialog box that appears contains many options for controlling how parameters are used and displayed on a report. For example, parameters have a name and a data type, though while these options are important, they are invisible to end users. The Prompt property, however, controls the text the user will see on the report next to the drop-down list. Therefore, this prompt could be changed from Category to Product Category, for example, to help make it more clear. Beneath the Prompt textbox are a number of check boxes, and one that is checked by default when building a parameter in Reporting Services against a cube source is the Multi-value check box. Unchecking this particular box changes the parameter drop-down box so that users can make only a single selection from the list. Allowing only a single selection removes the (Select All) option from the list, but the All Products element will still exist, since the query generated for parameters includes the All member by default.

In some cases businesses may decide not to have the All member in the list. This is most often done with parameters that allow multiple selections, because having both the (Select All) option and then an all members item is confusing for end users. Getting rid of the All member is a matter of modifying the query that was created when the Parameters check box was clicked. Remember that one of the things that will happen when you click the Parameters check box is the creation of a new dataset to fill the parameter list. You can see this new dataset by clicking on the Data tab and then looking at the Dataset list. The dataset will have the same name as the default name of the parameter. After selecting the query, notice that it creates a number of columns, such as ParameterCaption and ParameterValue. In the query, these columns are placed in the Columns clause in the query, but the Row clause contains the dimension, hierarchy, and then the AllMembers function.

In MDX, the AllMembers function returns all members including calculated members and the All member. If companies choose to remove the All member, the query can be changed, replacing AllMembers with the Children function.

Adding Expansion Capabilities

One of the most powerful methods of reporting is to use the matrix control to allow end users to examine lower levels of data in a report, using the rough equivalent of the expansion functionality found in ProClarity. This can be accomplished by adding multiple levels from the same dimension—to either the rows or the columns. The lower levels of detail are hidden by default and the end user can reveal them by clicking a plus sign next to the higher level member.

In order to add additional levels, the developer has to add new row or column groups to the matrix. An easy way to do this is by clicking on any cell in a matrix. Once this is done, grey borders appear along the top and left side of the matrix. This allows developers to select an entire row or column at a time to apply formatting. Right-clicking on any of these row and column selectors opens a pop-up menu that allows developers to add a column group or a row group.

In this example, years are the column headers. In order to also add the quarters to the columns, the developer right-clicks on a row or column selector and then chooses Add Column Group. This opens the Grouping and Sorting Properties dialog box. The General tab contains a section named Group on and it asks for an expression. Dropping the list down shows all of the fields available in the dataset. In this case, the report needs to include the quarters, so the developer picks the Fields!Calendar_Quarter.Value option. There are more steps that need to be performed, but if the developer closes the dialog box at this point, a new text box is added below the old Years textbox. If the report is viewed, the end result looks like that in Figure 10-11, with all the quarters displayed by default.

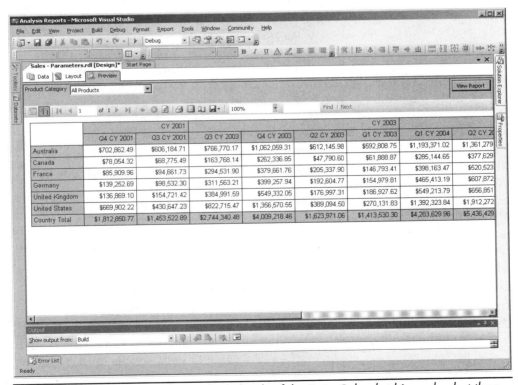

Figure 10-11 *The report now has multiple levels of the Date.Calendar hierarchy, but they are not yet interactive.*

In order to make this interactive, the developer has more to modify on the Grouping and Sorting Properties dialog box. Right-clicking on the textbox with the quarters in it and then choosing Edit Group reopens the dialog box. On the Visibility tab are the options needed to make the report more interactive. First, the initial visibility should be set to Hidden, which means quarters will not be shown by default. However, users should be able to view the quarters as necessary, so the next step is to check the box labeled Visibility Can Be Toggled By Another Report Item. In the Report item drop-down box, the developer chooses the item that can show or hide the quarters. In this case it would be the box named Calendar_Year.

Allowing users to expand from countries to the states or provinces that make them up would follow a similar path. The developer right-clicks on a row or column selector and then chooses Add Row Group. The expression for the Group On section would be set to Fields!State_Province.Value. On the Visibility tab, the initial visibility would be set to Hidden and the visibility would be toggled by the Country textbox.

Figure 10-12 shows how this report might look. The user has clicked the plus sign next to Australia and Canada to expand them. In addition, the year 2001 has been

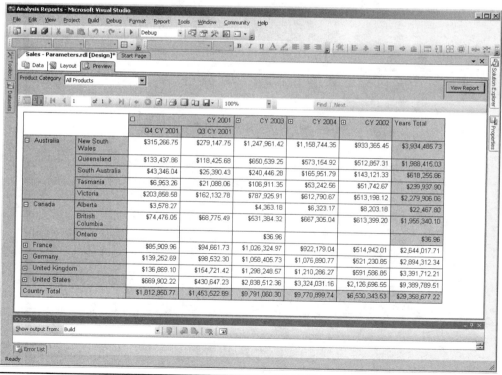

Figure 10-12 *This is a report featuring a parameter and a matrix control that allows users to expand members to lower levels of detail.*

expanded to show the quarters under it (there are only two quarters of 2001 in the data). Adding the capability for expanding members to lower levels of detail can be used in conjunction with parameters, just as is being done in this image. Subtotals can be turned on or off without affecting the functionality of the report.

Subtotals were added earlier, but they can be added for any group. This means that while there are country and year totals, there can also be totals for state/provinces and for quarters. The challenge is how these new subtotals are displayed, and it will ultimately be a business decision about whether or not to show them and how to format them if they are shown. Recall from previous discussion that the subtotals were given a light grey background. If subtotals are added to state/province and quarters and given the same light grey background, the entire grid will start out as grey when no members are expanded. That's because the total for a particular year is the sum of the quarters, so the number being shown will be counted as the subtotal and formatted accordingly. Figure 10-13 shows the results of the report if subtotals are added for both the quarters and the state/province, and the subtotals

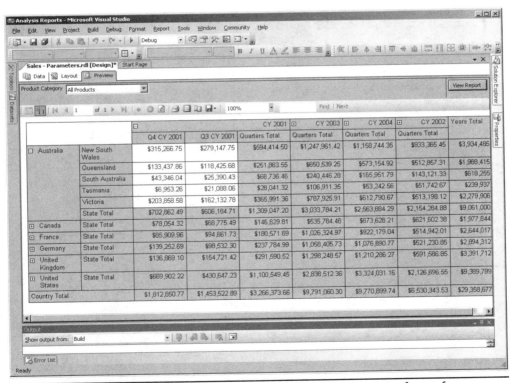

Figure 10-13 *Adding subtotals at multiple levels may lead to a more confusing format, especially if the formatting of subtotals is different from standard cells.*

were formatted to have a light grey background. The figure shows what the report looks like after expanding the year 2001 and Australia.

Accessing Relational Data

Most people think of Reporting Services as a reporting tool for relational reports, and there's no question this is how it is used the majority of the time. The flexibility of laying out reports goes well beyond the standard banded report writers that are familiar to many IT professionals, and the various output options, scheduling, and so forth make Reporting Services a strong contender for enterprise reporting needs.

In a simple example of how to work with a relational report, this walkthrough will cover the sales details for a product category within a country for a given year. Each individual order for both the product category and country will be listed for that year, so the report may be quite large.

The first step is to create a data source that accesses a relational database, which in this case is the relational data warehouse for the Adventure Works Company. This database, AdventureWorksDW, is the source for the cube used in most of the examples throughout this book. Creating the data source is done as before, by right-clicking on the Shared Data Sources folder and then selecting Add New Data Source. The Shared Data Source dialog box opens and defaults to Microsoft SQL Server connection, which is correct in this scenario. After naming the data source, the developer can click on the Edit button to open the Connection Properties dialog box, as seen earlier. After entering the server name, the developer should choose the AdventureWorksDW database. Figure 10-14 shows what the connection might look like, with the only difference between this example and that of the reader being the server name.

The next step in the process is to create a new report. Once again, the developer should right-click on the Reports folder and then choose Add, New Item, and Report (note that once again, the wizard is not being used.) Once the report has been created, the developer goes to the Data tab and chooses New Dataset from the Dataset drop-down list box.

On the Dataset dialog box, the dataset is given a name, and the data source is set to the data source just created (called AdvWorksDW in Figure 10-14). This ensures that the data source is the relational database and not the cube, as used in the previous example. At this point the developer could type in the SQL statement, but clicking the OK button opens the dataset in query mode.

The default view for a relational query is to show just a blank area at the top and a grid at the bottom. The blank area holds the text of the SQL statement and the grid will show the results if the query is executed. It is sometimes easier to use the graphical query builder, and the view can be switched back and forth using the

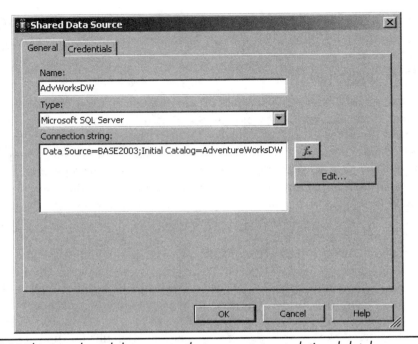

Figure 10-14 *This is a shared data source that connects to a relational database.*

Generic Query Designer button, which switches between the text box and a graphical display to which the developer can add tables and select fields.

For this particular query, there are a number of tables that need to be added. Right-clicking in the upper pane of the query designer opens a pop-up menu with the option Add Table. Selecting this option opens a list of the tables and views in this particular database. For this example, the developer chooses the following tables:

- ▶ FactInternetSales
- ▶ DimCustomer
- ▶ DimTime
- ▶ DimGeography
- ▶ DimProduct
- ▶ DimProductCategory
- ▶ DimProductSubcategory

The joins between the tables are read from the underlying database schema and put into place automatically. In this example a change is needed. There are three dates available in the FactInternetSales table, but only one will be used. Therefore, the joins between the TimeKey field in DimTime and the DueDateKey and ShipDateKey fields in FactInternetSales should be deleted. This means that TimeKey in DimTime will only be tied to OrderDateKey in FactInternetSales.

After selecting these tables, the developer chooses the following fields from the following tables:

- DimCustomer: FirstName, LastName
- DimTime: FullDateAlternateKey
- DimProductSubcategory: EnglishProductSubcategoryName
- DimProduct: EnglishProductName
- FactInternetSales: SalesAmount

It's certainly possible to add additional fields or combine the first and last names into a single column, but this example will remain simple in order to drive home a couple of key points.

As it stands, the query is rather simple in that it only selects a few fields, and then contains a number of inner joins between the tables. The last step in this example is for the developer to add some parameters. This can be done by simply adding a WHERE clause to the query and setting values equal to a parameter name, which in the case of SQL Server is a name preceded by an at sign (the @ symbol). The WHERE clause should filter on a product category, a year, and a country. The final SQL statement is shown below, with Figure 10-15 showing the final query as designed, albeit a bit compressed due to the constraints of space for screenshots.

```
SELECT DimCustomer.FirstName, DimCustomer.LastName,
    DimTime.FullDateAlternateKey,
DimProductSubcategory.EnglishProductSubcategoryName,
    DimProduct.EnglishProductName, FactInternetSales.SalesAmount
FROM FactInternetSales INNER JOIN
    DimCustomer ON FactInternetSales.CustomerKey = DimCustomer.
CustomerKey INNER JOIN
    DimTime ON FactInternetSales.OrderDateKey = DimTime.TimeKey INNER JOIN
    DimProduct ON FactInternetSales.ProductKey = DimProduct.ProductKey
INNER JOIN
    DimProductSubcategory ON DimProduct.ProductSubcategoryKey =
    DimProductSubcategory.ProductSubcategoryKey INNER JOIN
```

```
    DimProductCategory ON DimProductSubcategory.ProductCategoryKey =
DimProductCategory.ProductCategoryKey INNER JOIN
    DimGeography ON DimCustomer.GeographyKey = DimGeography.GeographyKey
WHERE (DimProductCategory.EnglishProductCategoryName IN
    (@ProductCategory)) AND (DimTime.CalendarYear IN (@Year)) AND
(DimGeography.EnglishCountryRegionName = @Country)
```

After adding the WHERE clause, three parameters are automatically created: ProductCategory, Year, and Country. Normally the developer would now create data sources to fill lists for each of these parameters so that users could select values, but this particular example will be used for other purposes in a moment.

The next step for the developer is to create the layout of the report itself. Clicking on the Layout tab opens the empty report in the designer, allowing the developer the freedom to place controls on the report as necessary. Unlike the earlier report that used the matrix control, this particular report will use a table—perhaps the most

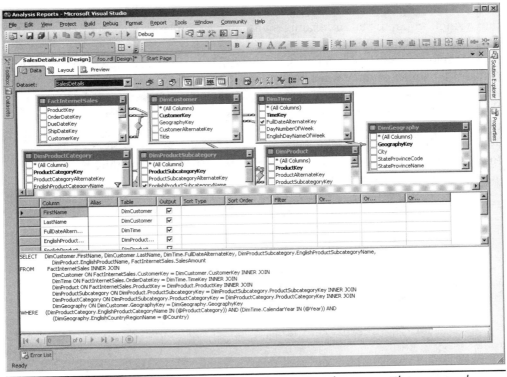

Figure 10-15 *The query designer after graphically creating the query. Changes can be made in the diagram at the top or by changing the text at the bottom.*

common way to show data in Reporting Services. This table automatically repeats all of the rows in a dataset and is often used in cases where businesses need a simple way to view the data. It's also very useful for allowing users to export the data to Excel for further analysis.

By default the table comes with just three columns, but right-clicking on any column selector allows developers to insert extra columns or delete the existing column, among other functions. In this particular example, the developer simply adds columns to the table and places all the fields in the table by dragging each field and then placing it in a detail cell in each column. The developer started by turning on the grid line, which was done by setting the BorderStyle property to Solid for all of the cells. Next, the developer applied some basic formatting by resizing columns, setting a background color to the header, and changing some of the text in header cells. After these changes, the report might look something like that shown in Figure 10-16.

At this point the report is ready to be viewed by clicking on the Preview tab. Because no queries were designed for the parameters, they appear simply as text boxes and the developer must know the correct values to type into the boxes in

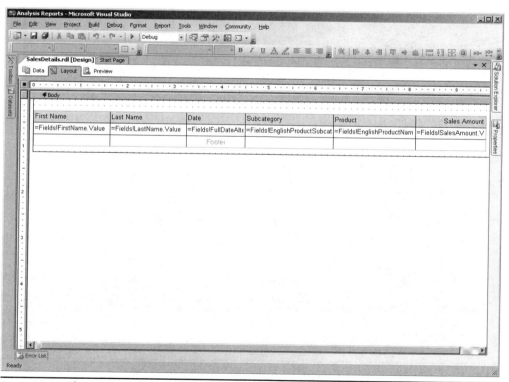

Figure 10-16 *This is a simple tabular report that will show data from a relational database.*

order to get valid results. This problem will be remedied in a moment, but for now, the developer can enter Accessories for the Product Category, 2003 for the Year, and Australia for the Country. Clicking View Report after entering these values executes the report, as shown in Figure 10-17. Examining the toolbar just below the parameters shows that this report contains 65 pages, so it is not a small report, by any means.

Linking Reports

Perhaps one of the most useful features when dealing with Reporting Services is the ability to link reports. Doing this provides the ability for someone jump from one report to another, often viewing greater levels of detail. This can be quite useful when working with data in cubes, which can be aggregated from a large volume of transactional data. Users sometimes want the ability to see all the records that make up what they are viewing in the cube. This particular example is a bit higher level than would be employed in most cases, but it works to show the technique in action.

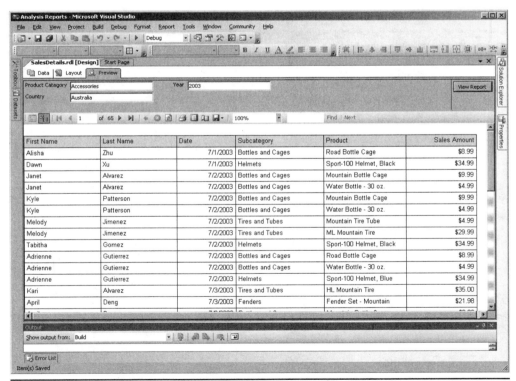

Figure 10-17 *This is the tabular report after the parameters have been entered and the report is executed.*

In order to show this, a new and very simple report will be created against the cube. The query will contain just the year level from the Calendar hierarchy and the Country level from the Customer Geography hierarchy. The report still has a parameter on the Product Category, as before, although the parameter does not allow multiple selections because the SQL statement in the relational report does not handle multiple selections (this can be modified by using the SQL IN statement).

The report uses a matrix control as before, with the years on the columns and the countries on the rows, and Internet Sales Amount as the measure. At this point the report can be run though, aside from selecting a category, the report is not interactive.

The key here is that each cell has an Action property, and this property is able to call other reports, among other things. Clicking on the data cell (the one containing the measure, Internet Sales Amount) and viewing the properties in the Properties window shows the Action property. Clicking in the cell reveals a button with an ellipsis and clicking that button opens the Action dialog box. The first option is to jump to an existing report, although the action can also jump to a bookmark (another section in the same report) or another URL entirely. In this case, jumping to another report is the desired behavior, and dropping down the list shows the reports available in this particular project.

Once the report has been selected, the developer can click on the Parameters button to open the Parameters dialog box. This dialog box lists the parameters on the report and allows the developer to choose what from the current report should be passed to the parameters on the linked report. The first parameter is the ProductCategory, and this should be set to whatever the user chooses as the parameter on the current report. Unfortunately, simply dropping down the list doesn't reveal the parameters from the current report, only the fields in the dataset. Clicking on the Expression option opens the Edit Expression dialog box and this does contain all of the parameters as well as the fields in the dataset, so the parameter can be selected here. However, a couple of changes are needed.

First, the parameters have both a value and a label. The value is usually the unique identifier in a cube, so it contains the dimension, hierarchy, and usually an index number for the item. The SQL statement in the linked report won't understand a product category of [Product].[Category].&[4] so the parameter will have to be changed to use the label instead, which is the text the person sees in the list. However, this introduces another problem; the values may be indented if they are at a lower level of detail. Therefore, the developer will have to wrap the LTrim function around the parameter, which removes all leading spaces from the value. Therefore, the final setting for the ProductCategory parameter will be:

```
=LTrim(Parameters!ProductCategory.Label)
```

The Year parameter should be relatively simple, but the label that is shown in the report for the year 2003 is actually CY 2003. In this case, it's necessary for the developer to strip off the leading CY and the space. This is done by using the Right function, which takes a certain number of characters from the right of the value; in this case the developer wants the four right-most characters, which are just the date. The final setting for the Year parameter will be:

```
=Right(Fields!Calendar_Year.Value,4)
```

Fortunately there is nothing special that has to be done with the Country parameter, so the final settings in the parameters dialog box are shown in Figure 10-18. Note that these changes are unique to this situation, and other cases may call for completely different manipulation in order to pass parameters.

After the developer sets the Action property, the data is clickable when displayed in the matrix. By default, the appearance of the numbers doesn't change to reflect that it is now clickable; instead, the developer will have to change text formatting if he or she desires underlining or color changes to cue the user in.

A final change that is often made is to hide the parameters on the linked report. Remember that the parameters were just text boxes before. On the linked report (in this case, the relational report) opening the Report Parameters dialog box shows the

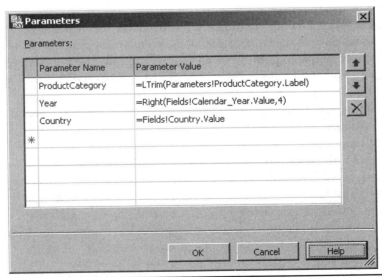

Figure 10-18 *This is the setting used to tie values from the current report to parameters in a linked report.*

various options for the parameters. One option is Hidden, which works well here. The end users do not see the parameters, but they are still available to be set by calling reports.

Summary

Many people assume that Reporting Services is a relational report writer and as such, ignore its place among the BI stack as an analysis tool. True, it is not as powerful as a full analytics client such as ProClarity, but that's not its target audience. The target audience for Reporting Services is much broader than that of ProClarity, and it can provide limited analytics to users throughout the organization with no training required. When it comes to working with cube data specifically, the abilities found in the matrix to expand data to show lower levels of detail is extremely useful for keeping the reports simple and uncluttered while also allowing users to see more detail if necessary. It's also possible to have a report that links to another report containing far more detailed information. Linking to other reports can mimic the drill-through capabilities found in Analysis Services and can present the data in a more pleasant format.

Reporting Services is yet another tool in the arsenal for BI developers. While this chapter has been a very brief introduction to its capabilities, it is important to get an overview of what Reporting Services can offer. Don't forget that one of the report types supported by PerformancePoint Server is a Reporting Services report, and you've now seen how useful those can be.

Index

Planning module
overview, 27–28, 215–216
PerformancePoint Add-in for Excel
creating reports and forms,
271–277
overview, 271
submitting plan data, 277–280
Planning Administration Console
applications, 217–220
Data Administrator role, 227–228
data connections, 229–231
Global Administrator role, 226
model sites, 220–223
Modeler role, 228–229
overview, 216–217
User Administrator role, 226–227
users, 223–225
Planning Business Modeler
associations, 271
Dimensions workspace, 234–256
Forms and Reports link, 261
Models workspace, 257–261
overview, 231–234
Process Management workspace,
262–269
Security and Roles workspace,
269–270
Planning Server, 229, 284, 289–292
plus sign buttons, 303
Point option, 178
portals, 12
ports, 292
Preview mode, 153
Preview tab, 322, 326, 339
previews, 129–130
Proactive Caching, 58
Process Management workspace, 262–269
Process Scheduling Tasks pane, 262, 268
processing cubes, 57–58
ProClarity
overview, 168–169
Professional client, 169–207
Standard client, 207–213

ProClarity Analytics Server. *See* PAS
(ProClarity Analytics Server)
ProClarity Corporation, 14, 25
ProClarity Desktop Professional, 25,
168–170, 203
ProClarity Professional, 14, 138, 207
ProClarity Standard, 138, 168–169,
206–209, 211
product categories, 184
product dimension, 42–43
Prompt textbox, 331
Properties tabs, 88, 96
Provision an Existing Database options, 287
Publish as Form Template dialog box, 277
publishing
objects, 90
to ProClarity Analytics Server (PAS),
202–207

Q

quality control, 10–11, 72
queries, 323–324, 326–327, 339
Query Designer, 323–324

R

Raw scores, 104
Read permissions, 85–86, 89
Refresh button, 140
Refresh option, 254
refreshing, 299
regulatory compliance, 72
relational data, 335–336
relational reports, 335–340
relational stores, 318
relational tables, 140, 163
relational warehouses, 42–43, 47–49, 51
Remove All button, 211
Remove button, 211
Report Builder, 318
Report item drop-down box, 333
Report Manager, 318
Report menu, 331

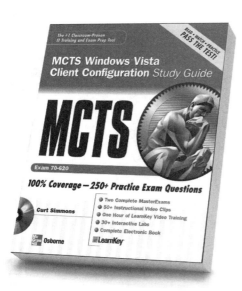

Stop Hackers in Their Tracks